Emerging Business Ventures under Market Socialism

The empirical case-study research literature on Chinese management is meagre. This rapidly changing market environment requires more research to provide an understanding of empirical processes of management practice and the business landscape in which they operate. This book adopts a holistic view to assess the impact of market socialism upon evolving economic enterprises and their ownership forms. It emphasizes the effects of market-socialist policies in shaping contrasting management patterns and behaviors in China between 2005 and 2010.

The book provides a comparative perspective on organizational development and management systems by focusing on three key emerging issues associated with the development of economic enterprise and market socialism in China: the emergence of different types of business venture; their contrasting management processes and patterns; and the impact of the political and institutional environment.

Based on longitudinal case studies between 2005 and 2010, the book explores the distinctive characteristics of emerging forms of economic enterprise. It identifies how rapid environmental and institutional changes in economic reforms are impacting upon their practices, particularly the role of government policy in shaping their ownership and management processes. Some general patterns in the development of business ventures are identified to outline the dynamics of industrial and organizational change under the transitional phases of a market-socialist economy.

Ping Zheng is Senior Lecturer in Business and Management at Canterbury Christ Church University, Canterbury, UK; ping.zheng@canterbury.ac.uk

Richard Scase is Emeritus Professor of Organizational Change at the University of Kent, Canterbury, UK; R.Scase@kent.ac.uk

Routledge studies in international business and the world economy

1 **States and Firms**
   Multinational enterprises in institutional competition
   Sally Razeen

2 **Multinational Restructuring, Internationalization and Small Economies**
   The Swedish case
   Thomas Andersson, Torbjörn Fredriksson and Roger Svensson

3 **Foreign Direct Investment and Governments**
   Catalysts for economic restructuring
   Edited by John H. Dunning and Rajneesh Narula

4 **Multinational Investment and Economic Structure**
   Globalization and competitiveness
   Rajneesh Narula

5 **Entrepreneurship in a Global Context**
   Edited by Sue Birley and Ian Macmillan

6 **The Global Structure of Financial Markets**
   An overview
   Edited by Dilip K. Ghosh and Edgar Ortiz

7 **Alliance Capitalism and Global Business**
   John H. Dunning

8 **Multinational Enterprises from the Netherlands**
   Edited by Roger van Hoesel and Rajneesh Narula

9 **Competition, Growth Strategies and the Globalization of Services**
   Real estate advisory services in Japan, Europe and the United States
   Terrence LaPier

10 **European Integration and Foreign Direct Investment in the EU**
   The case of the Korean consumer electronics industry
   Sang Hyup Shin

11 **New Multinational Enterprises from Korea and Taiwan**
   Beyond export-led growth
   Roger van Hoesel

12 **Competitive Industrial Development in the Age of Information**
   The role of co-operation in the technology sector
   Edited by Richard J. Braudo and Jeffrey G. MacIntosh

13 **The Global Restructuring of the Steel Industry**
Innovations, institutions and industrial change
Anthony P. D'Costa

14 **Privatisation and Liberalisation in European Telecommunications**
Comparing Britain, the Netherlands and France
Willem Hulsink

15 **Multinational Corporations**
Emergence and evolution
Paz Estrella Tolentino

16 **Foreign Direct Investment in Emerging Economies**
Corporate strategy and investment behaviour in the Caribbean
Lou Anne A. Barclay

17 **European Integration and Global Corporate Strategies**
Edited by François Chesnais, Grazia Ietto-Gillies and Roberto Simonetti

18 **The Globalisation of Corporate R & D**
Implications for innovation systems in host countries
Prasada Reddy

19 **Globalization of Services**
Some implications for theory and practice
Edited by Yair Aharoni and Lilach Nachum

20 **A Century of Foreign Investment in the Third World**
Michael J. Twomey

21 **Global Capitalism at Bay**
John H. Dunning

22 **Foreign Direct Investment**
Research issues
Edited by Bijit Bora

23 **Ford and the Global Strategies of Multinationals**
The North American auto industry
Isabel Studer Noguez

24 **The World Trade Organization Millennium Round**
Freer trade in the next century
Klaus Deutsch and Bernhard Speyer

25 **Consultancy and Innovation**
The business service revolution in Europe
Edited by Peter Wood

26 **Knowledge Economies**
Clusters, learning and co-operative advantage
Philip Cooke

27 **The Role of Resources in Global Competition**
John Fahy

28 **Globalization, Employment and the Workplace**
Diverse impacts
Edited by Yaw A. Debrah and Ian G. Smith

29 **Transnational Corporations**
Fragmentation amidst integration
Grazia Ietto-Gillies

30 **Growth Theory and Growth Policy**
Edited by Harald Hagemann and Stephan Seiter

31 **International Business and the Eclectic Paradigm**
Developing the OLI framework
Edited by John Cantwell and Rajneesh Narula

32 **Regulating Global Trade and the Environment**
Paul Street

33 **Cultural Industries and the Production of Culture**
Edited by Dominic Power and Allen J. Scott

34 **Governing Interests**
Business associations facing internationalization
Edited by Wolfgang Streeck, Jürgen Grote, Volker Schneider and Jelle Visser

35 **Infrastructure Development in the Pacific Region**
Edited by Akira Kohsaka

36 **Big Business and Economic Development**
Conglomerates and economic groups in developing countries and transition economies under globalisation
Edited by Alex E. Fernández Jilberto and Barbara Hogenboom

37 **International Business Geography**
Case studies of corporate firms
Edited by Piet Pellenbarg and Egbert Wever

38 **The World Bank and Global Managerialism**
Jonathan Murphy

39 **Contemporary Corporate Strategy**
Global perspectives
Edited by John Saee

40 **Trade, Globalization and Poverty**
Edited by Elias Dinopoulos, Pravin Krishna, Arvind Panagariya and Kar-yiu Wong

41 **International Management and Language**
Susanne Tietze

42 **Space, Oil and Capital**
Mazen Labban

43 **Petroleum Taxation**
Sharing the oil wealth: a study of petroleum taxation yesterday, today and tomorrow
Carole Nakhle

44 **International Trade Theory**
A critical review
Murray C. Kemp

45 **The Political Economy of Oil and Gas in Africa**
The case of Nigeria
Soala Ariweriokuma

46 **Successfully Doing Business/Marketing in Eastern Europe**
Edited by V. H. Kirpalani, Lechoslaw Garbarski, and Eredener Kaynak

47 **Marketing in Developing Countries**
Nigerian advertising and mass media
Emmanuel C. Alozie

48 **Business and Management Environment in Saudi Arabia**
Challenges and opportunities for multinational corporations
Abbas J. Ali

49 **International Growth of Small and Medium Enterprises**
Edited by Niina Nummela

50 **Multinational Enterprises and Innovation**
Regional learning in networks
Martin Heidenreich, Christoph Barmeyer, Knut Koschatzky, Jannika Mattes, Elisabeth Baier, and Katharina Krüth

51 **Globalisation and Advertising in Emerging Economies**
Brazil, Russia, India and China
Lynne Ciochetto

52 **Corporate Social Responsibility and Global Labor Standards**
Firms and activists in the making of private regulation
Luc Fransen

53 **Corporations, Global Governance and Post-Conflict Reconstruction**
Peter Davis

54 **Self-Initiated Expatriation**
Individual, organizational, and national perspectives
Edited by Maike Andresen, Akram Al Ariss, Matthias Walther and Karen Wolff

55 **Marketing Management in Asia**
Edited by Stan Paliwoda, Tim Andrews and Junsong Chen

56 **Infrastructure Development in the Pacific Region**
Edited by Akira Kohsaka

57 **The Globalization of the Executive Search Industry**
Professional services strategy and dynamics in the contemporary world
Jonathan Beaverstock, James Faulconbridge and Sarah Hall

58 **Global Strategies in Retailing**
Asian and European experiences
Edited by John Dawson and Masao Mukoyama

59 **Emerging Business Ventures under Market Socialism**
Entrepreneurship in China
Ping Zheng and Richard Scase

Emerging Business Ventures under Market Socialism

Entrepreneurship in China

Ping Zheng and Richard Scase

LONDON AND NEW YORK

First published 2013 by Routledge

2 Park Square, Milton Park, Abingdon, Oxfordshire OX14 4RN
711 Third Avenue, New York, NY 10017

Routledge is an imprint of the Taylor & Francis Group, an informa business

First issued in paperback 2018

Copyright © 2013 Ping Zheng and Richard Scase

The right of Ping Zheng and Richard Scase to be identified
as authors of this work has been asserted by them in accordance with
sections 77 and 78 of the Copyright, Designs and Patents Act 1988.

All rights reserved. No part of this book may be reprinted or reproduced
or utilised in any form or by any electronic, mechanical, or other
means, now known or hereafter invented, including photocopying and
recording, or in any information storage or retrieval system, without
permission in writing from the publishers.

Notice:
Product or corporate names may be trademarks or registered trademarks,
and are used only for identification and explanation without intent to
infringe.

British Library Cataloguing in Publication Data
A catalogue record for this book is available from the British Library

Library of Congress Cataloging in Publication Data
Zheng, Ping.
Emerging business ventures in China : entrepreneurship under market socialism /
Ping Zheng, Richard Scase.
pages cm. – (Routledge studies in international business and the world economy)
Includes bibliographical references and index.
 1. Entrepreneurship–China. 2. Socialism–China. 3. China–Economic policy.
 4. Organizational change–China. I. Scase, Richard. II. Title.
HB615.Z4834 2013
338'.040951–dc23   2013025151

ISBN: 978-0-415-50131-6 (hbk)
ISBN: 978-1-138-37684-7 (pbk)

Typeset in Times New Roman
by Sunrise Setting Ltd, Paignton, UK

Contents

List of figures xii
List of tables xiii
Preface xiv
Acknowledgements xv

1 Chinese market socialism: a summary account 1

2 Entrepreneurial growth and ownership 25

3 Management theory and practice in the Chinese context 43

4 The contradictions of state-owned enterprises 61

5 The emergence of privately owned enterprises 82

6 The impact of foreign joint ventures 99

7 Case studies: state-owned enterprise LTG, privately owned enterprise DAL and foreign joint-venture DSF 112

8 Emerging trends in Chinese market socialism 129

Appendix: the research investigation and the selection of case studies 137
Bibliography 155
Index 173

Figures

1.1	Annual FDI inflows to China, 2005–2011	17
2.1	Development in number of private industrial enterprises, 1995–2010	36
2.2	Development in number of employees in private industrial enterprises, 1995–2010	37
2.3	Development in total working capitals of private industrial enterprises, 1995–2010	37
2.4	Development in value added of industry of private industrial enterprises, 1995–2007	38
4.1	Contribution to profits by different markets, 2005	62
4.2	Structure of government administration responsible for LTG	65
4.3	Structure of organizational functions within LTG	67
4.4	Decision-making processes for the change of welfare regulation in LTG	70
5.1	The "supposed" structure of the DAL Company	87
5.2	The reality of the DAL structure	87
8.1	The analytical framework	140
8.2	The McKinsey 7-S framework	142

Tables

1.1	The percentage of economic components in total industrial production of China (%)	6
1.2	The percentage of economic components in retail commercial sales of China (%)	6
1.3	Percentage of transactions at market prices (by transaction volume) (%)	7
1.4	The percentage of economic components in China's GDP share (%), 1990–2001	9
1.5	The percentage of different economic components in China, 2003 and 2007	10
1.6	FDI stock from 1979 to 1991	15
1.7	FDI stock from 1992 to 2010	16
2.1	The private sector outpaces the public sector in China, 1998–2003	39
2.2	China foreign trade composition by enterprise ownerships in 2004	39
3.1	Institutional components of state and private sector enterprises	57
4.1	Drivers and barriers to SOE entrepreneurship	79
7.1	Entrepreneurial vs. administrative cultures	122
7.2	Organizational profiles of each of the three case studies according to the McKinsey 7-S framework	127

Preface

Hardly a day goes by when the economic transformations affecting China do not have an impact upon the global economy. Within a very short space of time, sustained and high levels of economic growth have pivoted China into its position as one of the World's leading economies, with direct consequences for all major regions of the globe. Not only has its growth contributed to the de-industrialization of Europe and large parts of the United States through its rapidly expanding manufacturing sector, but it has also affected less developed regions of the world, such as Africa, in its quest for raw materials and energy to fuel this economic transformation.

However, there is still limited Western knowledge as to the mechanisms that are related to this economic development. China continues to be a single-party dictatorship and yet this has nurtured a flourishing private economic sector and introduced sweeping economic reforms leading to the transition from state to market socialism. A dynamic private sector has emerged, which consists of a diversity of enterprise types that have developed alongside dramatically reformed state-owned enterprises.

This book discusses these different types of enterprise, highlighting how each is characterized by contrasting organizational types, business strategies, and leadership styles. The outcome is the appearance of different tensions between each of these business types and the dominant political order. Drawing upon case studies of enterprises in China, for which detailed longitudinal empirical evidence was collected, these are illustrated and interpreted according to contemporary theories relating to the economic and social transformation of China in particular and to social and economic change in general.

Acknowledgements

We would like to thank the managers and entrepreneurs in our case study organizations; without their commitment and continuous support over a six-year period, this longitudinal research would not have been possible. We would also like to thank Dr Jonathan Scott for his contribution to the discussion of Chinese guanxi business networks and Dr Wei Meng and Dr Zheng Li, who helped us access statistical data in China.

1 Chinese market socialism
A summary account

Introduction

The aim of this chapter is to introduce the main features of market socialism and the general environment within which organizations operate: the economic and political environment. Originally "market socialism" was the attempt by Soviet regimes to introduce market elements into their socialist economic systems in order to address the inefficiencies of their economies. It is the analogous system introduced in the People's Republic of China (PRC) by Deng Xiaoping in the late 1970s, which has evolved into what some economists, outside of China, would argue is modern Chinese capitalism.

The core difference between socialism and capitalism as far as the relations of production are concerned, is in the nature of ownership and control (Davis and Scase 1985). As Marx (1969) originally defined it, under capitalism, producers create the economic surplus, which becomes the personal wealth and property of non-producers; that means the capitalists exploit the proletariat. However, socialism is characterized by public ownership of the means of production, workers are masters or owners of the enterprises, so there is no exploitation. The distribution and deployment of social resources and economic surplus are conducted and determined by a centralized planning system of government rather than through market forces. Pierson (1995: 85) has outlined the core principles of market socialism:

> At its simplest, market socialism describes an economic and political system which combines the principles of social ownership of the economy with the continuing allocation of commodities (including labor) through the mechanism of markets. For market socialists, it is not markets but capitalist markets, that is, markets which inscribe the social and economic power of private capital, that are objectionable. They offer an alternative model in which markets are combined with varying forms of the social ownership of capital. Amongst its supporters, the market is recommended not only as a way of attaining greater economic efficiency under socialism, but also as a way of securing greater individual liberty or a more equal value of liberty, of increasing democracy and of enhancing social justice.

Socialism in China initially adopted the Marxist theory and the Soviet model when it was established in 1949. Through its own practices over decades, the Communist Party of China (CPC) has gradually developed its own socialist model and radically redefined many of the terms and concepts of Marxist theory from the Chinese point of view, to justify its economic policies. The Communist Party of China has proceeded from China's realities and integrated the fundamental tenets of Marxism with these concrete realities, developing new ways of building socialism in China. It has argued that socialism is not incompatible with economic policies such as markets, free trade, or anything else that appears to work. In current Chinese Communist thinking, China is in the primary stage of socialism, and this redefinition allows the People's Republic of China (PRC) to justify the existence of an economic market. China's transition from planning towards a market system has many surprising features. The Communist regime remains intact. Reforms have meant a gradual erosion of state economic control rather than a quick retreat from planning. Reforms began with no clear objectives other than a determination to improve performance. Even Deng Xiaoping's dictum—"seek truth from facts and just do whatever seems to work" (a guiding principle for reforms), presents a false image and a great deal of uncertainty. The goal of creating a "socialist market economy with Chinese characteristics" is itself an outcome of the reform process that has emerged well into the second decade of transition.

China's hybrid economic system is a political economy with both socialist and capitalist characteristics (Lichtenstein 1992; Opper 2001; Qian 2000). It is not simply a socialist economy like the old Soviet model or Stalin economy, nor does it imitate Western capitalism; it has hybridized both features. To understand this, it is necessary to grasp some knowledge of how the administration is structured and how power and control are wielded by the Communist Party.

The evolution of economic reforms in China

The essential content of China's reforms is the transformation from a planned economy to a market-oriented economy under the political regime of socialism. Initially the intention of economic reforms at the early phase only focused on adjustments of economic policies to improve China's economic performance. Until the middle 1980s, the objective of market-orientation appeared to be clarified, but the means to achieve it remained equivocal and controversial. Many policies were implemented as experiments, and often resulted in political conflicts. The evolution of economic reforms in China can be systematically clarified in three phases over the past half century (see Wu 1985; 2003), described below.

First phase: administrative decentralization 1958–78

Since New China was established in 1949, after three years of economic recovery from the distortion of civil wars, the Communist Party of China proposed the general route of socialist construction and reformation for the transition to socialism. Mao (1953a: 89) described this general route as follows:

> Firstly, during a quite long period, it was to gradually realize the national socialist industrialization, constantly expand socialist economic forces,

in order to construct the lagging agriculture country to be an advanced industrial country. Secondly, it was to gradually realize the state's socialist reconstruction in agriculture, handicraft and industry.

The objective of this general route was the reconstruction of the institutions from privatized production to a socialist-owned regime, with the aim of rapidly increasing productivity. In line with this general route, the state implemented the first *Five Year Plan* (1953–7). The principle task was to rapidly industrialize through the construction of 694 major industrial enterprises (Li 2004; Peng et al. 2004: 6). This built the foundation for socialist industrial construction. The annual average industrial and agricultural GDP (gross domestic product) growth in these five years (1953–7) was 10.9 percent (Ren and Ren 1993: 335). In this period, the centralization of administration appeared to be an effective means of allocating and distributing resources to where they were most needed for the country's reconstruction.

At the end of 1957, Mao Zedong launched the "Great Leap Forward" in order to push the speed of industrialization. The reforms in 1958 were supposed to decentralize administration and give autonomy to enterprises and employees, as well as to local governments. Liu Shaoqi and Shun Zhifang were the main representatives for this proposition. However, Mao always advocated the "spiritual incentive" and opposed the "material incentive" for people, as he regarded this as the distinctive difference between capitalism and socialism. Therefore, giving autonomy to enterprises and employees was a contradiction to Mao's main ideology, as the empowerment would inevitably involve material incentive for enterprise management. It was criticized as "Yugoslavian Revisionism" and "Capitalist Individualism," which should be abandoned. Decentralization focused only on local government, which was all about the distribution of authority from the central administration. This decentralization of authority involved seven elements: "planning," "enterprise jurisdiction," "resources allocation," "administration of approval," "investment and loans on construction projects," "finance and taxation," and "labor management" (Wu 2003). With the prerequisite of a planned economy regime remaining unchanged, the decentralization of authority in layers of hierarchy to local governments formed the institutional infrastructure for the "Great Leap Forward." Under this institutional support, different levels of local governments fully utilized the authority of deploying resources to launch basic construction projects, to employ labor and to freely use peasants' material assets, in order to complete Mao's unrealized and impossible missions, such as "Double steel production in one year' 'Exceed Britain in three years and overtop America in ten years," etc. (Bo 1993: 679). The inevitable consequence was failure. The negative effects appeared in many aspects of the economy, such as a reduction in production, large losses in industrial and commercial enterprises, serious scarcities in the supply of subsistence consumer products, and a slump of the whole economy. Between 15 and 30 million people died from starvation and famine in 1959–61 (Ashton *et al.* 1984).

In 1962, the Communist Party remedied the chaos caused by decentralization, and returned authority back to the centralized government administration.

4 *Chinese market socialism: a summary account*

This allocated and deployed resources by executive commands from the Central Committee of the Party. However, decentralization allowed for the growth of local market relations. For instance, the creation of township-village enterprises (TVEs) was the outcome of this period of decentralization. Local governors utilized the power they were granted from administrative decentralization to support funding for the development of their own regional enterprises, in order to pursue local benefits and achieve target performance (Qian 2000). TVEs were cooperative agreements between local governments and enterprises, which represented mutual benefits. It was argued by Boisot and Child (1996) that at this time, this was more a network than a market economy in so far as it was built on a tight web of interpersonal obligations based on trust rather than on atomized competitive relations. It later became clear that the emergence of TVEs became a major contributor to rapid growth in GDP in China for the later development of a market-oriented economy. By 1991 these enterprises were producing almost 60 percent of the total output in the countryside, as measured in market terms (Gabriel 1998).

Second phase: incremental reforms 1979–93

After the Communist Party had failed to reform the state-owned economic sector and faced a standstill in the growth of the state economy, the main force of reform began to focus on the non-state economic sectors in order to provide opportunities for growth. This was called the "Incremental Reforms Strategy" (Wu 2003).

The creation of this Incremental Reforms Strategy was initiated in 1976 after the collapse of the "Gang of Four." When political power returned to the right wing of the Communist Party, the concept of state-owned enterprise reform was advocated by Shun Zhifang in 1957 and became promoted by the Party at this stage. In 1979, Xue Muqiao published his work—*A study of the problems in China's socialist economy*. This had a big impact on ideas of reform at this time. He argued that:

> The economic reform needed to solve two problems – one was reform of administrative institutions in the state-owned enterprises (including collective enterprises); the other was reforms of the state administration in order to make it adequate for large social production.
>
> (Xue 1979: 185)

Influenced by these ideas, experiments on extending autonomy to state-owned enterprises were implemented in Si Chuang province. Between 1978 and 1979, over 100 state-owned enterprises were adopted as "experimental units" in this province, achieving significant improvements in performance as a result. The experiments were then expanded nationwide. By the end of 1979, 4,200 state-owned enterprises had been reformed. By 1980, this had increased to 6,600 units and their productivity accounted for 60 percent of total budgeted national industrial productivity, and 70 percent of total national industrial and commercial profitability (Wu 2003: 57). However, this positive effect didn't last for long; the limitation of these reforms soon appeared. The operation of these enterprises with their new autonomy did not trade according to the rules of market competition, nor in relation to normal "supply and demand" pricing mechanisms of mature market economies. Therefore, the exertion of power and autonomy by these enterprises was not propitious to the effective deployment of economic resources.

An important turning point in economic reform took place in September 1980. Headed by Deng Xiaoping, the Communist Party introduced policies that allowed peasants to contract land for farming on the basis of individual/family responsibility. This replaced the model of the "peoples communes."[1] The TVEs, on the basis of collective ownership, began to prosper after this change. Since then, China has launched a series of reform strategies and policies that have distinguished it from Soviet Russia and Eastern Europe with their focus on state-owned economic sectors. China abandoned attempts to reform the state economy and transferred its focus to non-state sectors, where the market-oriented enterprises were embedded. Since then, the growth of non-state sectors has driven the development of the whole economy.

Generally speaking, the success of reforms in the rural non-state economic sectors encouraged the Communist Party take further steps in other sectors to promote the growth of the non-rural, non-state economy. An increasing number of "mixed-ownership" enterprises emerged along the coastal areas, including foreign joint ventures, and these became the main force for China's economic growth. The performance of this incremental strategy can be illustrated in three dimensions:

Promoting measures for the growth of the non-state economy

Whether the existence and further development of the non-state economy should be permitted was a politically sensitive issue in China. The socialist doctrines of Mao's era, such as "more communes and the larger the better"; "the task of communists is to vanish capitalism." (Mao 1953b: 298), still shaped people's thinking for a long time. This changed with the legitimation of land being contracted to individuals and families. The growth of TVEs also opened up the possibilities of a new form of socialism. Because the non-state-owned enterprises were market-oriented, not planned, their emergence and prosperity gradually formed regional markets in which market forces started playing an increasingly important role in deploying economic resources. By the middle of the 1980s, production in the non-state sectors accounted for one-third of total national production. In the retail industry, its growth was even faster (see Tables 1.1 and 1.2).

Developing liberal economic policies to establish trading links between regions and the international market

The market infrastructure was weak due to over thirty years of planned economy and the extent to which market forces had been almost extinguished. However, the reform leaders of the Party adopted an "open" strategy using the world market and foreign direct investment (FDI) to rapidly reform the domestic market in some regions. These selected regions (particularly along coastal areas with geographical

6 *Chinese market socialism: a summary account*

Table 1.1 The percentage of economic components in total industrial production of China (%)

Year	1978	1980	1985	1990
State-owned	77.6	76.0	64.9	54.6
Collective-owned	22.4	23.5	32.1	35.6
Others*	0.0	0.5	3.0	9.8

Sources: *China Statistics Year Book* (selected from varying years).

*Others included private-owned and foreign-invested joint ventures.

Table 1.2 The percentage of economic components in retail commercial sales of China (%)

Year	1978	1980	1985	1990
State-owned	54.6	51.4	40.4	39.6
Collective-owned	43.3	44.6	37.2	31.7
Others*	2.1	4.0	22.4	28.7

Sources: *China Statistics Year Book* (selected from varying years).

*Others included private-owned and foreign-invested joint ventures.

advantages) were connected to international markets through tailored regulatory environments. Competitive forces were then injected to facilitate the future development of domestic markets. This forced enterprises to participate in market forces of competition and enterprise managers had to gain market economy skills. Market mechanisms reinforced the imperative to improve quality and cost of products in order to gain competitive advantage for survival. Within this atmosphere of relatively free markets, achieving greater enterprise autonomy and improving the quality of management became essential issues. Participating in import and export trading also impacted upon domestic pricing systems.

Establishing experimental areas for regional development

The methodology of regional development was adopted as an effective way to create small "regions" of free market economy along coastal areas.[2] This was implemented in order to test the new reform policies, to examine the outcomes, and to see how effectively the new system of market economy could operate. These regions were mapped out as 'economic development zones' (EDZs). How these experimental economic zones operated is elaborated upon in page 14 of this chapter. Their existence has shaped the fundamental characteristics of Chinese market socialism.

THE "DUAL-TRACK SYSTEM"

The "dual-track approach" was created to allow the two paradigms – planned economy and market-oriented economy to coexist. It created a "track" of the market economy to allow for the purchase of raw materials and sales of products

Table 1.3 Percentage of transactions at market prices (by transaction volume) (%)

	Retail commodities			Agricultural commodities			Producer goods		
Year	Market	State guided	State fixed	Market	State guided	State fixed	Market	State guided	State fixed
1978	0	3	97	6	2	93	0	0	100
1985	34	19	47	40	23	37	13	23	64
1991	69	10	21	58	20	22	46	18	36
1995	89	2	9	79	4	17	78	6	16
1999	95	1	4	83	7	9	86	4	10
2001	96	1	3	94	3	3	88	3	10
2003	96	1	3	97	2	2	87	3	10

Source: *National Reform and Development Commission and Price Yearbook 2005.*

for non-state enterprises, outside the unified state planning system. Such a dualistic system was particularly embodied in the pricing system and in ownership institutions (Opper 2001). This is a distinctive feature of the Chinese socialist market system. Until the middle of 1980s, the non-state economy accounted for 30 percent of total industrial outputs (Table 1.2). They could not survive if there was no free market exchange. In January 1985, the State Price Bureau and Material Assets Bureau officially issued "the legal notice for permission on opening industrial production materials and self-sell products" (Wu 2003). Since then the "dual-track economic system" has been formally in operation. This approach has fostered the basic market environment for the non-state economy's growth and prosperity. It has matched the general strategy as an institution to promote the formation of a dominant market-oriented economy. Gradually, prices in the domestic market matched prices in international markets as the share of the non-state economy grew. At the beginning of the 1990s, planned commodity prices no longer dominated the domestic commodity circle. A countervailing tendency also existed, where trade and investment barriers between provinces grew, inhibiting interprovincial competition. This potential Balkanization could be observed at times during the late 1980s and early 1990s as the dual-track pricing system gradually phased out price controls (Young 2000; Xu and Voon 2003) (see Table 1.3). Most economists (Qian *et al.* 2006; Morphy *et al.* 1992) agree that this dualistic approach has had more advantages for the transition of China's economy.

Third phase: the growth of reforms since 1994

The theory of integral reforms

Starting in the middle of the 1980s, the reforms were pushed forward by Deng Xiaoping. The theory of "reforms in an all-round-way" was generated amid the process of designing reform plans for systems of price, taxation, and finance. The CPC realized that reforms were needed in all aspects of the economic system. The market economy should be a "totality," requiring every aspect of the economy in harmony. The only paradigm that could replace the command economy was the market-oriented economy, as it was the only mechanism available for effective resources deployment and distribution. A market economy as an organic system, is comprised of three main systems: (1) independent enterprises with self-operating systems and self-responsibility for loss and profit; (2) competitive market systems; and (3) macro-control systems operating via spontaneous market adjustments. These systems should be integrated, so reforms should be synchronously exerted in these three aspects (Wu 1985).

The measures and executory schemes for "reforms in all-round-way"

In November 1993, the fourteenth Plenary Session of the Communist Party Central Committee decided how to build a socialist commodity market system. This consisted of the following elements:[3]

(1) Reform of finance and taxation: The old revenue-sharing system was replaced by the implementation of a unified "Tax-sharing system" and "VAT" for central and local governments based on their administrative authority. A system of taxation was established to meet the needs of the market economy, in order to facilitate fair market competition, particularly national taxation laws.
(2) Reforms of finance and banking: A unified, open, fairly competitive and strictly managed financial system was established. The national banks remained as the mainstay, while other types of financial agencies were allowed to coexist. Concrete reforms were as follows:

   (a) the establishment of a "Central Banking System', to execute currency policy under the administration of the central government.
   (b) national banks were to be set up to operate as professional commercial banks and provide various business and financial services.
   (c) the setting up of specialist merchant banks for imports and exports, agriculture, etc. These were made responsible for providing low-interests loans for government-assigned projects.

(3) The setting-up of a system of foreign exchange administration: The government determined two steps for the reform of the foreign exchange system. The first step was to eliminate the double standards of the foreign exchange rate between domestic enterprises and foreign enterprises; to realize the merger of dual-tracks of exchange rate, so that the currency of Renminbi (RMB) could be partially convertible. The second step depending on the actual situation at the time, was to abolish control over capital flows and to realize RMB currency as fully convertible currency.
(4) The reform of state-owned enterprises: This proposed the "further conversion of mechanisms of operation in state-owned enterprises, establishing them as suitable modern co-operations with manifest efficiencies to meet the increasing demands of the market economy."

Table 1.4 The percentage of economic components in China's GDP share (%), 1990–2001

Year	State-owned	Collective-owned	Private-owned*
1990	47.7	18.5	33.8
1995	42.1	20.2	37.7
1996	40.4	21.3	38.3
1997	38.4	22.1	39.5
1998	38.9	19.3	41.9
1999	37.4	18.4	44.2
2000	37.3	16.5	46.2
2001	37.9	14.6	47.5

Source: *China Statistic Yearbook* (selected from various years).

*Private-owned in this table means the all the privately-owned enterprises. In other words, all non-state and non-collective-owned enterprises. But it excludes foreign-owned enterprises.

(5) The establishment of a new system of social security: This created an institutional system that comprised social insurance, welfare, medical insurance, a retirement system, etc.

Since 1994, state-owned and controlled enterprises are no longer the determining force of the economy, and the rapid growth and emergence of private enterprises has taken precedence in the evolution of market socialism. Table 1.4 demonstrates the rapid growth of the privately-owned sector, of which GDP share has increased from 33.8 percent in 1990 to 47 percent in 2001; accounting for almost half of total GDP. Such mixed ownership and control under state planning is one of the distinctive characteristics of Chinese state socialism.

Table 1.5 illustrates the main indicators of four types of enterprise as emergent economic components by a comparison of the period between 2003 and 2007. In the 2000s, China's employment pattern and economy has been characterized by the downsizing of the state sector and the fast-growing share of foreign direct investment companies and owner-managed private firms. For example, according to OECD (2010d), annual average employment in foreign joint ventures has increased from 15 percent to 23 percent and 38 percent to 50 percent in owner-managed private firms from 2003 to 2007, whereas employment has significantly declined from 37 percent to 22 percent in the state-owned sector. Foreign joint ventures are major employers and as a result, their employment policies and practices have a strong bearing on reshaping the pool of human resources and the experience of work for a significant proportion of workers in China (Cooke 2004). Alongside foreign joint ventures, there has been a rapid growth of private-owned enterprises. Overall, between 2003 and 2007, government policies allowed for a dramatic rise in the industrial output of domestic-owned private companies (Table 1.5). These figures demonstrate that the private economy has become the mainstream in Chinese market socialism and the state sector has lost its dominant role.

10 *Chinese market socialism: a summary account*

Table 1.5 The percentage of different economic components in China, 2003 and 2007

Main indicators/ year	Number of enterprises		Value-added industrial output		Total capital (fixed assets + inventory)		Employment (%)	
Four types of enterprises	2007	2003	2007	2003	2007	2003	2007	2003
State-owned and state-holding (incl. direct and indirect)	6.08	16.22	30.93	41.36	46.89	58.86	22.36	37.71
Collective-owned (employee cooperatives)	4.36	10.60	3.73	6.39	2.54	3.91	4.19	8.14
Private-owned/owner managed firms (domestic)	74.57	59.39	44.67	33.03	32.02	22.70	50.27	38.28
Foreign-invested/ foreign joint ventures (non-mainland)	14.97	13.79	20.67	19.22	18.55	14.52	23.18	15.87

Source: OECD Economic Surveys: China 2010 (The Relative Size of State-Enterprise Sector), StatLink: http://dx.doi.org/10.1787/778043783675.

Government institutions in the transformation to market socialism

Administrative structure of the Communist Party of China (CPC)

The Communist Party of China (CPC) has both central and local organizations. At the top is the Central Committee. When it is not in session, the Political Bureau and its Standing Committees exercise the power of the Central Committee. Both the Political Bureau and its Standing Committees are elected by the plenary session of the Central Committee. The National Party Congress is the Party's organ of supreme power; it is held once every five years, and is convened by the Central Committee. Its functions are: to hear and examine the report of the Central Committee; to hear and examine the report of the Central Commission for Discipline Inspection; to discuss and decide on major issues of the Party; to revise the Party constitution and to elect the Central Committee and the Central Commission for Discipline Inspection. The Central Committee is elected by the National Party Congress. When the National Party Congress is not in session, the Central Committee leads all the work of the Party and represents the CPC outside the Party. It is elected for a term of five years. The Political Bureau, its Standing Committee and the General Secretary are all elected by the plenary session of the Central Committee. When the plenum of the Central Committee is not in session, the Political Bureau and its Standing Committee exercise the functions and powers of the Central Committee. Under the Central Committee of the CPC are such offices and departments as the General Affairs Office, the Organization

Department, the Publicity Department, the International Liaison Department, the United Front Work Department, and the Policy Research Office.

Local organizations of the CPC include congresses of various provinces, autonomous regions, municipalities directly under the central government, cities with districts, autonomous prefectures, counties and cities without districts, as well as districts of cities. The committees elected by the congresses listed above serve a term of five years. Grassroots organizations of the Party, where there are more than three full members of the Party, are set up in enterprises, rural villages, organizations, schools, research institutes, neighbourhoods, the People's Liberation Army, companies and other basic units. The presidency of the People's Republic of China, as the head of the state, is an independent organ of the state which, as an office of state power itself does not decide on state affairs, but exercises its power according to decisions of the National People's Congress and its Standing Committee. Mass organizations are an important component of China's political institutions. Despite the fact that they are non-governmental organizations, the All-China Federation of Trade Unions, the Communist Youth League of China and the All-China Women's Federation exercise, to a fairly large extent, some of the functions of the government. As a result, the tasks, organizational setup, and posts of leaders of some mass organizations are decided by organs of the central authorities. For the same reason, these organizations receive appropriations from the state treasury for funding.

There are two major ideologies that compete with each other within the Communist Party. One is the "state economy" approach, which emphasizes the need to maintain state control over economic activity (Aoki and Jin 1997). The other is the "market economy" approach, which argues that the state should develop the economy through encouraging market forces (Wolf 1988). This is achieved by the state supporting enterprises associations, financial agencies, agriculture unions, and other activities to encourage marketing functions in the economy. The present Chinese government favors this latter approach.

In the 1980s, state-sponsored reforms were intended to make the existing central planning system more flexible and efficient by decentralizing the administrative system and by making state-owned enterprises more efficient. This meant the prohibition and restriction of the private economy and the free market, and promoted the mainstream system of public ownership. The all-round shift toward market economic reforms took place in 1992, after Deng Xiaoping clarified the concept of the market economy as the cardinal plank of government policy, to replace the state-planned, socialist economy. Deng Xiaoping[4] said:

> From the very outset there are different opinions concerning the establishment of special economic zones, fearing whether this meant practicing capitalism. Shenzhen's construction achievements have answered those having worries of one kind or another, the special zone is "socialist," not "capitalist" in nature. Judged from the situation in Shenzhen, public ownership is the mainstay, foreign investment accounts for only one-fourth. Take that part of foreign capital for example, we can benefit from taxation and labor service! Don't

be afraid of the establishment of more Sino-foreign cooperative enterprises, Sino-foreign joint ventures and solely foreign-owned businesses. We need not be afraid so long as we are clear-headed. We have advantages, large and medium-sized State-owned enterprises and township enterprises, more importantly; we have the political power in our own hands.

(China Daily, 2002:1)

Regarding the Shenzen economic zone, Deng Xiaoping also said:

The "four small dragons" (Hong Kong, Taiwan, Singapore and South Korea) in Asia have developed very rapidly, so has your development. Guangdong should strive to catch up with the "four small dragons" in Asia. In a 20-years' time... not only should we develop the economy, we should also create a good social order and a good social mood. We should surpass them in material development and cultural and ethical progress. This and this alone can be regarded as socialism with Chinese characteristics. Singaporean social order is good, because the country is under strict control; we should learn from its experiences and should exercise better management of society.

(China Daily, 2002:1)

Deng Xiaoping's 1992 speech confirmed the political direction of economic reforms, the relevant supporting policies, and the removal of several state constraints in the economic sphere. FDI and private enterprises began to grow rapidly, and a market system based on hybrid forms of ownership emerged with the government's approval. At the same time, the government retained ownership over its four heavy and vital industries; the State security industry; the natural resources monopoly; the public service and communal products sector; and high-technology (*China Daily* 2002). As the progress of market reforms could not take place by itself, it has been sponsored by the government. The accession to membership of the World Trade Organization (WTO) further urged and spurred the progress of both economic and political reforms in China.

Some key characteristics of Chinese market socialism

The Chinese characteristics of market socialism as advocated by the Communist Party can be summarized as follows:

(1) The essence of socialism is to liberate and develop productive forces, eliminate exploitation and polarization, and finally achieve common prosperity. To reach this goal, the CPC is committed to adhering to socialist principles, which remain vital for public ownership and the system of distribution. However, these principles also incorporate the need for markets and private ownership. This redefinition permits features of capitalism to coexist within a regime of state socialist control.

(2) China is at the primary stage of socialism and will remain so for a long period of time, because of the nature of Chinese society and its present stage of development. China has a large population and disparities in levels of development in different regions. Productive forces are also far from developed.
(3) China's economic system combines the basic socialist system with a market-oriented economy. In the process of exploring socialism, the full development of a commodity market economy is a phase that cannot be surpassed during socialist economic development. This is a breakthrough from traditional thinking, which considers that a planned economy equals socialism and a market economy equals capitalism. Besides, it is believed that there is no fundamental contradiction between socialism and a market economy. A market economy is indispensable to the allocation of resources in socialized production. Combining socialism with the market economy is an innovation of Marxist theory in a socialist economy. This significant innovation is a distinctive feature of the "China Model," which generates a hybrid market structure encompassing both public and private ownership.
(4) China is still in the process of building "rules of the game" for a market-oriented economy. This means that the market legal framework is incomplete. The coexistence of the planned economy and the market economy means that the government stills greatly interferes in market exchanges and transactions, and political factors influence the direction of the economy. Though economic reforms have allowed enterprises to independently operate in the market place, production materials, land, investment, funds, and loans are still controlled by either central or local governments and are allocated through government administration.
(5) Regional imbalances in economic developments have been generated from the implementation of government policies. Coastal economic clusters have not been caused by the spontaneous tendency of business clustering, but are artificially engendered by government policies for "economic zones for foreign investment." Foreign investments are forced to operate in these tailored zones as part of the experiments in the market-economy. As the market economy matures, these zones will disappear. However, they are still operated at the current stage of market socialism and represent a distinctive characteristic.
(6) The Communist Party of China emphasizes the need to build a socialist spiritual civilization (socialist, cultural, and ideological progress). A socialist spiritual civilization is a significant feature of socialist society. It is seen as an important goal and guarantee of modernization in China. The Party believes that socialism with Chinese characteristics can only be built on both material and cultural and ideological grounds. Economic development offers the material basis for spiritual development, while, in return, cultural and ideological progress provides the ideological motivating force and intellectual support. Since Mao's time, the construction of spiritual motivation, other than material stimulation, has been stressed as the main task of civilization. This tradition has never changed under the market economy and although the material

incentive has been proposed, spiritual civilization is still the original emphasis in Chinese society. It can be regarded as a cultural characteristic of Chinese market socialism.

So far, a socialist market economy in the primary stage has been established. The public sector of the economy, as a dominant economic component, has contracted and the reform of state-owned enterprises has steadily advanced. Non-public sectors of the economy such as the self-employed and private-owned sectors, including the foreign-owned sector, have rapidly developed. Market systems are being built and the state continues to improve its macro-control mechanism. The reform of finance, banking sectors, housing and governmental structures is proceeding.

Foreign direct investment and economic development

China's Open Door Policy towards foreign direct investment (FDI) was initiated as part of the overall reform launched by Deng Xiaoping in 1978.[5] From a general overview of China's market conditions for the past ten years (1992–2002), it was elaborated as a basic and featured development of the Chinese economy. The present methods of driving China's economic growth are to attract FDI and issue national bonds (for government spending), as well as to encourage export growth. What does the Chinese government do to attract FDI? What kind of foreign policy does the Chinese government implement to promote FDI, while seeking to protect its national industry from the severe impact of FDI inflows? How does this Open Door Policy fit into a socialist market economy? Basically, foreign policies are exerted under the principle of gradualism and have only been implemented in tailored Special Economic Zones, which are sometimes also called Economic Development Zones (EDZs). These are experimental areas for foreign investment. They offer preferential tax and administrative treatment to foreign firms locating there. Moreover, for the first time in modern Chinese history, wholly-owned foreign enterprises are permitted in EDZs. The regulations and constraints over FDI disclose the role of the regulatory environment over foreign investment, which is an important feature of the governance of market socialism.

As shown in Table 1.6, FDI into China gradually increased in volume from 1979 to 1991. For instance, in contrast, the number of foreign-invested projects had seen a sharp rise from 638 in 1983 to 12,978 in 1991, which showed almost an almost twentyfold increase. However, in this period, foreign enterprises in Economic Development Zones had tight restrictions. They were permitted to operate only within the geographical area designated as Economic Development Zones. Naturally their businesses were confined to "passing trades," in which they bring in intermediate inputs from overseas, process them, and export the final products to other countries. Although they were given preferential treatment for imports and exports, foreign enterprises were not allowed to transfer the foreign exchanges they earned to the source country directly unless this was approved by the National Tax Bureau (NTB) and Foreign Currency Administration Bureau (FCAB). We

Table 1.6 FDI stock from 1979 to 1991

			Unit: US$ 100 million
Year	No. of projects	Contractual value[1]	Realized value[2]
1979–1982	920	49.58	17.69
1983	638	19.17	9.16
1984	2,166	28.75	14.19
1985	3,073	63.33	19.56
1986	1,498	33.30	22.44
1987	2,233	37.09	23.14
1988	5,945	52.97	31.94
1989	5,779	56.00	33.93
1990	7,273	65.96	34.87
1991	12,978	119.77	43.66
Total	42,503	525.92	250.58

Source: *China Statistics Yearbook 2000*.

[1] Contractual value means the value of contracts between foreign-invested companies and Chinese companies/governments signed for investment intention.
[2] Realized value means the value of foreign investments has been actually implemented and arrived according to the contracts.

may call this the first phase in China's open door policy towards FDI (Branstetter and Feenstra 2002).

The second phase corresponds to the period since 1992, when the decision to join WTO was made by the government. A series of deregulations on FDI were introduced in this period. There was a surge in FDI, as can be seen in realized value of foreign direct investment, which increased almost ten times from 110.08 in 1992 to 1088.21 in 2010 (Table 1.7). The trend of FDI inflows has steadily grown year by year, from 2005 to 2011 (see Figure 1.1). They totaled US$106 billion in 2010 and US$116 billion in 2011.

Foreign investment industries are classified into three groups: foreign capital encouraged industries, foreign capital restricted industries, and foreign capital prohibited industries. The first type of industry enjoys additional incentives beyond those that are already accorded to foreign investors, which include conservation of material and energy, and technology-intensive investments (such as agricultural and environmental technology); projects that improve product quality and raw-material efficiency; development of energy, communications, and essential raw materials; products in short supply and urgent need domestically; export-oriented industries; substitutes for imports (which save hard currency); and projects in central and western regions inland. "Restricted foreign investment industries" are those in which Chinese partners usually have to be the holding parties or play "leading roles" in any joint venture. Restricted projects include industries that already are fairly well established in China; sectors that are open on an experimental basis; the exploration of rare and valuable mineral resources; as well as industries subject to overall state planning, such as

Table 1.7 FDI stock from 1992 to 2010

Unit: US$ 100 million

Year	No. of projects	Contractual value	Realized value
1992	48,764	581.24	110.08
1993	83,437	1114.36	275.15
1994	47,549	826.80	337.67
1995	37,011	912.82	375.21
1996	24,556	732.76	417.26
1997	21,001	510.03	452.57
1998	19,799	521.02	454.63
1999	16,918	412.23	403.19
2000	22,347	711.30	593.56
2001	26,140	719.76	496.72
2002	34,171	847.51	550.11
2003	41,081	1,169.01	561.40
2004	43,664	1,565.88	640.72
2005	44,001	1,925.93	638.05
2006	41,473	716.48	670.76
2007	37,871	853.45	783.39
2008	27,514	1,130.15	952.04
2009	23,435	1,336.82	918.04
2010	27,406	1,430.92	1,088.21

Source: China Statistics Yearbook 1998, 2003, 2006, 2012: 233[6]

grains, pharmaceutical, wholesale and retail, financial services and broadcasting. Furthermore, for political, economic, or national-security reasons, foreign capital is not permitted into traditional indigenous industries, such as electricity and gas, and education and broadcasting, and those that are regarded as a threat to state security, as environmentally damaging, or as involving products made with national-proprietary technology (Schlevogt 2000).

There are two modes of entry for foreign affiliated enterprises in China: wholly-owned subsidiaries and joint ventures. Joint ventures (JV) can be broken into several sub-modes based on the percentage ownership of the equity: foreign majority-owned joint venture, equally-owned joint venture, and foreign minority-owned joint venture. These entry modes can be utilized by multinational corporations (MNCs) through their acquisition of an existing enterprise, or by setting up a new enterprise in the Economic Development Zones. However, foreign enterprises are not restricted to Economic Development Zones and their dividends are transferable. But their earnings need to be defined as net income after tax clearances by the National Tax Bureau and Foreign Currency Administration Council before they are allowed to be transferred to the foreign exchanges of their home countries.

The laws applying to FDI development in China are often unclear and are the result of its recent economic development. China, as a socialist market country, has

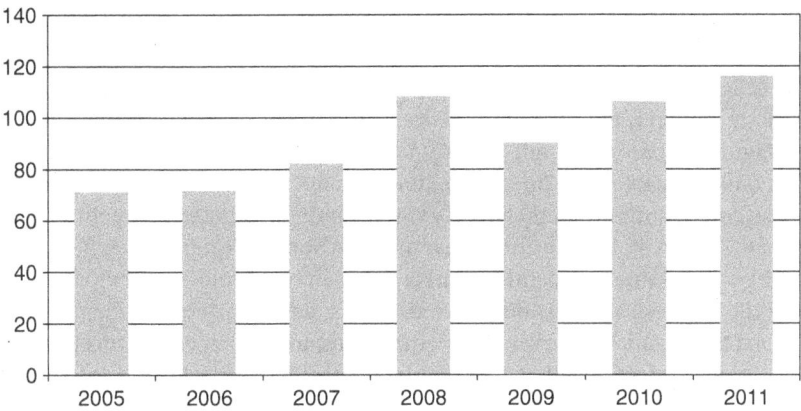

Figure 1.1 Annual FDI inflows to China, 2005–2011.
Source: United Nations Conference on Trade and Investment in China.
Note: Morrison, W. M. (2012), "China's Economic Conditions," Congressional Research Service (CRS), June 26, 2012 (www.crs.gov).

no available model of how to develop a successful socialist market economy. Deng Xiaoping has described the situation of China's Open Door Policy, as follows: "For the reform of Chinese economy, we have to grope the stones by our hands in this river in order to cross it," and "Whatever black or white cat, the one who is able to catch the rat is the best cat." These words simply describe the direction of China's Open Door Policy. Although it has no available model to adopt, the experiment of creating this model and gathering experience through a gradual "opening up" of the market is the method adopted by the Chinese government. It is the reason for setting up the Economic Development Zones in China, which are then used as experimental areas for new policies and developing models.

For the last two decades, China has had important policies to attract FDI such as beneficial tax policies, economic zones' policies, export promotion policies for foreign-invested enterprises, and a regulated value of the currency, etc. These policies have given foreign-invested joint ventures special treatment in areas such as profit taxes policy and intermediate-inputs import tariff remission. At the same time, important incentives for foreign-invested joint ventures to export their production have been also developed. However, China has imposed legal and de facto restrictions to limit foreign access to domestic markets. Indeed, many of the benefits just mentioned are conditional on export performance. Free Trade Zones (FTZs) are mainly located in Economic Development Zones (EDZs) where they have easy access to foreign markets. Meanwhile, domestic firms like state-owned enterprises (SOEs) and collective-owned enterprises (COEs) enjoy several protectionist measures but do not share many of the benefits directed at foreign firms. Native firms sell mainly in protected local markets and increasing competition from state-owned enterprises and collective-owned enterprises has taken place. To sustain its commitment to full employment and high production, the government has directed increasing amounts of credit to state-owned enterprises. A smooth opening up of domestic markets has been taking place, but the biggest step has yet to be implemented: the removal of special protective policies for domestic firms in general and state-owned firms in particular. However, the removal of all non-tariff barriers is not an easy task to complete due to China's dual-track economic structure. The opening of domestic markets to foreign production introduces competition in markets. This significantly affects the competitive position of native firms if foreign firms have more advanced technologies (Claro 2002). A larger, domestic competitive market will emerge. More competitors will come into the Chinese market and more domestic and joint venture companies will expand their markets to overseas. For the latter trend, domestic firms have to face the serious test of whether they are competent to compete in the international market.

About 65 percent of China's population lives in the countryside. And yet China's agricultural sector only generates 16 percent of the country's GDP—in sharp contrast to the 50 percent it generated fifty years ago. China's rural economic system has been guided by its mandatory grain-purchase system, with the production and cropping patterns determined and planned by the central government. This system has been changed gradually to a market-driven economy since liberal economic policies have been implemented. Chinese government support to agricultural products increased from 3 percent in 1995–7 to 11 percent in 2008–11, however, this is still well below the OECD average of 20 percent in 2008–10 (OECD 2012: 14). Since accession to the WTO in 2001, China has gradually engaged in free international trade of agricultural products, which means its agriculture is subject to global changes in prices, market accessibility, trade structure, and trade rules concerning agricultural products.

The impact on the agricultural sector is seen in the benefits from preferential treatment in free trade (especially in tariff reduction) enjoyed by all signatory countries to GATT (General Agreement on Tariffs and Trade). China can unconditionally obtain the most-favored-nation status in common with all WTO members. This gives China a better opportunity to tap international agricultural resources and markets. It also accelerates its agriculture reforms and establishes an agricultural macro-control system compatible with the market economy, thus enhancing the production of agricultural products and sharpening the competitive edge of China's farm products in the international market (Zhu 2006).

The negative impact on the agricultural sector is seen in the competition arising in the domestic market, created by the entry of foreign firms. As China has to open its domestic market and revoke all non-tariff restrictions on imported farm products, the government's protective policies on domestic farm products are being gradually phased out. Foreign agricultural products at lower prices are set to pose great challenges to their Chinese counterparts. The flood of foreign farm products into China puts heavy pressure on the country's foreign exchange reserve, the financial source of imports (Zhu 2006).

China's WTO tariff commitments vary according to products and industry sectors. The government has gradually reduced tariffs, non-tariffs measures, licenses and quotas. Between 2000 and 2005, applied Chinese tariffs declined on average by 7 percentage points, with a wide variation in tariff changes across manufacturing industries (Bas and Causa 2012: 8). This has implications for domestically-operated firms as they benefit from both a relative reduction in the costs of imported intermediary goods and the availability of new imported input varieties. Trade liberalization has inevitably affected processing and assembling trade through competition effects (Ge *et al.* 2011). China has used tariff-rate quotas (TRQs) to protect domestic production of some agricultural commodities, including wheat, corn, rice, soybean oil, cotton, and sugar. According to agreements with WTO, China must restrict domestic support to its farmers to 8.5 percent of the value of the specific crop. China maintains state import rights for some agricultural goods, including wheat, corn, rice, sugar, cotton, soybean oil, and tobacco. Foreign-invested enterprises in this sector have been able to distribute imported and domestically-produced agricultural goods since 2003. Foreign majority ownership was allowed in 2004, with no geographical or quantitative restrictions, and wholly foreign-owned enterprises were permitted in 2005. Foreign direct investment has played an important part in driving China's economic transformation in the past decades, accounting for as much as 17.3 percent of all investment in China in 1994 (EIU 2004: 32). During the 1980s and 1990s FDI was attracted to China by generous tax incentives provided by the government, and by a seemingly infinite supply of cheap labor. The attraction of these benefits seemed to be fading by the late 1990s, as investors realized that chaotic rules and poor infrastructure made it hard to turn a profit in China (Ma 2003). Entry into the WTO has created a more rule-based system as well as opening up to FDI previously restricted areas of the economy. This seems to have revived foreign investor interest in China. According to the Chinese government, annual FDI inflows into China grew from US$108 billion in 2008 to US$116 billion in 2011 (Morrison 2012: 12).

The challenges facing market socialism

China's transition is characterized by "gradualism" and "a market growing outside of the regime." Administrative decentralization and the expansion of managerial autonomy and incentives for state-owned enterprises has introduced major market-based reforms in the economy since 1979. This gradualist transition has led to the extraordinary development of the non-state sectors, replacing the role of the state sector in industry at the core of the economy, and to the governance of the economy, in large part, by market forces.

The extraordinary reforms in China have introduced huge changes to the economy. At the same time, it is quite natural that problems have emerged. Chairman Hu Jintao has admitted that: "China's economic infrastructure is weak, productivity is low and development is extremely unbalanced." This notwithstanding, China is still facing up to painful challenges such as further privatization of state-owned enterprises, institutional restructuring in the banking sector, tax reforms, actions on property right protection, and control of the growing economy. How successfully China completes these challenges will determine its international status not only in Asia but also on the world economic stage. The unfinished reforms of state-owned enterprises and the restructuring of the banking sectors are core challenges for the Chinese government at present. However, they remain demanding tasks for the Communist Party of China, since these require the application of international standards and laws in banking systems. The ultimate goal of China's reforms is to improve the efficiency of the utilization of resources. However, state-owned enterprises, as dominant forces in economy, have been operating with very low efficiency for a long time. Although the reforms of state-owned enterprises, began in 1978, producing greater operating autonomy to enterprises, their losses have increased due to institutional constraints. For example, losses for independent state-owned enterprises amounted to 42 billion RMB in 1978 but by 1997 the loss had significantly increased to 741 billion RMB (Lardy 1999: 42). The State Ministry of Finance and state-owned banks have extended loans to these loss-making sectors to keep them from bankruptcy. Such "soft budget constraints" within the financial sector can have disastrous effects for the entire economy (Stiglitz 1994). Kornai (1992) has pointed out that the major reason for the poor performance of state-owned enterprises is their "soft budget constraints" as the slow reform of state-owned enterprises and the slow reform of state-owned banks are closely linked. The transformation of state-owned enterprises and their structural readjustments have reached a crucial stage, filled with deeply-rooted contradictions and emerging problems. The major contradiction between a planned political regime and the demand for enterprise autonomous operations for a market-oriented economy is the cause for many of these problems. A considerable number of state-owned enterprises have not yet adapted to the demands of the market economy. They are not flexible in terms of structural change; weak in technological innovation; heavily in debt; carry social burdens; and have a large number of surplus employees and difficulties in production and business operations.

Gao, president of the Economic reform foundation in China commented:

> It is imperative to take practical and effective measures to solve these problems. This has a vital bearing not only on the success or failure of state-owned enterprises reform, but also on that of the overall economic restructuring of the country. Thus, a number of active measures need to be implemented in order to eliminate the barriers of further economic development, facilitate market competition, and promote technological progress so as to provide good management systems and a sound legal environment.
>
> (Wang 2000: 8)

State-owned enterprises have experienced three stages of reform over the last 20 years. The first stage started with an experiment in 1980, which focused on restructuring incentive systems for state firms and giving autonomy to managers to produce products for the market and outside the planning system (Hay et al. 1994). The second stage focused on the development of both products and markets, and property-rights reform. In contrast, the third stage corporatized state-owned enterprises (Lin 2001) and created a diversified ownership structure in the industry by implementing a 2-R reform strategy—*Retain* state ownership structure in strategic sectors for large enterprises, and *Retreat* from state control of small and medium size firms that operate in highly competitive markets (Liu and Woo 2001).

At the third stage of reform, corporate governance and clarity of ownership were major issues in the reform of SOEs. First, some serious problems were in need of further solutions. Lack of clarity of property rights and ambiguity of ownership were caused by the lack of relevant laws. Second, there was often little change in state-owned enterprises management structures after corporatization. The state still had full control and the capacity for intervention until 2001. This was directly administered by a government department. The directors/managers were actually more likely to be bureaucrats and not entrepreneurs, and were appointed by the administrative bureau. The selection of management was based on their rank in the state bureaucratic hierarchy. They often lacked management skills and incentives, and they were often politically motivated. This situation led to inefficiency, low productivity, and sometimes, corruption (Putterman and Dong 2000). Provinces within China, where the state controlled a large percentage of production, were notorious for their shoddy goods, high pollution levels, and ever increasing losses. Shanxi, Guangzhou, Yunnan, Qinghai, Ningxia, and Xinjang top the list of the least productive provinces with the state controlling 60–80 percent of the industry. Shanghai, directly controlled by Beijing, grew at an average of 6 percent, the lowest of all areas. Regions with less state control and more foreign investment reached 16.9 percent. While SOEs creating these problems were drastically over-staffed, they lacked the ability to reform and streamline their business structures. These were the main issues to be resolved in the third stage of reform.

Since these three stages of reform, some improvements are evident within the state-owned enterprise sector. For example, a more diversified ownership structure in the industrial sector has emerged since the late 1990s: wholly state-owned firms (44 percent of total industrial sales in 1997), collective-owned firms (26 percent of sales), and mixed state- and privately-owned firms (24 percent of sales, and wholly privately-owned firms (6 percent of sales) (Liu and Garino 2001: 35). The focus on enterprise autonomy, incentives, management, and competition has created a more market-oriented economy. Many large-sized, state-owned enterprises have achieved significant improvements in their performances in both domestic and international markets, for example, Haier, Lenovo, TCL, Cherry, and China Petrol. Between 2001 and 2010, these state-owned corporations have made successful mergers and purchases overseas with billions of US dollars. In 2010, Cherry Automobile was identified by Fortune magazine as one of the "Most Admirable Chinese Companies" for the fifth consecutive year. Haier Electronics has experienced strong growth from 2001 to 2010, and *Appliance Magazine* reported that its sales were up by 178 percent and net profit was up by 114 percent by the end of 2010 (*Appliance Magazine* April 12).

Despite the fact that the number of state-owned and state-holding enterprises has significantly declined by 57 percent from 64,737 in 1998 to 27,477 in 2005, and the number of employed persons has reduced by 50 percent, the gross industrial output value, total assets, and quality of management have considerably improved in the state-controlled enterprises (Zhang and Zheng 2008; Zou and Ouyang 2008). These figures reveal how reforms have improved the efficiency of production and effectiveness of management in the state sector. Total profits in state-owned and state-controlled enterprises have dramatically jumped sixteen times, from RMB 525.14 million (US$75.02 million) in 1998, to RMB 8485.46 million (US$1212.20 million) in 2006; and the total liabilities have also almost doubled in 2006 compared with 1998 (CYS 2007). This reflects the effect of profit-driven policies applied to state-owned enterprises, which has significantly pushed the profitability of the latter in the short term, but has also generated side effects and challenges for their long term competitiveness, such as myopia of the market, stunted governance structure, lack of sustainable competitive advantage, and over-dependence on government aid.

Although most centrally controlled state-owned enterprises have been corporatized and public-listed, they are subject to political interference and administrative responsibilities. They still undertake social responsibilities and staff welfare and whether this social burden can be stripped out depends on a series of changes in the external environment and in government policies. If problems such as price inflation, poor industrial structure and an undeveloped labor market cannot be dispelled through policy reform, the transition of state-owned enterprises can only cause inflation, unemployment and other problems (Otsuka *et al.* 1998; Lardy 2003).

The development of the market economy has been unbalanced, with most industries clustered in the eastern coastal regions, where most foreign companies have set up business. In 2010, the trend of economic disparities in regional development became even greater by comparison with 2002 (OECD 2012). This could disadvantage the whole development of the nation, and increase the disparity of income distribution. In 2011, exports in ten provinces account for 87.9 percent of the total exports of China with Sichuan, Xinjiang, Heilongjiang, inner-Mongolia, and Shanxi the fastest growing provinces (CYS 2011). The west of China and the inner-lands, especially the extreme north and the mountain areas, have remained undeveloped. This is not only caused by the poor transportation infrastructure, local bureaucracy and resource issues, but, in addition, telecom services and communication systems may also be of too poor a quality to attract foreign direct investment (FDI) and international trading. Furthermore, guided by the gradualist approach, the Chinese central government deliberately prioritized selected cities with geographical advantages (e.g. coastal areas and harbor cities) to experiment with its Open Door Policies in the early phases of "free" market development, which consequently created developmental gaps between the frontiers and those stunted regions. Due to this unbalanced infrastructural and economic development over decades, centralized government macroeconomic policies cannot be applied to all areas, which reinforces many existing regional imbalances.

Paradoxes in regulation and deregulation

Deregulation is urgently needed in many sectors, in order to achieve a complete market-oriented economy. In China, besides still the highly-regulated state sector, limited areas for entry of outsiders and foreigners exist. Constraints in foreign currency exchange create obstacles for the operation of foreign firms in China. The restricted foreign exchange capital market has hampered domestic enterprises from accessing international capital markets. Such high regulations lead to the existence of the so-called "informal economy," where a great number of firms operate "under cover."[7] For example, since China has severely restricted the exchange of foreign currencies, a black market has emerged to meet the market demand. This not only generates profiteering for speculators but also leads to the corruption of banking staff, who have control over foreign currency cash, because this business requires collaboration between them. There are more examples. When the market is highly regulated, not only can it create an informal economy, but it can also promote the abuse of power of State officials. When government officials have too much control over the rules and laws of the market, there is potential for corruption and illegal practices. For foreigners doing business in China the "Guanxi" network exists in the marketplace. This is often known as "no Guanxi, no business" (Zheng 2012). It cannot be denied that such a highly-regulated environment has played a crucial role in forming such relationship networks. According to the OECD 2002, the influence and function of "Guanxi" relationships seems to get weaker as market deregulation deepens and a more formal market environment emerges. It remains to be seen if this will occur in China. In Chapter 3, Guanxi, as an important concept of Chinese business networks, is further discussed in relation to different types of emerging business venture.

Concluding remarks

This chapter outlines the characteristics of market socialism in China in order to understand the multitude of variables and dynamics, institutions, characteristics, social, political, and economic systems that shape this market. Since China is formally a socialist country, it has a unique development history, constituting a hybrid model of capitalism and socialism, and the coexistence of both a planned and a market-oriented economy. Furthermore, this hybrid market model also has a historical and culturally rich inheritance, e.g. Confucianism, Taoism and Maoism, feudalism, etc. This explains why many Western theories and models of economic transition, to a certain extent, become inapplicable to the Chinese context, as these were developed in a different market context.

This chapter has reviewed key forces in the changing business environment in China. It has discussed how government politicians and policies are generating a socialist market economy with dynamic growth rates. Through decades of reform, a hybrid market structure has emerged, which encompasses both public ownership and private ownership, under a combined regime of both planned and market economies. By joining the WTO and continuously absorbing FDI, new opportunities and threats have been created that impact upon local business strategies and management styles. The inevitable trend of globalization and further market liberation, progresses towards the development of a more mature market economy. Under this changing macro environment, the process of state sector restructuring is ongoing and it remains a dominant force in shaping market competition. These characteristics of market socialism are the influencing factors that shape Chinese management practices, and the understanding of these is essential to understanding the characteristics of Chinese enterprises and management structures and processes; this is the subject of the next chapter. Macro economic transformations have led to the emergence of new types of business venture that will be examined from both macro and micro economic perspectives. The case studies introduced in Chapters 4, 5, and 6 will illustrate how these are characterized by specific and contrasting strategies and operational processes, but before these are discussed, theories and practices of enterprise management are reviewed by reference to their applicability to the conditions of Chinese market socialism.

Notes

1 The Communist Party of China (CPC) "Anthology of important literatures since the Third Plenary Congress" (1982) The People's Press, Beijing, p. 507. The people's commune is the regime of communal society, where all the people work in the communal village unit and equally share the surplus. All property, particularly the land and productive tools, belongs to the commune. The peasant does not own any piece of land. Under the new paradigm, contracted responsibility breaks this situation and allows the peasant to contract a piece of land based on the family or individual unit. He is responsible for both loss and gain, with the commitment of a fixed submission of annual gain.
2 The coastal areas of China have natural geographical advantages with the great convenience of transportation, communication and market infrastructures. Throughout history, these geographical advantages always lead to the advanced development of these areas compared with interior regions.
3 These are summarized and referenced from the literature archives on the official websites: www.chinatoday.com, www.china.org.cn and www.china-un.org (accessed 26 September, 2012).
4 http://app1.chinadaily.com.cn/highlights/party16/leaders/dengtour.htm (accessed 8 October, 2012).
5 The turning point was the eleventh general assembly of the Central Committee of the Chinese Communist Party, in which the legacy of the Cultural Revolution was officially repudiated and a resolution was adapted to the effect that emphasis would be placed on the modernization of socialism in the policies, to start in 1979.
6 *China Statistics Yearbook 2012*, 'Chapter 6-1 Foreign Trade and Economic Cooperation', National Bureau of Statistics of China, China Statistics Press, Beijing, p. 233.
7 The hidden dangers mean that unexposed illegal businesses exist informally in certain market segments, which are highly regulated, but such an informal economy contains danger and harm for the formal economy and becomes the counterpart for formal laws, although the dangers are apparently hidden.

2 Entrepreneurial growth and ownership

Introduction

The aim of this chapter is to explain entrepreneurship, privatization, ownership, and government policies in relation to institutional revolution in China's economic transition. The evolution of economic enterprises in China is examined in this historical context because this legacy has shaped many of the present features of management in the contemporary China. For decades there has been perennial interest in entrepreneurial growth from academics, practitioners, and policy makers alike. Entrepreneurship in emerging economies differs fundamentally compared with that in mature economies, where market orientation, economic development levels, market systems, and ownership configuration are contrasting differences that are likely to affect entrepreneurial interactions and outcomes (Bruton *et al.* 2008). China's institutional revolution has created a unique context for studying entrepreneurship and small business growth. The rise of the private sector and rapid growth of the "free" market economy entails diversified types of business venture whose interplay continuously shapes the specificity of market socialism. These are (1) indigenous entrepreneurial ventures; (2) foreign joint ventures; (3) collective-owned enterprises; and (4) reshuffled state-owned enterprises. These major types of ownership have evolved with economic reforms and are influenced by such forces as privatization, restructuring of state sector, technology advancement, World Trade Organization accession, globalization, and the infusion of foreign direct investment. The economic process in China is one of multifaceted and state-sponsored reform of market forces (Sheehan *et al.* 2000).

This chapter assesses the effects of privatization and entrepreneurial growth of different types of business venture under market socialism. It starts with an explanation of institutional change and the role of Chinese Communist Party and its policy development. It then provides a detailed account of the institutional and organizational change of state-owned enterprises in the state sector. The development and growth of private enterprises and foreign-invested enterprises in the private sector is further elaborated to depict an overview of growing entrepreneurialism in relation to changing government policies under market socialism in China.

The role of government policies and the Chinese Communist Party

It is evident that China's economy has achieved a rapid and sustained growth after nearly three decades of economic reform and revolutionary de-institutionalization, during which the state has played a crucial role (Zheng and Scase 2013; Milana and Wu 2012). Free enterprise and entrepreneurship are essential for sustainable economic growth, particularly in China, where entrepreneurial growth in association with the emergence of the private sector has been a driving engine for the establishment of a "free" market economy. Institutions influencing entrepreneurial development are undergoing a significant transformation in China. Before 1978, private enterprises and free-market exchange were regarded as "capitalist tails" that were forbidden and punished by the state (Wu 2003; Kshetri 2007). Since 1979, the Chinese Communist Party, headed by Deng Xiaoping, has officially launched reforms in the direction of a market economy. This was a breakthrough in the old totally planned economy and it endorsed the role of free-market functions under socialism. The first phase of transition was from 1979 to 1993, and this marked the initial formation of a market economy in which management practices with diversified ownership forms emerged under a "dual-track" economic system. This was consolidated after 1993, following the adoption of open-door policies, and foreign direct investment absorption. Despite the Open Door Policy and advocacy of "market elements" in the economy during the 1990s, "entrepreneurs" were often regarded as pertaining to an "inferior class" and particularly referred to those who were not able to find other jobs (e.g. those with criminal records or the poorly educated) (Nair 1996). Nowadays (since 2000), China has earned a reputation as one of the world's most entrepreneur-friendly countries (America 2007; Kshetri 2007). Indeed, entrepreneurialism is booming in China (Gangemi 2007). From 2000 to 2010, business start-up rates have increased twelve-fold (see Figure 2.1). This contrasting ideological change over three decades reflects the institutional revolution that has been led by the Chinese Communist Party and its policies.

Clearly, one of the most notable features of China's transition to a state-controlled market economy is the liberalization of market relations. However, its model distinctively differs from those of its counterparts in Eastern Europe, such as Russia, Romania, and Bulgaria. Chinese political leaders have chosen an "incremental" approach in deregulating price controls and allowing the emergence of competitive markets (Opper 2001; Yang 2002). Since 1978, previously prohibited enterprises of private and foreign forms of ownership have been permitted to compete against state-owned enterprises (SOEs) (Wu 2003; Steinfeld 1998). In order to develop a market economy, China's reform-minded policy makers have sought to realize the potential gains from furthering the transformation of enterprise ownership within political "command" parameters. By permitting the partial divestiture and privatization of a majority of state and cooperative-owned enterprises, as part of the process of institutional development (Sheehan *et al.* 2000), the Communist Party has created a quasi-competitive market environment that involves a variety of players (Peng *et al.* 2004; Liu and Garino 2001).

Unlike Western capitalist economies, key actors in China's socialist market economy are a significant number of state-controlled and state-owned economic institutions. These are, for example, dominant in such sectors as banking, telecommunications and the media industries, all of which are protected from private ownership (OECD 2010). There are also majority government stakes in larger, newly-formed limited liability corporations (state-owned enterprises, SOEs), which are subject to supervision of the state-owned State Assets Supervision and Administration Commission (SASAC) and various government ministries. These SOEs derive many advantages from government ownership, since they have direct contacts with decision-making ministerial bodies. Such direct dealings can lead to laws that reduce taxes, restrict competition in the domestic markets, and curb the import strategies of foreign companies (Lai 2010). It is also possible, because of these "intimate" relations between SOEs and central government bodies, these enterprises are able to influence the government-controlled Central Bank to preserve a low-valued RMB and thereby protect Chinese exports (Kennedy 2005; Langlois 2004).

China is a single communist party system that has entrenched political controls over resources at both national and local levels. At the same time, local provincial authorities have considerable power in law enforcement, market regulation and economic management. This is enabled by the central government retaining direct control over the appointment of provincial leaders and closely monitoring their performance (Lai 2006; Huang 1996; Li 2004). Even so, this "duality" of organizational processes can lead to corruption and bureaucratic inefficiencies. Local officials have considerable discretion in collecting taxes, providing health care and controlling funds for regional development projects. Corruption is regarded as one of the most damaging political side effects in the reform era of China's market socialism. For example, between 1997 and 2002, 846,000 Party members and ninety-eight provincial or ministerial-level officials were disciplined for corruption, up by 27 percent from 1992 (Lai 2006: 249).

The distinctiveness of Chinese market socialism means that government policies shape general market forces, the macro-business environment, and the legal rules of the game (Child and Tse 2001). Socialist values are deeply embedded in Chinese society and their institutional heritage is significant in shaping the nature of the market economy (North 1990). For example, all senior managers in state-owned enterprises must be Communist Party members and they are required to participate in intensive training programs of socialist ideology and Party ideas on a regular basis each year in order to have a firm grasp of socialist values. This historical heritage and the specific Chinese institutional characteristics are uniquely different from those of Western capitalism and other post-communist countries (Davis and Scase 1985; Giddens 1971). Russia's "big bang reform" strategy, for example, led to the sudden collapse of state socialism, with the effect that its economy is now dominated by oligopolies run by former state bureaucrats and senior managers of state enterprises (Lai 2006). China's gradualist policy has navigated a steady path towards diversified ownership structure. Its piecemeal adoption of the institutions of a market economy has, on the one hand, ensured stabilized and continuous economic growth but, on the other, created economic disparities between regions, cities, and provinces (Huang *et al.* 2003; Li 2010). Although the state-owned sector of the economy has been dramatically reduced, SOEs still constitute a significant share of the total economy. According to OECD (2010: 106), by 2007, despite only accounting for 6 percent of firms, SOEs produced 31 percent of the value-added industrial output, employed 22 percent of the workforce and controlled 47 percent of the stock of fixed assets, suggesting that they are prone to being relatively large and capital intensive. The extent of state control in China and Russia is more than twice as high as any other OECD country, as a result of the high degree of both state ownership and government involvement in business operations (OECD 2010: 113). This reflects a major objective of Communist Party policies. Tensions between "state" and "market" socialism are, nevertheless, becoming prominent as market reforms deepen and, as such, challenge the political and cultural underpinnings of the centralized political regime.

It is evident that the policy focus on enterprise autonomy, incentives, management and competition has created a more market-oriented economy. From 1999 to 2007, labor productivity growth is higher in the state-owned industrial sector than the private sector—5.6 percent versus 3.6 percent per year respectively (OECD 2010d: 110). Many large state-owned enterprises have achieved significant improvement in their performance in both domestic and international markets. As witnessed, for example, by the success of the Haier Group, Changhong Electronics Group, Shanghai Haixin Group, Huali Electronics Group, Shenzhen Mingda Electronics Co., TCL Electronics Corp., and Petrol China. These state-owned corporations have made successful mergers and purchases overseas worth billions of US dollars (Zhang 2003: 64).

The restructuring of the state-owned sector: political, institutional, and organizational changes

Historically, following administrative decentralization in the 1960s, the state-owned enterprises and collective-owned enterprises were managed by local governments and they were given a certain degree of operational autonomy. The contract-responsibility system was replaced by a modern corporate system in which the state was entitled to a dividend on its shares in state-owned enterprises' assets. Having fulfilled their compulsory delivery obligations, state-owned enterprises were allowed to sell their above-quota outputs to markets at market-determined prices. State-owned enterprises and collective-owned enterprises were also permitted to purchase inputs from markets to increase production or to expand production capacity.

Before 1999, when a considerable number of state-owned enterprises had not yet been reformed to the market economy, they were inflexible in structure and governance, weak in technological innovation, heavily in debt, had over-committed social burdens, were overstaffed, had low productivity, and lacked managerial skills in business operations (Lardy 1999; Wu 2003). Boisot identified four characteristics of state-owned enterprise management in 1987: (1) enterprise performance was hard to define and measure; (2) definitions of responsibility were vague; (3) rewards for good performance were low; and (4) and a cost center mentality prevailed. The organizational culture that prevailed within state-owned enterprises was inward-looking and non-performance oriented. These problems within state-owned enterprises reflected the challenges that the state sector had to overcome in the transformation of the market economy. Traditional state-owned enterprises were the heritage of particularistic "feudal" relations rather than universalistic "market," which reforms had to change (Boisot 1987; Boisot and Child 1988).

The managerial evolution in state-owned enterprises from the transition of a command economy to a market-socialist economy had gone through the birth pangs of coping with rapid and severe fundamental changes. When the reforms started in 1979, most state-owned enterprises were profitable. Taxes and revenues from state-owned enterprises and collective-owned enterprises were the government's main sources of fiscal income. However, in spite of a significant increase in productivity, the profitability of the state-owned enterprises had declined substantially since the market-oriented forms started. In the late 1990s, more than 40 percent of state-owned enterprises were operating at a loss, despite large amounts of implicit subsidies from low interest loans and other state policy protections. The decline in profitability of state-owned enterprises was partly attributable to the dissipation of their monopoly rent. However, increases in wages and other worker fringe benefits were other important reasons. The average annual growth rate of the state-owned enterprise wage fund in the state sector was 16 percent in 1978–96, while the average annual growth rate of output in the same period was 7.6 percent (Lin *et al.* 1998).

Prior to economic reforms, managers of state-owned enterprises in China were rewarded primarily on their success in meeting physical output targets set by the government. There was basically no autonomy in firms with respect to many economic activities. The state specified detailed directives for all the state-owned enterprises and collective-owned enterprises to follow, and the exercise of performance evaluation was nearly non-existent, or at least, extremely unimportant (Boisot 1987). Since the beginning of the reforms, enterprises have increasingly been given more decision-making power concerning production, supply, marketing, financing, pricing, personnel, wages, and bonus (Zhou 1988). Such changes were reported to have been triggered by the demands of managers in state-owned enterprises and collective-owned enterprises in order to gain increased autonomy. Equally, the government was also convinced that more delegation of power to the enterprise level would increase operational efficiency (Wu 2003).

With reforms, rewards were instead based much more heavily on firms' tax payments and accounting profits. While the tax rate on firms remained high by Western standards, in practice more than three-quarters of retained profits went to firms' managers and workers. The link between accounting profits and employee compensation might, if anything, have been stronger than in Western firms (Gordon and Lienesch 1991). However, Gordon and Lienesch suggest that, due to the large difference between accounting prices and market prices, the amount of tax evasion increased quickly during the period as market prices grew with inflation, while official prices remained relatively constant.

In 1986-7, the resulting loss in tax revenue led the government to shift to a contract responsibility system in which each firm signed a contract with the government, typically for three to five years, agreeing to minimum tax payments during each year of the contract. It was also designed as a performance evaluation system of the enterprise, in order to minimize the loss of control brought about by autonomy decentralization (Liu 1995). The function of the contract responsibility system was to achieve three objectives (Xie and Lin 1992):

- assure a stable growth in government income;
- change government's control over enterprises from direct to indirect intervention; and
- create an environment for the emergence of entrepreneurs.

The main objective of the system was to encourage entrepreneurialism and stimulate people's inventive to work by specifying certain targets to be achieved and by linking their achievements to their reward systems. Basically, this is similar to the budgetary evaluation system in a modern firm (Liu 1995). Under this system, the Government contracts the enterprise out to a contractor, which may be an individual, a group of individuals, or an entire enterprise. Normally, the contractor will be the chief executive officer of the enterprise (Tang *et al.* 1994). The contractor commits to fulfilling various targets or production indexes, of which a profit target is normally the major one. A base amount of profit has to be ascertained as a reference for setting the profit targets in each year within the contract period. The contractor may also be rewarded or penalized by means of pecuniary remuneration. Targets and remuneration are negotiated between the government and the contractor for each enterprise, so that the terms of contracts are always different from each other (Li *et al.* 2004).

The contract responsibility system emerged at a time when there was virtually no system of performance evaluation for state-owned enterprises. It has played a role of introducing the concept of performance evaluation during the course of managerial evolution in China. The system normally works best in profitable enterprises. Those enterprises that are suffering losses are incapable of taking out a contract with the government, because it is difficult for them to guarantee future profits. Moreover, after the government gives the partial right of control and recourse of surplus to the contractor, the boundaries of property rights in state-owned enterprises and collective-owned enterprises becomes even more ambiguous. Consequently, it exaggerates the conflicts between the contractors of enterprises and the government in the extent to which the tort to the state benefits is susceptibly occurred (Wu 2003). Therefore, in late 1993, the contract responsibility system was abandoned by the Chinese government, but the payroll remained linked to profitability. The total income of employees increased or decreased with the ups and downs of their company's profits.

Generally speaking, the effects of autonomy decentralization and profit retention have been very limited due to the untouched infrastructural administrative institution of the state-ownership system. These measurements have improved state enterprise efficiency, particularly in terms of motivation and decision-making, as well as in information transparency. The reduced degree of government direct intervention in the daily operations of enterprises has facilitated the efficiency and effectiveness of enterprise management. However, it cannot solve the in-depth structural problems of state-owned enterprises, such as "soft budgets," multi-objectives, and conflicts of interest. Another negative effect of these reforms is "insider control" (Masahiko and Hyung-Ki 1995), as a certain degree of autonomy is decentralized to enterprises, that is, de facto, to top management. This inevitably leads to a loss of control by the Party over the managers of state-owned enterprises. The only way to inhibit "insider control" is administrative intervention from the supervisory bureau of the government. However, this would then mark a return to the shortcomings of the centralized administration system. Enterprise directors are under the supervision of the Party Committee of the enterprise, but the division of responsibility is vague between them, which often results in inefficient governance. Corruption is frequent when supervision is weak and irresponsible. Under such conditions, some directors with the power of autonomy in management can transfer state capital to personal accounts, causing the loss of state-owned assets. Such corruption has been described as "rent-seeking activities" (Wu 1993). Steinfeld (1998) has drawn attention to two main causes for rent-seeking behavior in China—one is agencies having to seek new roles for themselves in the transition from central planning, and the other is the absence of formal institutions and governance, which are essential requirements for a functioning market economy.

In November 1993, the fourteenth Communist Party Delegates Congress determined several key answers to the construction of a socialist market economy, which stressed the necessity for enterprise reforms. It proposed a new system of "modern corporate institution" to replace the old "autonomy decentralization and profit retention." The Corporation Law was implemented on July 1, 1994 and in consequence, a range of 100 state-owned enterprises was selected for the experiment of reforms in institutional corporatization. Until 1997, the party further clarified the need of reforms in corporatization by extending this to medium-sized state-owned enterprises. One of the primary aims was to reduce government interference in the running of large state-owned enterprises and to encourage them to behave in a more entrepreneurial fashion, enabling them to become internationally competitive firms, structured along the same lines as Western corporations with Boards of Directors accountable to shareholders rather than being subject to the political authority of the Communist Party (Sheehan *et al.* 2000). In 1999, some emphases on corporate governance and multiple-investor structure were proposed. Corporatization of state enterprises included the following processes:

- The achievement of the divorce of government administration and enterprise management: under the command economy, the Chinese government collapsed the role of governance and role of ownership into one body.

- The restructuring of state monopoly enterprises into competitive modern corporations: Under the planned economy, to achieve the required economies of scale, there was usually one monopoly enterprise in each industry. Under the market economy, in order to create competition in the industrial environment, the state reorganized and restructured state enterprises to create more competitors to break down these monopolies. Take the petroleum industry as an example. Prior to the reforms, the state set up two bureaux—the Petroleum Industry Bureau and the Petroleum Chemistry Bureau—to manage all the petrol businesses nationwide. After the reforms, these two bureaux were gradually reorganized into three competitive commercial companies—SINOPEC, CNPC, and CNOOC. Their business operations are under state supervision, but they do not have the administrative functions of government organs.
- The listing of domestic and international security and stock markets through the reorganization of assets: To improve their performance and management, the core assets are stripped from the original state enterprises, and reorganized for initial public offerings (IPO) and listings. The non-core assets, bad debt and redundant staff are retained in the original enterprises, so that the newly-created enterprises can possess the feasibility of IPO and listings with the prerequisite of a good record of performance and quality assets. Normally acquisitions and mergers are often employed by state-owned enterprises to gain strategic growth, IPO and stock market listing.
- The establishment of a system of independent directors in state owned enterprises: Independence is the key element for the functioning of this system. Directors should be independent business partners and they should be independent of the major shareholders. They should not hold a large percent of company shares or represent any of the main shareholders' interests. In accordance with the investigation of the Organization for Economic Co-operation and Development (OECD) in 1999, independent directors in public listed companies accounted for 62 percent in America, 34 percent in Britain and 29 percent in France. China has initiated this system as a compulsory requirement for all public companies in 2001.

As Sheehan and colleagues (2000) point out, "reform in this way is intended to make those large corporations subject to a greater degree of market discipline, while avoiding the still very politically sensitive step of privatizing any of the 'commanding heights' of Chinese heavy industry." But although the Party leadership is keen to stress that this is not a program of privatization for the largest state-owned enterprises, the modern enterprise system (MES) and the group company system (GCS) reforms are very much concerned with questions of ownership and property rights, suggesting that Chinese leaders have at least "internalized the logic" of Western European-style privatization strategies (Steinfeld 1998). Furthermore, since 1995, the reform and restructuring of small- to medium-sized state-owned enterprises (also called "grasp large and release small"—"zhua da fang xiao") was launched. This allows individuals and private enterprises to buy out small-sized state-owned enterprises, as they are regarded as non-strategic enterprises in the state's economic planning. Some actions, such as the selling-off of enterprise housing to workers, and the sale of shares to individual investors, bring the program closer to at least partial privatization than the central government seems willing to admit (Zhang 2000).

Haier Corporation

Haier is a successful large collective-owned multinational corporation with a state-owned background. It is a good example of the outcome of managerial evolution in the state sector. Haier began as the Qingdao Refrigerator Factory, originally an importer of refrigerator production technologies from Germany. From modest beginnings, the company has grown and expanded into a prospering Chinese multinational corporation whose brand name has become more recognizable in the world community over the last decade. Haier now manufactures a wide range of household electrical appliances in eighty-six categories with 13,000 specifications, and is now an exporter of these products to more than 160 countries. Haier's global sales in 2002 totalled RMB 71.1 billion (US$8.6 billion). The development of the Haier company reflects its success in its managerial evolution. Haier's success can be attributed to its prompt response to environmental changes and its implementation of managerial reforms. The first opportunity to Haier was from autonomy decentralization and the introduction of market mechanisms. As one of the outcomes of this transformational opportunity, Zhang Huimin was appointed as the CEO (chief executive officer). His leadership and managerial talent guaranteed the first step of Haier's success. The second opportunity was suggested by Deng Xiaoping's speech in 1992, which confirmed the direction of market development policy. This inspired Zhang Huimin to form a growth strategy for market competition. To gain the necessary economies of scale, he planned to develop Haier as a giant in the household electrical appliances industry, with an investment of 80 million RMB (US$9.7 million). But Haier could not get this large loan from the state banks. As a solution, and supported by the government, Haier issued bonds and raised 36.9 million RMB (US$4.5 million) on the stock market, which could be regarded as the third opportunity to boost its outgrowth in a modern corporatized format. Then, China's rapid economic expansion brought about the fourth opportunity for fast expansion. Haier bought out the Qingdao Refrigerator Factory, the Qingdao Air-condition Corporation, and the Guangdong Aide Company in 1996. These acquisitions allowed Haier to enlarge its market share in the electrical appliance industry and to restructure corporate management and culture. All of these steps in its development gradually formed the resources and capabilities for Haier to compete in the global market place. As a consequence of its growth in size, Haier installed information systems to re-energize its business management system so that the company could react to the market promptly. Within two years, Haier successfully integrated a management information system (MIS) across the corporation. The early adoption of this information system was the fifth opportunity for Haier's success. Following the further opening-up of the market, Haier's CEO believed that global expansion was the sixth opportunity for its future development. Therefore an international strategy was vigorously promoted. Armed with this strategy, Haier evolved its management in a global perspective. It built its competence in both price and quality and established strategic alliances with many international rivals. Haier constructed a learning organization culture to constantly advance its management knowledge to cope with the rapidly changing environment. Its famous logistics innovation in supply-chain management provided a pattern and an example for successful Chinese management (Chen *et al.* 2004). Valuable lessons can be learned from Haier's success in relation to how state-owned enterprises can be restructured and reformed to be entrepreneurial and competitive in order to fit into the market economy.

The development of the private sector and entrepreneurial growth

The development of the non-state economic sector initiated in 1978, started to break down the ideological obstacles of the Soviet model after 1997. This sector's prosperity made a remarkable contribution to the growth of the whole economy. In general, the gradual evolution of the non-state sector into a market structure proceeded through the following paths (Garnaut *et al.* 2001; Ho 1994):

(1) The liberalization of individual businesses: In 1979, after the Cultural Revolution, a good deal of intellectual youth who were sent to the rural counties for re-education, returned to the urban cities. This generated pressure on employment and so the government opened up the economy for entrepreneurship. In July 1981, the State Council issued laws to clearly define the boundaries of enterprises as "businesses employing fewer than 8 as the divide between individual enterprises and private enterprises." As in the early 1980s, enterprises hiring more than EIGHT employees were regarded as "exploiters" and not part of a socialist economy.
(2) The prevalence of 'the contract farm' on the basis of the peasant's family: From 1980 to 1982, the contract responsibility system prevailed in rural areas after the commune system was dissolved. Peasants with contracted responsibilities were permitted to set up their own family farms on the collective-owned lands in their villages. Officially it was called a "collectively-owned corporation economy," although, de facto, it was a private ownership economy.
(3) The development of township-village enterprises: During the 1980s, the development of township-village enterprises prospered and became an important component of the national economy, as well as the key supporting force for economic growth in the 1990s. Total industrial production of township-village enterprises reached RMB 160 million (US$19 million) in 1992, accounting for 35 percent of total national industrial production. Employment in township-village enterprises exceeded 100 million people and equaled total employment in state-owned enterprises in the same year (Chen, 1994). There is consistent evidence that township-village enterprises out-performed state-owned enterprises in productivity growth (Wu 1995; Jefferson 1999), even

though township-village enterprises in general had low-technology production methods and obtained technical expertise from state-owned enterprises (Peng 1997). Many township-village enterprises adapted an export-oriented development strategy. The exports of township-village enterprises had an annual growth rate of 10 percent for five successive years from 1995 to 2000. In 2000, the total value of exports by township-village enterprises reached RMB 867 billion (US$105 billion), accounting for one-third of China's total exports.

Township-village enterprises in different areas illustrate different characteristics, and their ownership structures are variable. Based on their sources of initial investment, structure of ownership, industrial orientation, income distribution, and management systems, Chinese economists (Chen 1998; Zuo 2001) have classified township-village enterprises into three models:

- the southern Jiangsu model (Sunanmoshi), characterized by a dominant initial investment by township and village government;
- the Wenzhou model (Wenzhoumoshi), featuring private ownership under the disguise of the "red hat," i.e. officially "socialist"; and
- the Pearl River Delta model, (Guangdongmoshi), distinguished by foreign direct investment and export-oriented manufacturing.

(4) The legitimatization of private-owned enterprise: After this process of reform in the early 1980s, China's economy was finally opened to foreign investment and individual businesses. But private businesses (which hired more than eight employees) were still regarded as abandoned capitalism. Following the growth of the market, however, private enterprises expanded significantly in the mid-1980s. The Communist Party, headed by Deng Xiaoping, was determined to admit to the existence of a private economy. Until 1988, the development of the private sector economy was subsumed in an amendment of the Constitution in the seventh People Delegate Congress (Qian 2003).

Private enterprises were initially permitted as a supplement to the state and collective sectors. Private enterprises first took hold in the rural sectors, as an outgrowth of the virtual privatization of agriculture, and in small-scale individual enterprises in the urban sectors. During the mid-1980s, large private enterprises grew out of these rural and individual enterprises, and also out of collective-owned enterprises and state-owned enterprises. Some were sole proprietorships that grew and hired more employees. By 1988, when private firms were officially recognized, China had 500,000 individual enterprises that could be called private firms (Gregory and Tenev 2001). The change in political sentiment following the voice of protest from some conservative socialists opposed to the emergence of private enterprise caused a temporary setback to the growth of private enterprise. But Deng Xiaoping's famous "south talk" and "south tour" in September 1992 opened the way for renewed growth. During the 1990s, the government encouraged the privatization of smaller, non-strategic state-owned enterprises and allowed collective-owned enterprises to transform into private enterprises. In 1997, 4,180,000 laid-off workers and employees in the state sector found new work in the private sector (Zhang 2002). The number of registered private firms rose from 655 thousand in 1995 to 12 million in 2005, the average growth rate of these reached 94.5 percent. By 2010 the number of these registered firms more than doubled to 27 million; a phenomenal growth of the private sector. Likewise, employment in the private sector increased from 9.56 million in 1995 to 169.2 million in 2005, and 331.2 million in 2010; an almost thirty-four times increment in a fifteen-year period. Relevant production and value added of private industry all mounted up dramatically (see Figures 2.1, 2.2, 2.3, and 2.4). As Gregory and Tenev (2001: 15) comment:

> It is evident that new employment in the private sector has exceeded the combined total for state, collective, and township-and-village enterprises. This explosive development is in sharp contrast to the decline of the State-owned Enterprises and Collective-owned Enterprises. The Private sector has become an important source of job creation, absorbing a significant number of workers laid off from State-owned Enterprises.

According to an OECD Economic Survey of China in 2005, private-owned companies, which are controlled neither by state nor collective shareholders, are responsible for as much as 57 percent of the value-added production of the non-farm business sector in 2003. Overall, between 1998 and 2003, the progressive evolution in government policies allowed a fivefold rise in the output of domestically-owned private companies. By contrast, the output of the state sector rose by just over 70 percent in this period (see Table 2.1).

Nevertheless, policy discriminations against private-owned enterprises still persist. Although the private-owned enterprises have been permitted to have import

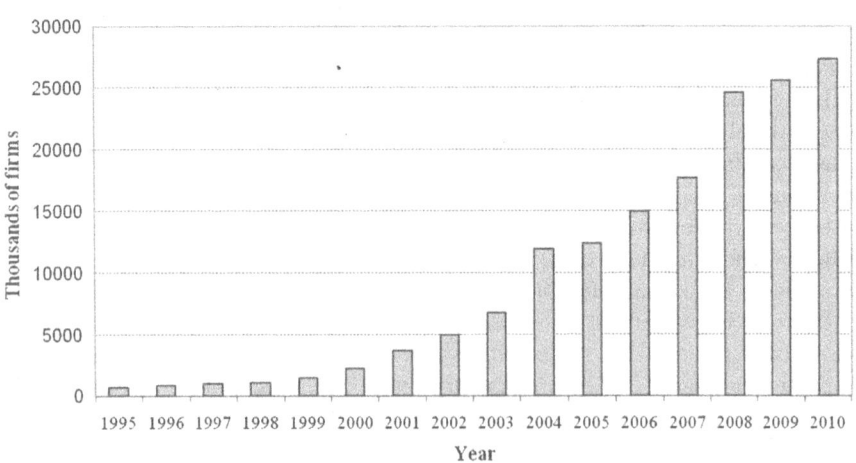

Figure 2.1 Development in number of private industrial enterprises, 1995–2010.
Source: China Statistics Yearbook 2006, pp. 536–538; and 2011, p. 526.

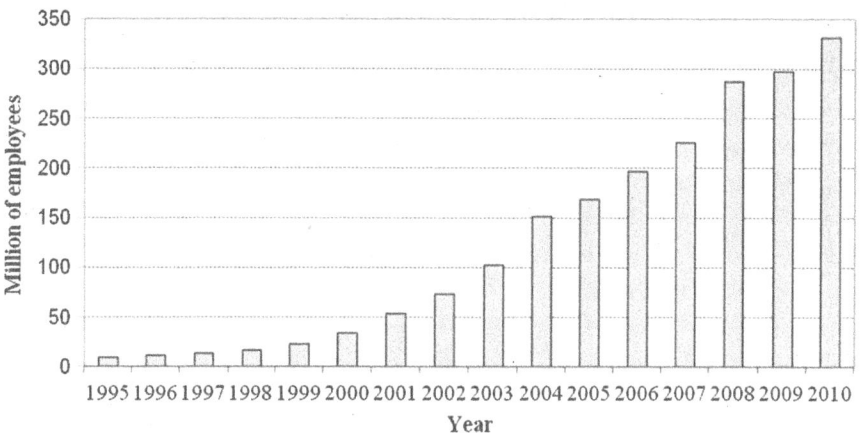

Figure 2.2 Development in number of employees in private industrial enterprises, 1995–2010.

Source: *China Statistics Yearbook* 2006, pp. 536–538; and 2011, p. 528.

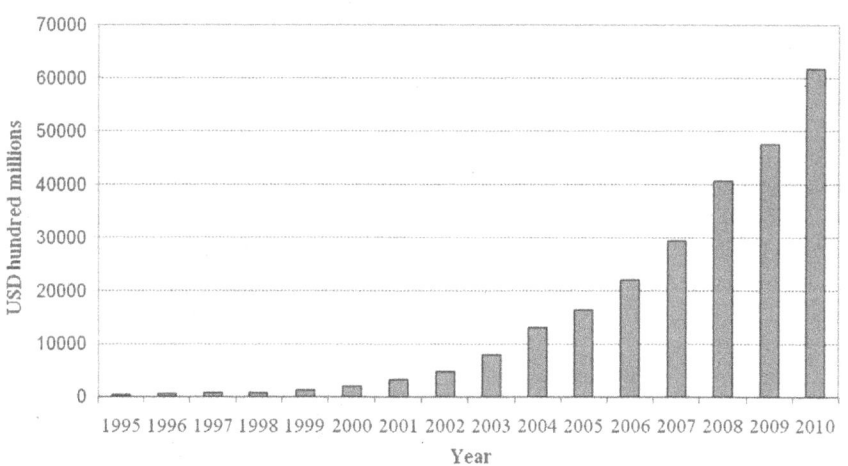

Figure 2.3 Development in total working capitals of private industrial enterprises, 1995–2010.

Source: *China Statistics Yearbook* 2006, pp. 536–538; and 2011, P. 526.

Notes: Working capitals refer to capitals that an enterprise can cash or use during one year or one production cycle that may exceed one year, including cash and savings deposits of various forms, short-term investment, money receivable and prepaid money, inventories, etc. (*China Statistics Yearbook* 2006, p. 574).

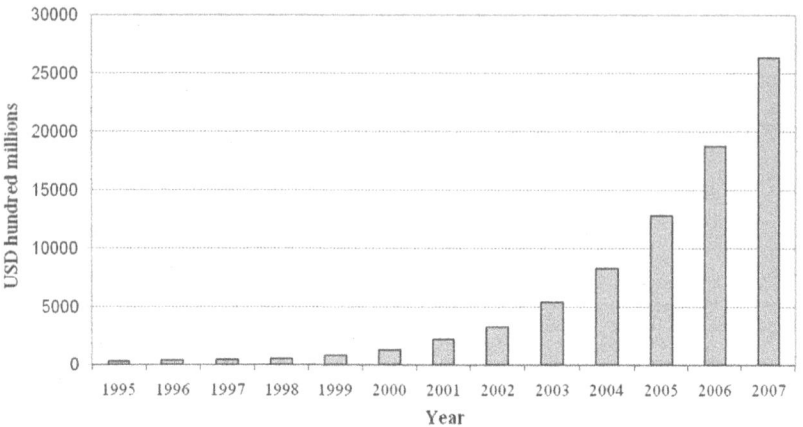

Figure 2.4 Development in value added of industry of private industrial enterprises, 1995–2007.

Source: *China Statistics Yearbook* 2006, pp. 536–538; and 2009, P. 514.

Notes: 'Value added of industry' refers to the final results of industrial production of industrial enterprises in money terms during the reference period. Value added of industry in the *China Statistics Yearbook* (2006, p. 574) is calculated by production approach as follows:

Value added of industry = gross industrial output − industrial intermediate input

+ value-added tax.

The statistic data of value added of industry of private industrial enterprise is only available up to 2007 according to China's statistic yearbooks in various years between 2006 and 2012.

and export licenses since 1998, the government has set higher entry barriers on private owners for the granting of import and export licenses. For instance, according to the "Provisional Stipulation for Self-managing Licenses for Imports and Exports by Private-owned Enterprises," by the Ministry of Foreign Economy and Trade, the conditions for the granting of licenses to private-owned enterprises, must be: (1) net assets above RMB 850 million (US$103 million); (2) net annual sales revenues above RMB 300 million (US$36 million); (3) the possession of teams of professionals and specialists in the import and export business (Sun 2005). These higher entry barriers have restricted the growth of private-owned enterprises in international markets. As Table 2.2 illustrates, it is obvious that private-owned enterprises only contribute a small portion of exports (US$692.5 billion) and imports (US$419.8 billion) by comparison with state-owned enterprises, which saw US$1535.9 billion of exports and US$1764.5 billion of imports in 2004. The dominant players in foreign trade are foreign-owned enterprises, which account for the majority share of exports and imports. The growth rates of exports and imports (99.3 percent and 70.8 percent) for the private enterprises are significantly higher than is seen in the state sector (11.4 percent and 23.9 percent respectively), which demonstrates the huge potential of the competitiveness of private-owned enterprises for future growth (see Table 2.2).

Table 2.1 The private sector outpaces the public sector in China, 1998–2003

	1998	1999	2000	2001	2002	2003	Change (over 1998 & 2003)
Non-farm business sector							
Private sector	43.0	45.3	47.7	51.8	54.6	57.1	14.1
Public sector	57.0	54.7	52.3	48.2	45.4	42.9	−14.1
State-controlled	40.5	40.1	39.6	37.1	35.2	34.1	−6.4
Collective-owned	16.5	14.7	12.7	11.2	10.1	8.8	−7.7
Total (79% of GDP)	100	100	100	100	100	100	
Economy-wide							
Private sector	50.4	51.5	52.8	55.5	57.4	59.2	8.8
Public sector	49.6	48.5	47.2	44.5	42.6	40.8	−8.8
State-controlled	36.9	37.1	37.3	35.7	34.6	33.7	−3.2
Collective-owned	12.7	11.3	10	8.8	8.0	7.1	−5.6
Total (100% of GDP)	100	100	100	100	100	100	

Source: *OECD Economic Survey of China 2005*.

Table 2.2 China foreign trade composition by enterprise ownerships in 2004

				Unit: billion US$ and (%)
	Export		Import	
Economic components	Amount	Growth rate (%)	Amount	Growth rate (%)
Total	4922.0	35.4	5010.2	36.0
State-owned enterprises	1535.9	11.4	1764.5	23.9
Foreign-invested enterprises	3386.1	40.9	3245.7	40.0
Collective-owned enterprises	317.9	26.5	177.2	33.9
Private-owned enterprises	692.5	99.3	419.8	70.8

Source: *China Foreign Economy and Trade Yearbook* (2005), p. 64.

Notes: The level approach is applied to calculating percentage of growth rate in this table, which is derived by comparing the level of the last year of the interval with that of the beginning year. The statistics in this table are adapted from the *China Foreign Economy and Trade Yearbook (2005)*, compiled by the Committee of Inspection and Administration of State Assets, State Council, China Economy press, Beijing, p. 64.

Foreign direct investment and joint ventures: strategies, policies, and rationale

The expansion of foreign joint ventures during market liberalization

In 1979, the enactment of the Corporate Law of Sino Joint Ventures ("Zhongwai Hezi Qiye Fa") marked the turning point in the market transition from forbidding foreign direct investment (FDI) to encouraging FDI into China. The main focus of this strategy was to gain advanced technology and to learn modern management experience from foreign companies, in order to enhance the competitiveness of indigenous firms. The old strategy of import substitution for China's industrial development was then replaced by an export-oriented strategy, driven by liberalization and foreign direct investment. From 1979 to 1988, the Chinese government established five Economic Development Zones and initially designated fourteen coastal cities as experimental frontiers for the implementation of its marketization policy.

Since the mid-1990s China has been the second largest recipient of foreign direct investment worldwide (after the US). This is due to two factors: investment incentives offered by the government and the country's abundance of low-cost labor (Branstetter and Feenstra 2002; Luo and O'Connor 1998). The expansion of foreign joint ventures in the market has brought new Western management concepts into indigenous firms, and improved their competitive advantage (Warner 2004; Wong and Salter 2002; Jiang 2006). In the 2000s, China's employment pattern and economy has been characterized by the downsizing of the state sector and the fast-growing share of foreign direct investment companies and owner-managed private firms (OECD 2010d).

Before 2010, foreign enterprises enjoyed "tax holidays" and preferential tax treatment in imports and exports, access to raw materials, and the use of property. Corporate income tax for these enterprises was at a preferential rate of 15 percent; even lower than the 18.5 percent seen in Hong Kong. Resource inputs and the purchase of equipment for production were exempt from import restrictions. These foreign joint ventures (FJVs) enjoyed a 100 percent tax exemption for the first two profit-making years and a 50 percent tax reduction for the following three years for production-oriented FJVs (Lin 1999: 82). In January 2010, government policies toward FDI changed direction, as the "holidays" on tax exemption and reduction were removed in competitive, low-tech-based manufacturing industries (Chen *et al.* 2011). Instead, the State Council issued a statement to encourage overseas investors to invest in new energy, environmental protection, high-technology, and advanced manufacturing sectors (*Xinhua News* 2010); thus demonstrating how China's efforts to boost more foreign investment in high-technology and new energy sectors is linked to its strategy to become a global leader in these "advanced" sectors. However, the success of Party policies in attracting foreign-owned joint ventures has created vulnerabilities for both parties. The economic prosperity of cities and regions is vulnerable to the strategic decisions of foreign-owned companies, as these are mobile in their production, with sales and marketing sites situated in different countries around the world. Similarly, these same companies are vulnerable to changes in Party policies in terms of tax benefits, labor laws, and funding policies. Their competitive advantage of having production and sales facilities in China can suddenly be eroded as a result of national and local government decrees.

The emerging business ventures

As a result of these institutional reforms, government policies shaping the development of market socialism has led to the emergence of four distinctive types of enterprise ownership: (1) the restructured state-owned enterprises (SOEs); (2) reformed cooperative-owned enterprises (COEs); (3) foreign joint ventures (FJVs); and (4) owner-managed entrepreneurial firms (private-owned enterprises) (POEs). State-owned enterprises are highly policy-led and characterized as reactive to restructuring demands, as they are inclined to conform with institutional arrangements. Their resource-focused competitive advantage is built upon on a grant-aided policy (Hassard *et al.* 2010). They have enjoyed privileged access to state bank finance. Mergers and acquisitions are taking place between medium- to large-sized SOEs across sectors, which enable diverse state-owned businesses to agglomerate to form larger industrial clusters. Such a strategy is creating quasi-monopoly industries that dominate vital sectors of the Chinese economy, such as, for example, telecom and real estate sectors. This is possible under market socialism because of the Party's control as it is exercised over state-owned enterprises. However, this stringent political control also creates acute tensions between free-market forces and government supervision systems; bearing in mind that the primary objective of reforms in the state sector is to transform state-owned enterprises into market-oriented modern corporations.

Collective-owned enterprises are literally owned by employees but, de facto, are controlled by local authorities. They generally lack government policy support, since they are regarded as a secondary component of the state sector and do not benefit from policy aid in the same way as state-owned enterprises. They have ambiguous property ownership rights and remain peculiar off-shoots of the socialist planned economy. The reforms in the 1990s were attempts to resolve the issue of whether they were owned by local authorities or by employees (Chen *et al.* 2008; Sanders and Chen 2005; Yano and Shiraishi 2004). In the transition process, they have become a "mixture" of private investment ventures and socialist-inspired cooperative organisations (Wang and Han 2008). As economic reforms deepen, their significance is in decline. This type of ownership is likely to wither with the further development of market socialism.

Foreign-owned joint ventures are major employers in China, and, as a result, their employment policies and practices have a strong bearing on reshaping the pool of human resources and the experience of work for a significant proportion of employees (Cooke 2004). They are often regarded as a "best practice" benchmark. Furthermore, foreign joint ventures are the dominant force of the non-state economic sector because of their capabilities, based as these are upon a combination of local skills and knowledge with foreign-imported technologies and advanced management practices. This gives them competitive edge and enables them to position themselves at the high end of the industry chain. They are proactive in responding to market demands because of their creative and deliberative attempts to be at the forefront of market threads. It remains to be seen if this will continue to be the case in the future as the development of indigenous managerial, technological, and scientific skills reduces the need for the Chinese economy to be dependent upon the import of these skills. At present, the state and foreign joint ventures have a symbiotic relationship; they are dependent upon each other for the pursuit of their own separate objectives and agendas. The outcome is market socialism, consisting of a dialogue and accommodation between Western capitalist corporations and a growth-oriented Communist Party.

Private-owned enterprises have demonstrated considerable initiatives in pursuing and securing opportunities under institutional constraints (Yang 2002; Kshetri 2007). Due to the fact that government policies still heavily favor state-owned enterprises, indigenous entrepreneurial firms are forced to cluster in low-value and low-cost-based manufacturing sectors. They suffer restricted access to financial resources since the state-owned banking sector is reluctant to lend to them. Although they share many characteristics of entrepreneurial counterparts in the West, the dynamics of market socialism compels them to occupy "niches" in the market that are not catered for by other types of enterprise. They are regarded by both the state and other market actors as marginal or peripheral to the future development of market socialism. However, entrepreneurs act as institutional change agents since they are extremely adaptive and flexible; their pursuit for new opportunities and collective actions for achieving their own interests have created unintended consequences for the development of market socialism in China.

Despite the fact that the institutional features of China's market socialism shape each of these type of ventures' ownership characteristics, their continuing evolution is generating tensions between Communist Party control mechanisms and market-driven economic processes. Chinese market socialism is a specific type of socioeconomic and political system; it defines the strategic and operational characteristics of the reformed state-owned sector as well as the rapidly growing private-owned sphere of the economy. We will discuss each of these ownership types with case illustrations in the next chapter, as they possess features that are the direct outcome of ongoing tensions between Communist Party political objectives and the imperatives of market relations. It is likely these will become more acute as the Chinese economy continues to be integrated into the global marketplace. At the very least, the discussion demonstrates the importance of taking into account the specificities of macroeconomic and political institutional forces for understanding the role of economic enterprises as the key market players that may appear to have cross-national global similarities but in fact (empirically) are very different.

3 Management theory and practice in the Chinese context

Introduction

This chapter reviews the development of management concepts under China's market economy in the past decades. The economic reforms of injecting free-market mechanisms into a socialist economy is a radical and pioneering innovation that was initiated by China's Communist Party under the leadership of Deng Xiaoping in 1979. Xiaoping described this revolutionary change as "China's economic reform is like crossing a river through probing into the bottom of river which no one knows what is in there and how deep it is." His proposed approach revealed the huge challenges of tackling the prominent problems that China's socialist economy had long suffered. Deng drew a famous analogy between his pragmatic concept and a cat—"no matter white cats or black cats, the cat that catches rats is the best cat." This idea has guided experimental reforms to encourage economic growth and develop a "free" market economy with specific Chinese characteristics. In 2013, the new Chinese Communist Party leader, Xi Jinping, also used a metaphor to describe continuous economic reforms as "shoes"—"the shoes that fit your own feet are the best shoes." This reinforces the pursuit of Chinese market socialism and distinguishes it from Western market capitalism.

As we discussed in the first two chapters, the characteristics of Chinese market socialism are distinctive in the way the Party has developed a state-controlled market economy with market resource allocations and regulatory policies, navigated and directly administrated by the state under the total control of a single party rather than by a Western process of multiparty democracy and free-market transactions. Thus, Chinese market socialism as a specific type of socioeconomic and political system, defines the strategic and operational features of a reformed state-owned sector as well as a rapidly growing, private-owned sphere of the economy which, itself, engenders distinctive outcomes for different types of enterprise ownership. Each of these economic enterprises possesses characteristics that are the direct outcome of ongoing tensions between Communist Party political objectives and the imperatives of market relations. They are interactive in order to shape the specificities of the socioeconomic and political framework of market socialism in China. Hence, any discussion of Chinese management theory and practice must take into account these specific political, economic, organizational, and cultural factors. To neglect these is to render impossible any understanding of the hybrid nature of management practices in the Chinese context.

Given nearly three decades of development of market economy, Chinese management theory and research is an emergent process whose outcome is difficult to predict. Most of the established theories that are applied to the Chinese context have been developed in a Western context. In this chapter, we highlight the key issues associated with contemporary Chinese management practice in relation to business growth and entrepreneurship as well as to business networks. The relevant management issues will be discussed by reference to the different organizational contexts and ownership forms—state-owned enterprises, private-owned enterprises, and foreign joint ventures. Following this discussion, in subsequent chapters, we illustrate each type of management pattern and organizational characteristic by reference to each type of organization.

Entrepreneurship and growth

A central issue in the literature on entrepreneurship is firm growth theories. Despite substantial empirical research and theoretical development in this field, a comprehensive understanding of the complexity and heterogeneous nature of firm growth phenomena is still very limited and inconsistent (Leitch *et al.* 2010; McKelvie and Wiklund 2010). A recent review (Shepherd and Wiklund 2009) found over eighty empirical studies in leading management and entrepreneurship journals published over the past fifteen years and noted that there was a lack of attention to the potential qualitative differences in firm growth paths, since most of the studies focused on the question of "how much?" before providing answers to the question of "how?" (McKelvie and Wiklund 2010: 216). There is insufficient research evidence explaining firm growth processes and outcomes. Within this development process, variations such as intentions and goals and resources and opportunities in organizations may change over time, which will ultimately affect the modes of growth over different periods and contexts. That said, the "how" aspect of growth is a fundamental question that needs to be better understood and requires more research (McKelvie and Wiklund 2010; Leitch *et al.* 2010).

Entrepreneurship has been described as complex; a contextual event and the outcome of many influences (Gartner *et al.* 1989). It has been defined in different ways, but essentially it emphasizes a creative process of extracting social and economic value from the environment (Scott *et al.* 1997). Different researchers give prominence to a different blend of factors, but at its core are the ideas that the entrepreneurship process is opportunity driven, resource efficient, and owner dependent. Storey (1994) postulates on the characteristics of growing entrepreneurial ventures and suggests that there are three integral components that drive small firm growth: characteristics of the entrepreneur, characteristics of the firm and characteristics of growth strategy. However, it is argued that although it may be possible to identify key success factors that affect the growth of small- and medium-sized enterprises (SMEs), it is unlikely that a comprehensive model with predictive capability will emerge (Smallbone *et al.* 1995). Deakins and Freel (2006) comment that the inclusion of individual variables and organization ownership factors in this characteristic approach is compelling and, in aggregate, they probably impact upon firms in much the way that Storey envisages. Salancik and Pfeffer (1980: 655) claim that "ownership as a source of power can be used to either support or oppose management depending on how it is concentrated and used." The firm's growth can be viewed as an attempt by owners and managers to utilize its resources (Penrose 1960; Peng 1997; Peng *et al.* 2004).

From a resource-based perspective, entrepreneurship can be regarded as a process of identification, acquisition and accumulation of resources to generate unique organizational capabilities for competitive advantage (Bergmann-Lichtenstein and Brush 2002; Man *et al.* 2002). In a limited resource environment (such as emerging economies like China), knowledge and rationality are extremely complex (Guo and Guo 2011; Long and Long 1992), and knowledge is highly interdependent on resource availability (Kodithuwakku and Rosa 2002). Resource restraint in an entrepreneurial setting is not just a matter of financial or physical resources, but includes the capability to make frequent decisions about which opportunities are worth pursuing among various strategic choices. The owner–entrepreneur as the "prime mover of the process" (Behave 1994) constantly provides direction, leadership and enthusiasm to keep the business going, thus their time and capability are often as critical and as scarce as money (Ravasi and Turati 2005). Gupta and colleagues (2004) point out that value-based entrepreneurial leadership emphasizes building commitment through active, creative and discovery-driven engagement, based on the opportunities presented by the environment (e.g. customers, product opportunities, etc.) for the purpose of achieving results and wealth creation. Despite the varied range of factors being studied in entrepreneurial processes, the question that remains unclear is: What are the specific factors that may determine strategic choices between high and low value-added product strategies? McKelvie and Wiklund (2010) also suggest that there should be more research to determine what specific strategy leads to specific outcomes, rather than discussing strategies in general. China's economy is driven by the growth of its manufacturing sector, but most Chinese firms are located in the low-value chain of the industry. This raises many questions: Does this mean that the low value-added strategy will handicap firm growth or result in a less sustainable growth mode? Also, how do we explain the burgeoning SMEs in the low-value chain industry sector and how do such firms gain their competitive advantage? Empirical evidence on the development of specific growth modes and the formulation of capabilities serving different strategy choices is inconclusive. One notion addresses the importance of knowledge management and learning capabilities as the key for the ongoing development of new resources and as a source of sustainable competencies (Starkey *et al.* 2004; Guo and Guo 2011; Carayannis *et al.* 2006). Some studies focus on the critical role of leadership that provides direction and develops new resources for enabling strategy choice in the entrepreneurial management process (Ng and Thorpe 2010; Diamante and London 2002), while others emphasize that structural and strategic formulation of internal business management processes determines the outcome of the entrepreneurship process (Lyles *et al.* 1993; Ireland *et al.* 2001; Hitt *et al.* 2001).

The entrepreneurial process model

The entrepreneurial process is one of the core aspects of entrepreneurship research. Wickham (2006) advocates an entrepreneurship process model that encompasses four interacting contingencies in the process of entrepreneurial value creation; (1) the entrepreneur; (2) a market opportunity; (3) a business organisation; and (4) the utilization of resources (also see Behave 1994, for the basis of this concept). Wickham's work emphasizes the interactive effect of these four dimensions in a dynamic process that "success fuels success" and failure feeds back into the learning of success. It posits that the entrepreneurial organization should be a learning organization. That is, it should reflect on and learn from its success and failures in order to modify future responses in light of experience and knowledge acquisition. Leadership and direction from entrepreneurs is the core of the organization process. It uses a resource-based view that argues that capability is developed from how organizations access and manage resources. This model has illustrated key aspects of entrepreneurship process that have been discussed in this field of literature, such as opportunities, entrepreneurs, leadership, resources and learning. However, the model does not provide an answer to the contextual and developmental effect on these key contingencies in the process. Nonetheless, this framework defines a recognized scope of what is involved in the business venture process and can act as an analytical tool for considering the question of how these contingencies are developed and interact over time. Even Wickham (2006: 229) suggests that in support of these theories, further research should use case studies of each type of business venture to identify how this process differs in each ownership form. To advance the understanding of this entrepreneurial process model, as Porter (1980: 110) suggests, ownership structure exerts a strong influence on the goals and structure of organizations. Indeed, a large body of literature has emphasized the important implications of the ownership factor in the formulation and deployment of firms' strategies and resources (Yang 2002; Tan 2002a; Peng *et al.* 2004; Ghobadian and O'Regan 2006; Zahra *et al.* 2000). This consideration has therefore guided the selection of the case studies in the present research in order to reflect the representation of major ownership forms in both the state and private sectors under Chinese market socialism. It draws upon firm growth literature with a focus on the entrepreneurial and organizational process approaches as the main framework underpinning this research. However, many sub-fields have developed as areas of study around the entrepreneurship process including resource-based theories, the concept of business networks, access to and leverage of resources, knowledge as a specialized firm resource and the role of entrepreneurial leadership with attention on individual entrepreneurs.

Growth of indigenous Chinese entrepreneurs

Chinese entrepreneurs have emerged amongst these changing economic conditions along with the development of private enterprises since the 1990s. These new entrepreneurs have often moved from secure jobs in state-owned factories, with hopes of making personal fortunes (Djankov *et al.* 2006). They have been keen to exploit market opportunities and have reacted skillfully to take advantage of ambiguous government policies, taxes and regulations (Yang 2004; Yang and Li 2008). In short, they are "buccaneer capitalists." There are two types of entrepreneurs that have emerged from different phases of market transition. The early-emerged entrepreneurs are often poorly educated and manage their businesses very informally, on a rule-of-thumb basis (Schlevogt 2001). This is in contrast to those late emergent, high-tech-based business ventures, whose owner–entrepreneurs are often highly skilled and well educated with knowledge advantage (Chen *et al.* 2011; Guo and Guo 2011). Consequently, they all operate in a similar manner to their Western, small business counterparts (Holt 1997). These indigenous entrepreneurs have shown impressive flexibility and dynamism in expanding their businesses in the absence of secure legal frameworks, and with very limited access to bank loans (Gregory and Tenev 2001; Dorn 2001; Djankov *et al.* 2006; He 2009). They are characterized by a strong entrepreneurship orientation, the extensive use of business networks (Krug 2004), the exploration of informal funding sources and an organic management structure (Schlevogt 2001; Yang 2007). The private-owned enterprise detailed in the following case study demonstrates these distinctive characteristics.

Impact of foreign joint ventures

Foreign joint ventures are the outcome of foreign direct investment (FDI) in China. The government has granted a series of privileges and tax treatments to attract FDI since 1978, and, as a consequence, this has been a significant pushing force in the growth of China's market economy (Chung and Bruton 2008). Some studies reveal that, to a large extent, the management practices of foreign joint ventures have developed a hybrid model, combining characteristics of Western management and Chinese cultural and human resource features in order to be adaptive in the local business environment (Cooke 2004; Gamble 2000; Melvin 1997; Yan and Warner 2001). Taylor's study (2001) points out that managers in foreign joint ventures seek to use a variety of local and "universal" strategies and practices to control and utilize labor within the constraints of the local institutional context. Cooke (2004) asserts that managers who are delegated power and autonomy play an important role in shaping management practices of foreign joint ventures. Their decisions and knowledge determine the performance of businesses (Legewie 2002).

Davidson (1987) pinpoints the factors that determine foreign joint ventures' performance as organizational cultures, administrative structures and management philosophies. Child (1998) has argued that wholly-owned foreign enterprises have relatively lower profitability when compared with Sino-foreign joint ventures. Knowledge of local governmental issues, culture and markets, is critical to both indigenous firms and foreign investors. Foreign partnerships enable access to advanced knowledge and external resources that may be transformed into competitive advantages for small businesses in China (Basu and Yao 2009). The research in this paper focuses on small-scale joint ventures that are run by overseas Chinese entrepreneurs. It aims to explore the impact of foreign-engaged ownership in shaping small business development.

The privatization of collective-owned enterprises

Collective-owned enterprises in China are owned by employees but controlled by local authorities (Walder 1995). They are regarded as a component of the state sector but secondary in scale to state-owned enterprises. They have ambiguous property ownership rights and remain peculiar offshoots of the socialist planned economy. The reforms in the 1990s were attempts to resolve issues of whether they were owned by local authorities or by employees (Chen *et al.* 2008). Property, employee rights and productivity performance have been at the center of ongoing debate with regard to collective ownership (Sanders and Chen 2005; Yano and Shiraishi 2004). Market reforms have changed the ownership form of traditional collective-owned enterprises as privatization has become incorporated within them (Peng 2001). Since 2005, government reform policies have encouraged the transformation of COEs into limited liability, private-owned, and shareholding companies (Wang and Han 2008). Thus, they are a "mixture" of private investment ventures and socialist-inspired cooperative organisations. According to a report from the All-China Federation of Industry and Commerce (ACFIC 2007), approximately 20.3 percent of private enterprises grew their businesses through mergers with state-owned or collective-owned enterprises in 2006. These types of mergers and acquisitions (M&A) form an important aspect of entrepreneurship practices under market socialism. Access to substantial resources, such as land, facilities, finance, and skilled labor forces, are critical issues for private entrepreneurs (Yang 2002). Hence, private enterprises are rather keen on tendering for such M&A as a means of low-cost expansion (Wang and Han 2008). Through the privatization process, this type of business venture has gradually evolved into sole private ownership and its historical significance is decreasing and will eventually wither.

The restructuring of state-owned enterprises

Given the changing nature of market socialism, many state-owned enterprises are realizing that they need to be more innovative and flexible than perhaps they have been in the past. The reform of state-owned enterprises has long been restricted by the Communist Party's socialist ideology but, even so, they have undergone various reforms. Changing values and behavioural patterns are a priority in order to get SOEs operating in new ways. Despite a growing body of research on Chinese business practices and entrepreneurship development (Reeder 1984; Shen 1994;

Naughton 1994; Child 1995; Schlevogt 2001; Warner 2004; Luo et al. 2005; Tang et al. 2007; Yang 2007; Kshetri 2007; Yang and Li 2008), there appears to be an absence of critical insight into the significance of entrepreneurship within state-owned enterprises or indeed on the influence of Chinese industry structures and economic reforms in approaches to strategic entrepreneurship development within these enterprises. Yet, assumptions are made about entrepreneurship being the main driver for efficiency gains and the improvement of effectiveness of state-owned enterprises which are caught between the traditional pressures of maintaining the status quo of state administration and the demands of a global market economy (Baark 2001; Wang and Zang 2005; Phan et al. 2008).

Building on the basic notion of entrepreneurship as the "identification of market opportunity and the creation of combinations of resources to pursue it" (Guth and Ginsberg 1990: 5), a firm-level perspective focuses on those organizational characteristics and behaviors aimed at innovation and strategic renewal (Zahra and Covin 1995). Such studies reveal that corporate entrepreneurship has significant consequences for firm survival, performance, and growth (Barringer and Bluedorn 1999; Zahra 1993). Tang and colleagues (2007), investigating 166 firms in northern China, confirm the positive influence of entrepreneurial orientation on performance. In particular, they find that the relationship between firm performance and entrepreneurial orientation is more positive among state-owned enterprises than among private-owned enterprises. The findings of an empirical research project among Chinese large firms by Luo and colleagues (2005), indicate that internationalization, firm size and age, and market orientation all impact on the practice of entrepreneurship in organizations, and that this in turn contributes to superior performance. Chen (2004) argues that, for China, the corporate governance structure results in the inefficiency of SOEs and that the creation of an effective corporate governance mechanism requires the development of the country's market-oriented institutions. Since entrepreneurship within organizations (including entrepreneurial activities and orientations at the level of an established organization) has been recognized as an important element in organizational and economic development, performance, and wealth creation, an advocacy of corporate entrepreneurship development in state-owned enterprise is leading to ownership diversification and structural change in recent reform progress, resulting in privatization and a minor degree of private ownership involvement in state-controlled enterprises. However, Antoncic and Hisrich (2003) argue that ownership structures with substantial state involvement could inhibit the development of entrepreneurship activities and are not beneficial for organizational growth and profitability.

A resource-based view (RBV) of the firm suggests that the essential aspect of entrepreneurship is that of developing and configuring organizational resources and capabilities. It asserts that heterogeneous endowments of resources and capabilities shape organizations and form the main sources of competitive advantage (Barney 1986; Grant 1991; Hamel and Prahalad 1993). An extension of RVB is that of the knowledge-based view (KBV), which models organizations as knowledge-bearing entities (Nonaka and Takeuchi 1995) that leverage knowledge for competitive advantage (Barney 1986; Grant 1996; Foss 1996). In line with KBV research, knowledge can be uniquely retained by an organization and thereby yield sustainable profit. A core premise of this perspective is that growth within companies occurs through entrepreneurial activities that exploit and create knowledge (Foss 1996; Kogut and Zander 1996; Grant 1996; Spender and Grant 1996). Following this perspective, Guadamillas and colleagues (2008) explore the way an established firm uses resources and capabilities, and especially its accumulated knowledge, through case study research. They identify some of the most important factors contributing to the success of this strategy, such as the internal development and integration of relevant technological knowledge, human resources policies, organizational flexibility, knowledge management tools based on IT, and purchase of companies and cooperation agreements for the acquisition of external knowledge.

A contingency perspective addresses interrelations of organizational change and highlights the interaction between structure, strategy, systems, culture, and human capital (Peters and Waterman 1980; Triandis 1994). As Dessler (1976) noted, complexity, uncertainty, and diversity emerge as important determinants of organizational form. These determinants, in turn, mirror the type of task the organization must perform, with entrepreneurial, creative tasks resulting in greater uncertainty, complexity, and diversity for the organization. The organization, process-based contingency view addresses the integrity of the organization and interactions of organizational factors. For instance, structure shapes strategy and vice versa; the characterization of structure can be revealed by the ways in which staff work; the style of the manager's behavior reflects the culture and beliefs of the organization. This view can build up a profile of organizational characteristics, which allows the importance of organizational performance to the implementation processes to be examined (see Chapter 4 for a case illustration and analysis of this view).

Chinese organizational behavior: "Guanxi" networks

The Chinese business network is subject to debate in Western practitioner and academic discourse, generating a host of questions focusing on the way in which Chinese enterprises behave differently from their Western counterparts, how Chinese society is distinctively characterised by Guanxi culture, and whether Western firms should understand and adopt Guanxi practice in order to achieve superior competitive success in the Chinese market. In China, Guanxi is characterized by the combination of political connections and social capital in the transitional market economy, which means that more complex and dynamic relationships are involved in Chinese business networks (Guo and Miller 2010; Park and Luo 2001; Martinsons 2008; Simmons and Munch 1996; Buttery and Wong 1999; Bian and Ang 1997). In one dominant stream of studies, Guanxi is labeled as the most distinctive feature of the Chinese style of networking that resonates well in Asian culture, where it is regarded as an essential strategy for Western firms to adopt as they enter the Chinese market (Wong and Chan 1999; Standifird and Marshall 2000; Jenkins 2000). The growing literature on Guanxi emphasizes a mix of wisdom and cultural distinction—the ancient roots of Chinese social networking—with the embedded heritage of Confucianism (Yang 1994; Cheng and Rosett 1991; Tan 2002a; Wang *et al.* 2005), suggesting that Guanxi, in traditional clientelism, may be associated with corruption, with others questioning its appropriateness to a modern society (Guthrie 1998; Fan 2002; Anderson and Lee 2008). Little attention has, however, been paid to how Guanxi practice varies across ownership forms: although Guanxi is used to access resources including, *inter alia*, political power, licenses, information, and finance (Yang 2004) by leveraging the value of political connections to secure opportunities and advantages (Nee and Opper 2010), access, most crucially, is determined by whether a firm is either state-owned or private-owned (Yang 2002; Yang 2004; Tan 2002b; Zheng and Scase 2013). State-owned enterprises (SOEs), as distinct from private-owned enterprises (POEs), derive many advantages from government ownership, since they have direct contacts with decision-making ministerial bodies, which can lead to laws that reduce taxes, restrict competition in the domestic markets, and curb the import strategies of foreign companies (Lai 2010; Kennedy 2005; Langlois 2004). Indeed, politically connected firms can secure positional advantage over unconnected firms under tight resource constraints (Nee and Opper 2010), and yet political connectedness can have both positive and negative effects on firm value subject to firm ownership (Wu *et al.* 2012). We thus contend that the dynamic of changing Guanxi relations should be assessed across different ownership forms to distinguish the political and social elements in business network relationships. Institutional changes and the free-market economy continue to shape people's cultural and ideological perceptions; and political games have different impacts on different types of entrepreneurs and organizations depending on the degree of political connections between the business and the government authorities. The changing market conditions and institutional environment continue to either preserve or reduce the value of political capital. In today's increasingly dynamic business world, many more firms are focusing on supply chain networks and innovation activities instead of political connections, as they seek complementary resources and develop new capabilities through collaboration with other firms to ensure superior competitive performance.

The trend of cultural convergence and entrepreneurship

Small entrepreneurial businesses (wherever located) are over-dependent upon the owner-manager's energy, risk-taking capacities, and ability to obtain external resources for survival and growth—hence they deploy expedient, short-term, opportunistic and pragmatic business strategies, which reflect a potential lack of internal resources and access to external resources to enable longer-term business plans and clearly defined, coherent business strategies. Conversely, their larger counterparts, particularly cross-border or multinational companies (MNCs), can access resources and expertise and have a cadre of experts and professional managers with in-depth knowledge in functional specialisms and hence their greater business credibility facilitates access to a wider range of external resources (e.g.

strategic business partners, expert consultants, financial assets, loan or equity capital etc.) Networks and connections are universally important in both social and business contexts, especially to obtain resources, to secure opportunities, and to maintain connections with their suppliers and clients. In this regard, Chinese entrepreneurial firms operate analogously to those in the West and have the same objectives, but how they reach the outcome—whether by giving gifts, banquets, or exchange of favors—varies considerably. National cultural differences distinguish Chinese Guanxi practice from Western networking behavior (Holden 2002) and, despite many differences and numerous arguments against convergence, many more similarities exist than one might expect (Miner et al. 1991) such that the processes inherent in economic development and industrialization have led to universal attitudes, values, and beliefs regardless of the national or cultural context, for example when comparing US and Russian respondents (Bailey and Spicer 2007; Alexashin and Blenkinsopp 2005; Holt 1997). Although the dynamics of market transition have led to a divergence of management practices, the influence of international "best practice" (particularly the universal rules of the free market) promotes a convergence of management practices, especially to an ideal "culture free" entrepreneurial economy (ibid.). It implies that, despite different cultural roots, the market economy imposes standardized capitalist and international practices, which increases the use of social capital to build market-oriented relationships.

The development of market socialism and Guanxi: an institutional perspective

The Communist Party of China has gradually developed its own socialist model and has radically and innovatively redefined many terms and concepts of Marxist economic theory in the Chinese context to justify its economic policies, perceiving no fundamental contradiction between socialism and a market economy, which is indispensable to the allocation of resources in socialized production. As a distinctive feature of the "China Model," which generates a hybrid market structure encompassing both public and private ownership (Naughton 1994; Opper 2001; Wu 1993), the communist regime remains intact, and reforms have gradually eroded state economic controls rather than quickly retreating from planning (Peng et al. 2004), revealing a hybrid economic system representing a mixed political economy with both socialist and capitalist characteristics (Lichtenstein 1992; Morphy et al. 1992; Naughton 1994; Opper 2001), with continuing intervention in market exchanges and transactions, and political factors influencing the direction of the economy (Gao and Tian 2006). This hybrid "market socialist" economy enables rent-seeking[1] by officials (and others) who exploit discrepancies between the two price mechanisms (Wedeman 2003) by gaining from it and their political control of resources, thus engendering the orientation of corruption and dependency on Guanxi (Wu 1993), and an administrative monopoly representing a unique power exchange for goods in transition economies (Guo and Hu 2004), leading to rampant rent-seeking Guanxi (Lin et al. 1996; Dorn 1998). The market, when politically manipulated, can promote the abuse of power by State officials; with two suggested types of Guanxi: (1) culturally rooted "favor-seeking" Guanxi; and (2) institutionally defined rent-seeking *quanli Guanxi*, based on power dependence relationships of power exchange which reflect the authoritarian-based state's organizational hierarchy and institutions (Su and Littlefield 2001). Entrepreneurs are, consequently, under the constraint of institutional rules when they try to take advantage of institutional holes and seek opportunities (Yang 2004). Indeed, the utilization of personal connections, particularly in private firms, can substitute for formal institutional support in the absence of a complete legal framework for a private economy in transitional societies (Xin and Pearce 1996). Political capital becomes more important for firms to invest in, in order to secure advantages when governments restrict resources and information transparency. Yet political capital is, arguably, fungible in all types of economies, and China does not differ fundamentally from established market economies (Nee and Opper 2010), such that SOEs with close connections to the political elite perform worse than private firms (Fan *et al.* 2007; Wu *et al.* 2012) and purely market competitive players—often active in privately organized markets and knowledge-intensive sectors—refuse to invest in political networking in preference to product and technology competency, which they regard as key to their success. Nevertheless, political capital still can yield valuable economic advantages (Nee and Opper 2010) for entrepreneurs and firms who frequently transact in those markets and who will, therefore, have strong incentives to maintain and cultivate political connections.

However, power exchange Guanxi may lead to corruption and illegal deals that may be destructive to business development in the long run. Corruption is regarded as the most damaging political side effect in the reform era of China's market socialism, as evidenced by large and increasing numbers of Party members and provincial or ministerial-level officials being disciplined for corruption (Lai 2006: 249). Increasing ethical concern over the use of political connections has raised critical questions about its appropriateness and legitimacy. Some studies point out that Guanxi's negative effect could lead to personal gains rather than organizational benefits in the long run (Chen and Chen 2009; Dunfee and Warren 2001) and challenge the morality of business practices (Snell and Tseng 2002). So we contend that the use of "political" Guanxi is less likely to build organizational core competency in the long run, being based on short-term transactions and sometimes having a detrimental effect; whereas the use of "rational" market-based Guanxi is likely to contribute to a firm's long-term sustainability.

Globalization and emerging forms of business venture

Globalization involves the exchange of enormous quantities of capital, labor, goods, and services across national borders (Marcussen and Kaspersen 2007), and existing hierarchical structures of governance have been challenged by the increased velocity, intensity, and extensiveness of global transactions, while states have undergone a process of transformation, undertaking new functions (Held *et al.* 1999). Chinese Government systems have been gradually reconstructed to create new functions of public services, whilst democratic, functional, and servant-oriented governance mechanisms are the major objective of reforms in order to focus on free-market and business activities, which depart from the state's central government that formerly had a direct mandate and control of its economic systems. In the age of globalization, private actors (Boli and Thomas 1997), transnational corporations (Scholte 2008), international governmental organizations (McNeely 1995), and networks play an increasing role in driving the process of liberalization, deregulation, and Westernization.

State-owned enterprises

Unlike Western capitalist countries, China's gradualist transformation proceeded through the dynamic interplay of state-guided and entrepreneurial capitalism (Baumol 2007), in which market-oriented firms, such as state-owned enterprises in the state sector and private-owned enterprises and foreign joint ventures in the private sector, play critical roles in developing the market economy. In the early 1990s, enterprise reforms were identified as institutional innovations, hence the new system of "modern corporate institutions," which replaced the old system of "autonomy decentralization and profit retention." This was implemented in the (experimental) 1994 "Corporation Law," leading to 100 SOEs being reformed. In 1997 these were extended to medium-sized state-owned enterprises. This innovation aimed to reduce Government interference in, and encourage entrepreneurialism within, large SOEs so they could become internationally competitive firms, structured along the same lines as Western corporations, with independent Boards of Directors accountable to shareholders rather than the government (Sheehan *et al.* 2000), with an emphasis on corporate governance and a multiple-investor structure being proposed in 1999 (Wu 2003; Chen *et al.* 2008). With SOEs being rife (China Statistics Year Book 2005), many large SOEs have achieved significant improvements in their performance on both domestic and international markets; for example Haier, Changhong, Shanghai Haixin, Huali, Shenzhen Mingda, TCL, and China Petrol which, between 2001 and 2003, have made successful lucrative overseas mergers and acquisitions (Zhang 2003) (see Chapter 4 for a case illustration).

Private-owned enterprises

Organized in a very informal way because of how the domestic private sector emerged historically in the shadow of the state economy, many POEs possess only vague property rights, ownership structures, corporate governance mechanisms, financial records, and rights to market access. The policy environment to date has favoured state-owned enterprises, whether in providing access to markets, or to resources and finance, and policy discrimination is still significant towards private-owned enterprise (Li *et al.* 2004), when compared with foreign firms with granted policies and privileged benefits. In light of the institutional perspective, entrepreneurs everywhere are under the constraint of institutional rules when they try to take advantage of structural positions and institutional holes (Yang 2004), but they use Guanxi to identify opportunities in institutionally separated niches exploit poorly defined and enforced rules, and obtain resources (see Chapter 5 for case illustration).

Foreign joint ventures

Foreign direct investment (FDI) has driven the growth of China's economy and generated greater global economic integration. Additionally, mobile labor has bridged the cultural, institutional, and contractual differences across nations (Wu 2003; Child and Tse 2001) providing an increasing number of jobs (Cooke 2004; China Statistical Yearbook 2005: 526), diversifying the economy, and facilitating technology transfer. Notably, early-established Western MNCs have adapted their more sophisticated management practices to the Chinese environment (Bjorkman and Fan 2002), and are often hailed by the Chinese media as good models to be followed by domestic firms (Cooke 2004). The ability of Chinese indigenous firms to adapt to change and develop core competencies of product quality and management skills has become increasingly important in market competition, whilst the traditionalist value of Guanxi has changed accordingly alongside institutional and market development. Thus, a more universal principle of business networking, based on the transaction-market, has emerged to replace the old value of Guanxi, although to a certain extent it may still retain certain features of the Chinese style (Anderson and Lee 2008). Under an increased degree of globalization and market economy, the influence and function of Guanxi has appeared to weaken as market deregulation deepens and a more formally regulatory market environment emerges (OECD 2002). This review gives rise to the belief that Guanxi is likely to play different roles in different types of businesses at different phases of their growth path, as the strategic emphases of network activities vary in relation to ownership and industry (see Chapter 6 for case illustration).

Institutional change, network relationships and firm growth

As the Chinese economy continuously transforms itself towards a freer market and sound legal framework, the monopolized interests based on public property will decline, leading to less dependence on such *quanli* (power) or rent-seeking Guanxi. Chinese governance mechanisms are in the process of being transformed to a servant-oriented function, rather than authoritarian-based control. Ostensibly, the continuously increased transparency of information and improved communication mechanisms will reduce power exchange activities; e.g. the nationwide reform of China's customs structure and system from 1998 to 2001 (LNCIQ 2011), which aimed to implement international standards of customs service and eliminate "red-tapism." The Guanxi phenomenon is more likely to be an outcome of political and institutional settings, as cultural values and norms gradually change and as institutional and political structures transform from one state to another (see Table 3.1). Table 3.1 demonstrates how regulative, normative, and cognitive values in the state and private sectors have changed over time alongside economic reforms and institutional revolution. According to Organizational

Development (OD) theory, three factors—resource, process, and value—affect organizational response to different types of change (Rollinson and Broadfield 2005; Grieves 2000; Zheng and Scase 2013) starting in resources then moving to visible, articulated processes and values, and finally migrating to culture— implying that organizational processes, internal resources, and capabilities also determine firms' performance. Our empirical case study findings suggest that Guanxi connections seem to play a more critical role at both the start-up stage and later in the market, depending on government-controlled resources, such as government contracts, state-controlled licenses as high entry barriers, and state bank finance. However, political application becomes less important when firms move to the fast-growth stage, whilst they increasingly depend on technology, product quality, organizational capacity, and profitability as the core competency in their market competition (consistent with Park and Luo 2001; and Nee and Opper 2010, suggesting that organizations with advanced skills and resources are less dependent upon Guanxi connections). The use of Guanxi sometimes overrides Government rules and regulations, including gift giving, Guanxi, and corruption. For example, the supplier–buyer relationship between UK and Chinese companies is subject to significant levels of bribery and illicit payments, which are concerned with individual gain rather than corporate benefits (Millington *et al.* 2005) and the impact of such Guanxi practice may be expected to undermine the long-term relationships that are essential to Just-in-Time systems (Brand and Slater 2003). *Quanli* (power), or rent-seeking Guanxi in particular, tends to involve bribery, which puts firms in jeopardy (Su and Littlefield 2001). Moreover, power exchange activities that are based on short-term transactions, such as government tenure, will be altered on a three- to five-year basis and will have a detrimental effect on building organizational competency. Our longitudinal case study of SOE from 2005–10 demonstrated that the political Guanxi culture causes organizational inertia and affects human capital development, which presents a challenge for future development and growth (see the case illustration in Chapter 4).

Managerial implications of management and behavioral issues in China

The political-ideological system of market socialism continues to influence all aspects of society, including the operation of enterprises and economic transactions. However, the extent of such influence is subject to the type of ownership (Zheng and Scase 2013; Tan 2002a). Managing business and organizational dynamics can be a huge challenge to managers as the business environment in China has become increasingly competitive and complex. Business concepts and management methodologies in different types of emerging business venture have evolved over time both on organizational and institutional grounds (as Table 3.1 illustrates). Understanding these changes is crucial in order to gain an insight into the characteristics of Chinese management practice. The area of knowledge management in entrepreneurship research has been a growing field, with increasing attention being paid to the role of new competency development. Resource-based

Table 3.1 Institutional components of state and private sector enterprises

Institutional components		State sector	Private sector
Regulative			
	Past (before 1978)	State-owned enterprises (SOE) are the dominant force and have a special privilege monopoly position in the market.	Private enterprises only existing in market gap and institutional holes (Yang 2004); regulation slack to private property and entrepreneurs, and the absence of institutional support (Yang 2002).
		High political Guanxi activities due to dominant state ownership and socialist regime with command economy.	*High Guanxi dependence activities to obtain resources and seek the umbrella of political protection.*
	Present (after 2000)	Retreat from the dominant force of market economy but still retain major components in strategically important industries; SOEs characterized by economies of scale, policy-directed, administration-controlled and with a lack of flexibility and ability to respond to market change.	Substantial force of market economy; institutional change towards the completion of legitimacy, granted privileges and promotion of the growth of private enterprises and foreign-invested enterprises. POEs dominate low value-added manufacturing activities and FJVs occupy high value-added activities
		Reduced political Guanxi activities and increased reliance upon technology and knowledge-based competency and market rules.	*Reduced dependence on personal Guanxi and institutional holes and increased extension of market exchange activities and international markets.*
Normative			
	Past	Complete dependence on government planning, administration, soft budgets and political power; little management autonomy under planned economy.	Survival of private businesses closely linked to the firms' relationships with local authorities and powerful individuals who control market resources. POEs seek informal institutional support from Guanxi networks.
		Political relationships with upper authorities are critical for job security and resource allocation in SOEs.	*Relationships with powerful bureaucrats and politicians are likely to determine the success or failure of business operation due to the absence of an institutional and legal infrastructure.*

Continued

Table 3.1 Continued

Institutional components	State sector	Private sector
Present	Management restructuring creates ownership diversity and reduced state-controlled governance and granted management autonomy to SOEs. Adoption of modern corporation system and separation of enterprise management and political administration enhances market-orientation incentives, which lead to profit-driven objectives in SOEs. *Policy-directed and profit-driven value becomes the dominant norm in SOEs' market activities, and managers' belief in political Guanxi has changed to be complementary.*	The improvement of formal institutions towards the private sector provides supportive policies to the rapid growth of private firms and promotes increasing recognition of the importance of entrepreneurship. Private-owned enterprises and foreign joint ventures become the dominant force in the market economy. *Entrepreneurial culture, increased market value and globalization are likely to direct business activities focusing on long-term sustainability depending on core competency and market-oriented relationships, while the traditional Guanxi influence has been significantly reduced to merely a facilitating role rather than a deterministic factor.*
Cognitive		
Past	Privilege to work in state-owned enterprises and a symbol of being middle class and having a high social status. *Access to market resources and opportunities are the prerogative of those who are in power, which leads to dependence upon Guanxi with powerful people.*	Objection to the private economy and no recognition of private entrepreneurs; "getihu" (individual business or private small company) are looked down upon as the low class of the social hierarchy. *The survival of private business has to rely on who you personally know, favoritism and rent-seeking activities.*
Present	State economy has retreated from the market component and there is a changing perception of SOEs' declining position and their shrinkage in competitive industries, in which they have been replaced by private businesses.	Private businesses gain their legitimacy in the market economy. They are recognized as a symbol of success and an inspiration of entrepreneurship. Chinese private entrepreneurs can formally participate in the Government election system as an innovative measure of market socialism.

Table 3.1 Continued

Institutional components	State sector	Private sector
	Profit-making ability becomes more essential in SOEs, whilst political relationship and who you know have declined despite the latter still existing; however, economic emphasis and materialist values have changed the mission of SOEs in the market economy.	As the role of institutional infrastructure and policy increases, R&D ability, technological innovation and "green enterprise" criteria become more important in the private sector.

competency is increasingly seen as a knowledge-based view of a firm with knowledge emerging as the most valuable of resources, and how to access, manage, and apply knowledge becoming a major research issue (Lockett *et al.* 2009). A firm's competency can be dependent upon external factors, such as its network with suppliers, customers, and government agencies, which can provide input and resources not available to it (Von Hippel 1988; Freeman 1991). Guanxi can be viewed by the firm as a resource, while the cost (in terms of time and effort) of acquiring and maintaining it can be significant to the organization. Its appropriate application, relevant contexts, and long-term effects on organizations need to be understood and taken into consideration when assessing opportunities and resource allocation. Otherwise, it can result in detrimental effects and liabilities (Vanhonacker 2004).

Although we have discussed studies conducted in China, there are some generic issues that hold true for any business organization, irrespective of the context. For example, whether a company is located in a capitalist or socialist country, there is frequently an excessive over-dependency upon the energy, innovative risk-taking ability, and capability of the manager to obtain external resources. These qualities frequently shape the extent to which a business will survive and the manner in which it can grow. The top managers' decision-making capacity and shareholders' relationship also have a critical impact on the success of any business venture. Becoming a learning organization has been strongly advocated in management practice across the world. Networking strategy is prioritized externally through partnerships and strategic alliances, which entrepreneurs and managers can draw on for reciprocal expertise, knowledge, and technology to compensate for their limited internal resources (Lall 1992; Romijn and Albaladejo 2002). However, for small businesses, the focus should be upon developing internal knowledge management systems, including investing in staff training and nurturing a learning culture, as this affects organizational capabilities for accumulating and retaining knowledge gained from external networks (Zheng 2013; Malerba 1992; Wallin and von Krogh 2010). A balance between external and internal knowledge acquisition should be maintained as the latter is often neglected by entrepreneurs and managers.

Most Chinese firms have placed themselves in labor-intensive industries to access a low-cost advantage (Li and Qian 2009), which may make them vulnerable to external changes. However, it is evident that the strategic focus of these emerging business ventures is shifting towards a more innovation- and technology-oriented development process (Fu 2012; Zhao 2006). Chinese firms use the means of increasing product portfolios and advancing production technology to improve their competitiveness and elevate their supply chain positioning (Zheng 2013). However, managers need to be aware of the conditions required for the choice of diversification strategy as this needs not only market knowledge, but specialized staff skills and high management competency. This suggests that managers and entrepreneurs must possess the skills together with open-mindedness towards the constant learning of new knowledge in order to help the business in an appropriate way. A well-designed integration and diversification strategy may enhance a firm's competitiveness and profitability (Campbell 1995; Chatterjee *et al.* 1992; Rommer 1990). Such managerial implications would help entrepreneurs and managers to appropriately formulate their strategic choices with relevant understanding of conditions and processes acquired. To understand how organizations learn, and to be able to apply this to maintain a sustainable competitive advantage, is likely to facilitate the achievement of a successful growth outcome.

Note

1 Defined as economic rent referring to the returns over and above the costs of employing a monopolistic resource (e.g. bureaucratic power) by manipulating government policy (Su and Littlefield 2001).

4 The contradictions of state-owned enterprises

Introduction

Studies of business organizations in China have yet to focus on the impact of different types of ownership upon management styles and organizational behavior. Clearly, different ownership types can lead to different organizational processes, giving rise to variations in strategy, structure, systems, values, management style, and decision-making. In addition, the legal context and regulations, as these relate to different types of business venture, create organizational differences in the market environment in which business ventures operate. This is a distinctive feature of market socialism that cannot be neglected.

Private-owned and foreign-owned joint ventures that have emerged under market transformation are continuously changing. State-owned enterprises (SOE) are also undergoing management restructuring, corporatization, and ownership diversification. The reform of state-owned enterprises has long been restricted by the Communist Party's socialist ideology but, even so, they have undergone various reforms. So, too, have collective-owned, cooperative enterprises as these have evolved from town and village businesses under earlier state socialism. We discuss these issues by reference to case studies of different enterprises. The first of these is LTG, a state-owned enterprise.

LTG history: a state-owned enterprise

The case of LTG is a state-owned public corporation that was legally "spun-off" from a large state garments trading company in 1998.[1] Its history reflects re-structuring progress since 1955 by administrative reforms, from "centralization," to "decentralization," and a market-focused organization. It was originally a broader Import and Export Company. It then specialized in the textile industry and became the China Textiles Import & Export Corporation in 1960. It was an adjunct of the State administrative system, managed by the Central Party Committee. In 1987, it developed as a market-focused trading company with an emphasis on the import and export of garments and related products.

Changes in the global economy and China's accession to the WTO provided the company with the opportunity to reform and become the organization of

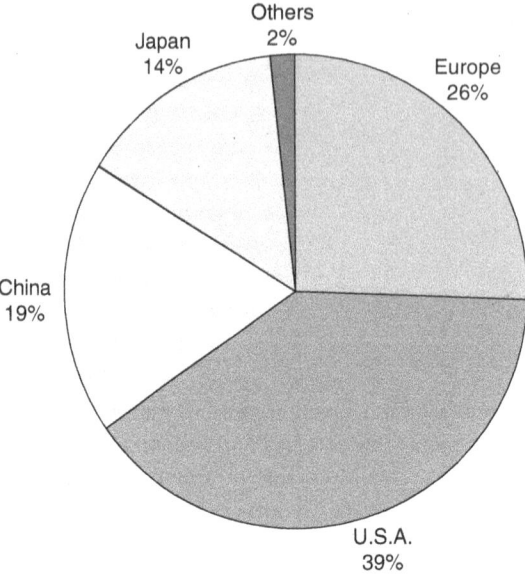

Figure 4.1 Contribution to profits by different markets, 2005.

today: a public company listed on the "A" stock market of Shanghai in 2000. In August 2001, it became legally incorporated with an independent board of directors. It consisted of six wholly-owned, and partly-owned factories, and its operational functions included fabric dyeing and garment production. Its annual production was more than two million garments and 105 million meters of dyed fabrics. On the basis of this core activity, the company was gradually diversifying into different industries, such as real estate, property management, and retail services. It was also attempting to gain a foot in the capital market for investment management.

In the light of LTG's performance, the statistics demonstrate steady but slow growth in profitability and a dramatic improvement in shareholder equity. Its fixed assets have significantly increased from 291 million RMB (US$35 million) in 2000 to 830 million RMB (US$100 million) in 2005. The main trading business, Times Garments Export and Import (TGIEI), contributes to the majority profit of LTG's total annual gains. Its profit share has increased from 75 percent in 2002 to 90 percent in 2005. The major profit from TGIEI is from overseas markets, basically from the three areas of Europe, the US and Japan. The profit from China's domestic sales was only 19 percent in 2005 (see Figure 4.1).

LTG is a good example of a state-owned enterprise that has successfully transformed from a production unit under the planned economy to a market-focused enterprise operating in a competitive environment. Through restructuring and corporatization, it has become a public company and a leading force in the textile

Contradictions of state-owned enterprises 63

industry and it plays a dominant role in both domestic and overseas markets. It represents an epitome of how state-owned Chinese enterprises have evolved and it mirrors the evolution of management in the state sector in general. During the fieldwork, senior management's reluctance to answer some questions reflected political sensitivity and how government attitudes still affect management behavior and decision-making within the enterprise. This is despite its claims that restructuring has divorced the administration of the State Authority from enterprise management. The interviews and observations indicate that although LTG is a market-oriented conglomerate corporation, it is still directly influenced by the state and by political forces.

LTG has strategic planning for five-year, short-term objectives and ten-year, long-term goals. The statement of strategy is explicit at both the corporate and operational levels. Like the company's formalized management systems, the strategy is officially documented and elaborated. It reflects political direction and government policy as well as LTG's development from continued market reforms. The ten-year development goals of LTG (2002–2012) are:

> To enhance the company's innovative capacity in business diversification; to grow the total profitability by 1.5 times on the basis of 2002, and to achieve one hundred million RMB in 2012. To develop LTG as a large-scale conglomerate with strong assets and competitiveness; and to diversify into trading and manufacturing industries.
>
> (Author interview, 2006)

State-owned enterprises are highly policy-led and characterized as reactive to restructuring demands as they are inclined to conform to institutional arrangements. Their resource-focused competitive advantage is built upon on a grant-aided policy (Hassard *et al.* 2010). They have enjoyed privileged access to state bank finance. Mergers and acquisitions are taking place between medium- to large-sized SOEs across sectors, which enables diverse state-owned businesses to agglomerate to form larger industrial clusters. Such a strategy is creating quasi-monopoly industries that dominate vital sectors of the Chinese economy. For example, in this case, LTG merged with one of the largest national state-owned real estate company's in 2008–9. This is possible under market socialism because of Party control, which is exercised over state-owned enterprises.

The structure of this state-owned enterprise, at both administrative and governance levels, reflects the impact of state ownership over the formation of its structure. The Administration and Inspection Committee of State Assets (AICSA) was set up in 2002 by the sixteenth Congress of the Communist Party. This was followed by the issue of a Provisional Decree of the Enterprise and State Assets Administration and Inspection, which provides the basic infrastructure for the administration of state assets. The Decree defines the role of AICSA to be that:

> In accordance with its authorization, AICSA fulfils the owner's duty to implement discretion in State owned and controlled enterprises in terms of

independence, merger, purchase, bankruptcy, dismissal, decrease or increase in capital, issue of bonds, cessions of shares, etc. and other such grand proceedings. It also appoints at all levels of senior posts, such as the president, vice president, the general manager, vice general manager, principle accountant, and Board of Directors.

(Li 2004: 4)

This new administrative agency—AICSA—is responsible for the administration and supervision of State assets after the separation of political and enterprise governance. It has the role of "Boss" or the "representative of the owner" in order to fulfill owner responsibilities; that is, election of management, claims on profits, major decision-making, and the disposal of assets. However, as Fang from The State Finance Ministry says:

The degree of this function and how far this administration can go are not specified in detail. For example, there is no current law on how to distribute the profits of State-Owned Enterprises although there is a proposal for operational budget planning. But it does not explain clearly the relations between the operational budget of State assets and State finance at the extent to whether the gains of State assets should be included into the revenue of State finance.

(Fang 2004: 8)

As a result, some conflicts and undefined relations still confuse its implementation. The present Party Secretary of LTG, Ms Liang, says in an interview in this case study:

As a state-owned enterprise, the current management structure of LTG is still inefficient and the reforms have not had much significant effect upon improving our management efficiency. We still have not established the appropriate mechanisms in relation to the market. The old management systems in conjunction with the State administration still remain the same. If you ask the former Party Secretary, who was in the post at the company from 1987 to 2004, you would find that the current structure of LTG is quiet similar to what it was before. Personally, I think the quality of management in this state-owned enterprise is far behind that of the advanced foreign enterprises. Moreover, there is so much uncertainty and confusion in many of the guiding policies from the central authority. As an enterprise, we are still waiting for how to move to the next step in structural reforms. It tells you that nothing is certain at this time. What I say today might change later. Especially my personal opinions need to be in concordance with central authority, but we now wait for new instructions. The state-owned enterprise is not very flexible like private-owned enterprises, as there are many restrictions on our operations and management. For example, in our marketing and sales, the strategy and plans are fixed and settled without flexibility, so we are unable

Contradictions of state-owned enterprises 65

to adjust and adopt changes in line with demands that arise from customers and the market. We have a different structure in place as a state-owned enterprise.

(Author interview, 2006)

Interviews with the former Company Party Secretary, Mr Qi, Vice General Manager, Mr Li, as well as other divisional managers, also demonstrated similar attitudes of inflexibility and "constraint" within the company's complex and multi-dimensional structure. The organizational chart, provided by the company's planning department, is shown in Figure 4.2.

It is a rigid hierarchy, controlling personnel, finance, and corporate strategy. The AICSA represents the State and the Communist Party and exercises direct administration over both wholly-owned and share-holding enterprises. The central

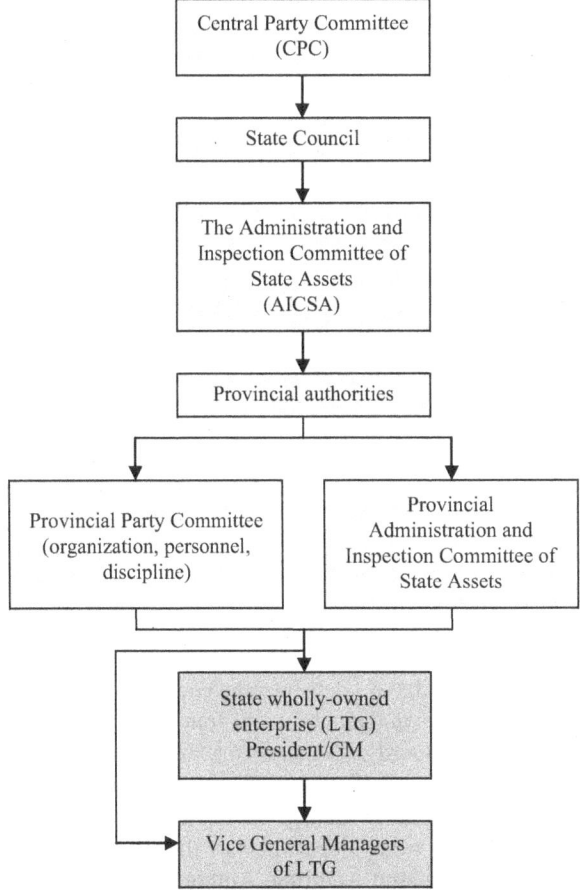

Figure 4.2 Structure of government administration responsible for LTG.

66 *Contradictions of state-owned enterprises*

State Authority still has holistic and tight administrative control over state-owned enterprises, but its power is aggregated in one body—AICSA. This top-down administration restricts the enterprise's ability to respond to changing markets and customer demands. Instead, political issues dominate the nature of management in state-owned enterprises. Although the Party Committee has parallel power to AICSA, it has a weaker impact. As the current Company Party Secretary, Ms Liang says:

> As the Party Secretary, our role is to smooth the management, and help people stay in the same direction as the party. We hold frequent meetings and discussion sessions for the consistent education of the Party's ideas as well as for the assurance of political concordance. We solve conceptual conflicts in management, and spiritually motivate them for the maintenance of high moral and ethics at work. We normally don't get involved in business operations, except for board meetings at the corporate level for big decision-making. We usually support the general manager's decisions.
>
> (Author interview, 2006)

The former Party Secretary, Mr Qi, also says:

> I was the Party Secretary from 1987, and retired from this post in 2004. The role of party secretary becomes weaker and less important in State enterprises after the market transformations. Market values and competition have gradually taken over from the old concepts of equality and life-security. The focus of work has shifted dramatically. In the past, the party secretary was superior to the general manager and determined all the decisions in the enterprise, but after the market reforms, our function and power of influence have faded away. We have become a necessary but insignificant figure. The work involved in our routine is with personnel, focusing on moral and ethics, carrying Party ideas to employees and conveying new concepts from the central Party authority to senior management. However, the principle work in the enterprise today is to focus on the market and so that management can generate profits for the higher authorities.
>
> (Author interview, 2006)

Since 2001, Boards of Directors have been introduced in almost all public companies. The formal structure of management is illustrated in Figure 4.3. This consists of the Board of Directors, Board of Supervision, President, and General Manager. Final decisions are made by the Board of Directors, which is overseen by the Board of Supervision. The General Manager and Vice General Managers exert direct control through their functional departments—the General Manager's Office, Finance, Personnel, Planning, and Auditing. Authority and hierarchy are the key features of the LTG structure. The General Manager is basically the final decision-maker with relevant consultation with Vice General Managers. He also

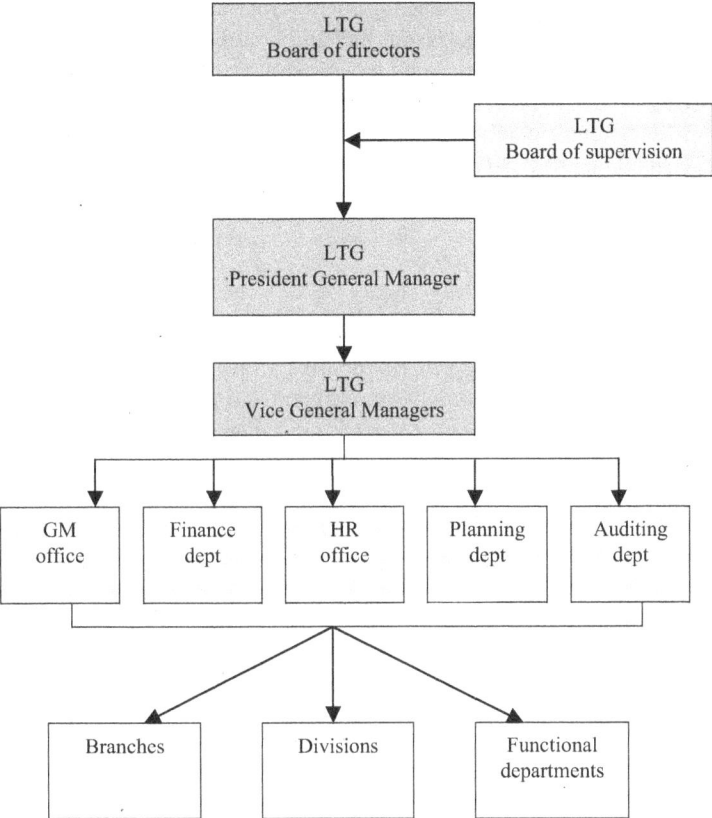

Figure 4.3 Structure of organizational functions within LTG.

reports to AICSA for authorization on key decisions that relate to corporate strategy, financial investment, and key personnel appointments. His job is not only about management at the corporate level but also about reporting to the higher authority—AICSA. Maintaining good relations with this higher authority is essential for senior managers, as AICSA has the discretion to appoint or dismiss them. In interviews, they are very cautious in what they say and practice discreet behavior. This is because AICSA stresses they should not give media interviews and should not disclose any information in public without authorization. In this case study, we obtained an interview with the Vice General Manager, Mr Li, because of a personal contact. When asked about the most significant change in LTG reforms, he says:

> The most significant change in state-owned enterprise is organisational restructuring in terms of management autonomy and corporatization. By learning from western companies, we have created the modern corporate

company to replace the old administrative unit. Tripartite governance formalizes the company's efficiency for the market economy: the board of directors, the board of supervision and the board of senior managers. Big decisions at corporate level, such as investment and strategy, need to get authorization from the AICSA. However, daily operational and divisional business decisions are delegated to lower-level managers. If we are compared to western companies, we are still far from complete corporate independence but compared to the state-owned enterprises of the past, it is a distinctive change in its regime.

(Author interview, 2006)

At the end of the interview, Mr Li emphasizes that I should treat him as an anonymous interviewee because AICSA doesn't allow him to speak to external agents. He mentions that AICSA is very powerful and places very tight controls and restrictions over senior managers in state-owned enterprises.

The Labor Union (LU) has a role in this state-owned enterprise structure. It holds an Employee Congress and has the right to speak for employee rights and welfare in LTG. As the former Party Secretary, Mr Qi says:

We hold a large Employee Congress once a year. Employees can freely express their opinions, proposals and suggestions. We put valuable opinions to the management for adoption. It is an organisation to protect employees' rights and benefits in accordance with the "Labor Law." Social events and activities for employees are held on a regular basis to improve their social and corporate life, and to make them feel part of the company. The Labor Union also provides help to solve problems in employee's personal lives. Greeting cards from the General Manager as well as gifts for all their holidays are organised for them by the Labor Union.

(Author interview, 2006)

Compared with private sector organizations, the Labor Union seems to have more functions and a much greater impact in this state enterprise. Take welfare as an example: a housing fund only exists in state-owned enterprises, but only sometimes in foreign joint ventures, and it is non-existent in the other private types of enterprise. Life security and employee benefits are well embodied in LTG. Extra hours at work are paid at a fair rate in line with the Labor Law. Annual increments in salary, as well as the offer of long-term stock equity to senior management, are implemented and guaranteed by formal contracts. This is in dramatic contrast to the insecurity of employee benefits and welfare in private-owned and collective-owned enterprises, where only minimal levels are promised. Employees' rights are ignored in these companies. The Labor Law is often breached, and employees work at weekends for long hours without extra pay. State enterprises are still operating in the same way as government agencies in that they have almost the same rules for staff and employee contracts.

In order to strengthen competitiveness in the market and to implement government requirements, LTG has invested one-and-a-half million RMB for the adoption of International Standards Organization (ISO) 9001 in 2000 and Quality Management System (QMS) in 2001. This system further formalizes the routine and management procedures for quality control in service and products. To quote what interviewees said about the QMS:

> We are required to implement QMS in order to improve the efficiency of management, as it specializes and clarifies the responsibilities and procedures for product and service management in each division and office. It constructs a formal procedure in company management, which regularizes the flow of supervision in terms of series of procedures and processes, makes quality control more predictable in planning. But the problem for this quality control system is that it is too complex to follow and these compulsive procedures are inflexible sometimes.
> (Mr Liu, Director of Planning Department; author interview, 2006)

> We think it is essential for us to have ISO 9001 and Quality Management System, as LTG is a very large company and we do need to have formal procedures in place to clarify everything to avoid confusion and argument. In my view, this system has improved our routine management, so that product and service are controllable and manageable. We don't have to worry about the person who is in charge of the work if he leaves, because the records and procedures of work are filed in documentation. This system implementation has solved such problems.
> (Mr Chen, Manager of International Co-Operation Department; author interview, 2006)

> The reforms in this SOE are intended to make for more efficient management to prevent inefficiency in the State sector. Responding to State administrative requirements, most SOEs are encouraged to adopt advanced QMS for managerial improvement. We spend RMB one and half million for the implementation of QMS. This seems worthy as it noticeably redefines and formalizes our management processes and fortifies LTG's competitiveness to fit in the market systems that are demanding better management.
> (Mr Qi, Past Party Secretary of LTG; author interview, 2006)

Management authority is decentralized to subsidiary companies and divisions through a Performance Control System, which monitors results instead of routines. According to the Director of the Planning Department, this control system is designed according to three methods—"Contract," "Rental," and "Stock-sharing." The branches and divisions in the "Contract" and "Rental" systems are given the autonomy to run their own businesses. They control their operations and determine their own strategies for markets. Each branch is responsible for its profit and loss and reports to the headquarters of LTG on an annual basis. The "Contract"

70 Contradictions of state-owned enterprises

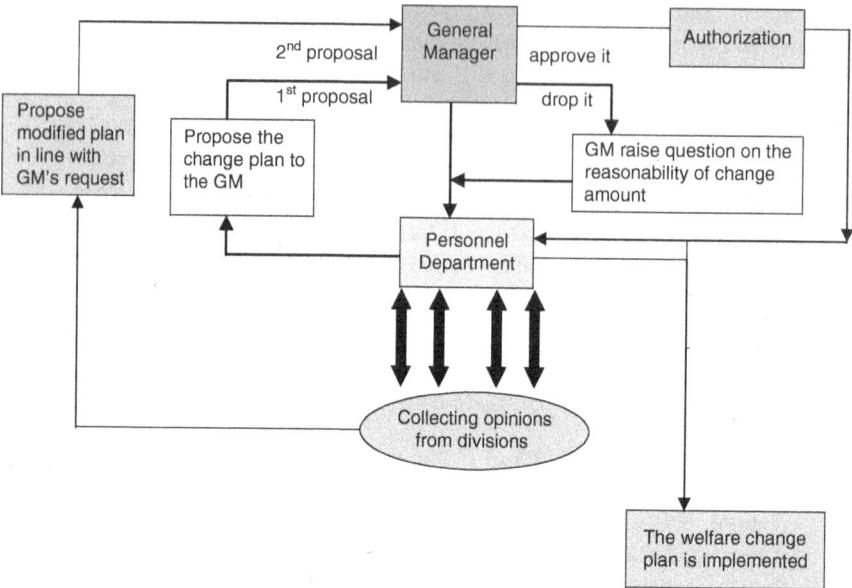

Figure 4.4 Decision-making processes for the change of welfare regulation in LTG.

method is to fix a target for profits and production that the branch has to achieve at the end of each year with agreed terms and conditions. The "Rental" method is to lease the facilities and assets to the subsidiary companies based on an agreement to pay rent each year. Headquarters retains control over these relatively independent branches by monitoring results in accordance with their accomplishment of profit targets. But if the contracted targets are not achieved, headquarters replaces the managers of the divisions/ branches.

The decision-making process is determined by the hierarchy level and the degree of authority. Simple and small decisions that do not relate to the whole organization can be made at the middle management level, without approval authority from the top. Operational decisions that relate to the strategy and finance of the whole organization require approved authority from headquarters—the General Manager. Big decisions in relation to strategy and institutional change require authorization from both the Board of Directors and AICSA. Mr Liu, Director of Planning, gives two examples of such decision-making. The first is for an operational decision—a change required in welfare regulation in terms of the annual heating fee for the employees. The following diagram (Figure 4.4) illustrates how this decision is made. The Personnel Department proposes this change plan to the General Manager, but he thinks the amount of change is unreasonable and passes the proposal to the Personnel Department for revision. The Personnel Department then passes this request to the subsidiary companies for the collection of opinions. Revisions are made on the basis of these suggestions. The second proposal is then handed to the General Manager for approval. Authorization is given and the Personnel Department then implements the final plan. Normally such a cycle requires one week for final decision-making.

Communication procedures and routine processes in LTG are formalized by rules and documentation. Paperwork is heavily used for information flows. Formal operational meetings as well as Party meetings are all held on a regular basis for both horizontal and vertical communication across middle line management and divisional heads. Senior management is very much engaged in all kinds of meetings for both organizational management issues and state administrative matters. Tight control from AICSA also requires frequent reports from the senior management of LTG. The Vice General Manager says that they are always busy in meetings with AICSA as this is not only part of their duties but they also need to maintain good relations with their ultimate political "boss."

The systems of LTG are still changing as it is in a process of market transformation. As a market-oriented SOE, LTG is further diversifying its product range across industries and continues to construct a better management capacity suitable for operating in a dynamic changing environment. The market economy requires efficiency and competitiveness, which is a big challenge for SOEs that have operated under a planned economy over such a long period of time. Structural change, ideological shift, and institutional transformation to a free market are very demanding for them. As China is still evolving its ownership patterns, it generates chain reactions for further changes in the configuration of organizations. Ownership is a practical issue at the current stage. As the Director of Planning, Mr Liu says:

> The central State authority will continue to reform ownership equity and stock equity, as these are two main issues in state-owned enterprises restructuring. We all know there will be changes coming soon, but we don't know how it will be. This worries us. These changes will require management innovation and new systems, but we don't have the professional knowledge for it. We are in the middle situation where the old systems are eliminated and new ones are not formed completely yet. At both top and middle management, we don't know how to change management to achieve what is expected after the ownership is further diversified. It is a significant difference in comparison with western public companies, as state-owned enterprises issue three types of stock to insure state ownership protection—State shares, Legal Corporate shares, and General shares. The total shares of LTG are 106 million, but only 30 million general shares are in public circulation for purchase. There are 70 million State shares and 6 million Legal Corporate shares that make up 66% of the total are not released for public purchase by the government, which insures the security of the State ownership. Although we have changed in many aspects in structure and management, the reality is that we are not a complete market company yet. We are still seeking for the best practice for state-owned enterprises.
>
> (Author interview, 2006)

Strategic decision-making is determined by upper political authority rather than by market demands. Despite management autonomy and ownership diversity, middle management is still tightly controlled through a culture that reflects the continuing dominance of the Party and centralized state ownership. A distinctive feature of the senior managers of this SOE is that more than one-half of them are from a military background; all held military rank above "Captain" before being transferred to LTG. This is a significant and common feature in all state-owned enterprises because a military long-term education ensures accordance with the attitudes of the Communist Party. As a rule, those from a military background are transferred to either government agencies/administration or to state-owned enterprises. Seventy-eight percent of management staff have university degrees, usually in foreign languages, international trading, and finance. However, they do not have qualifications in management education. This is a problem as the restructuring of management systems requires key staff to understand global management methods if it is to improve efficiency and innovation. Human resource management is a new concept in SOEs and conventional state bureaucracy personnel policies still dominate methods of managing labor. Despite reforms, old ideas and working practices still prevail, with a continuing focus on hierarchy, job description, and bureaucratic routines and procedures. Take the recruitment system, for instance – to quote what Mr Liu, Director of Planning says:

> The recruitment system is backward in LTG although it is explicitly established for market-orientation. We have all the policies and criterion for market recruitment and the selection of capable talents. But they are only policies in wording and not implemented by management. It is an inevitable problem as well as a cultural tradition of SOEs. There is an underlying way of doing things in SOEs, especially in personnel issues. LTG has not opened-up recruitment after autonomy was delegated to the enterprise in 1994. Before this delegation, the Ministry of Foreign Trade and Economy Committee (MFTEC) was responsible for both appointments and recruitment for all SOEs. After enterprise autonomy was introduced, self-recruitment was authorized to be the responsibility of LTG, but we still rarely have open recruitment, because the upper authorities continue to make recommendations to appointments. Moreover, inside arrangements for filling vacancies also often happen in LTG.

> Generally speaking, most of the staff in LTG have personal relations with someone in either senior management or in the upper authorities of government. Sometimes, there is waiting list for vacancies from employees with personal contacts. However, the people who fill these vacancies often don't have the required qualifications for the posts, but they are assigned on the basis of personal connections. For example, I feel I need an assistant with an MBA degree, but the person who has been assigned to my office is a personal contact of the General Manager, has an irrelevant qualification, and that does not help me in the way I expect. Furthermore, even though we have

Contradictions of state-owned enterprises 73

open recruitment policies on the talent market, selection is not done by a scientifically-designed system, but is personally controlled by managers. So the candidates who have personal connections will be selected regardless of their formal qualifications and capability.

Because hierarchical authority is an unshakable force and culture in LTG, you cannot challenge this practice. This tradition generates problems in our management capacity, because the quality of staff is not adequate. This results in failure or poor performance in the execution of management plans. That is why the plan is always right but the results are often not achieved.

(Author interview, 2006)

Recruitment in LTG seems to be based entirely on personal contacts without fair competition and scientific selection. Open recruitment is rarely adopted due to the tradition and culture of LTG, although a market-focused business requires selection on the basis of meritocratic capabilities. Such a pattern of personal contacts also results in a process whereby sanctions on employees are hardly implemented due to personal ties that are deeply embedded among government officers, senior managers, and lower levels of staff. Those who make mistakes can always be excused from punishment through personal relations. This is the culture of state-owned enterprises. Mr Qi, the Company Party Secretary, comments on this problem:

Because of the poor quality and qualification of management staff, the execution of rules and regulations cannot be carried out completely. There is always a broken sequence between the processes of decision-making and implementation. Frequent deviations in execution commonly happen. The staff in the functional departments are often inert and inactive. They have a passive attitude to work and only when their leaders push them will they move forward a bit. Some of the new graduates being recruited are capable of talking but incapable of acting. They are not motivated and stimulated at work, and they lack a responsive attitude and crisis awareness. They have no ambition in pursuing their careers.

(Author interview, 2006)

As the head of International Business Development says:

The problem for state-owned enterprises is how to deal with competition on the market, and talent management is a key part of competition. How to retain capable talent and how to motivate talent is a big challenge for an SOE. The new mechanism of talent management will challenge the existing culture of SOE. It is like an organism without fresh blood. The people being hired in the enterprise in the past ten years have all been through personal connections with ties to provincial authorities and top management. Many of them are the children of these officials and political leaders. They are hired because of their contacts not for qualification. I worry about this enterprise because it will die in the absence of talent in the future. I describe LTG as a "diabetic without awareness." I am a diabetic, but I have awareness of diabetes so I am taking proper treatment and improving my condition. But a "diabetic without awareness" is dangerous as it is a chronic disease but if you don't realize it and still think of yourself as a normal person, the day of the total collapse will happen sooner or later.

(Author interview, 2006)

Personnel management in state-owned enterprises seems to be a major problem due to their culture. There is no explicit staff development policy and there is a lack of a proper motivation mechanism. Training is supposed to be an effective way to improve the quality of staff and the skills of a profession, but these are not well developed through systematic mechanism in LTG, and they operate on a random basis. Staff awareness of the importance of training is not established and employees don't pay too much attention to training courses when these are offered to them. Absence and carelessness are common among staff. The control and planning of training is poor, as there is no analysis and evaluation of what training is needed. It simply happens whenever there is an issue arising from the demand of work or from the higher authorities. State enterprises are particularly distinctive in the ways they recruit staff. The influence of a personal relations culture is more powerful in state-owned enterprises than in other types of ownership, *overriding market demands and rules.* Such a difference between the state enterprise case and the other types of enterprise reveals that political power and hierarchical political authority are much greater in state-owned corporations.

Leadership is a central feature of any organization. The General Manager and Vice General Managers have the most influential impact on the style of management. Thanks to their military background, their leadership style is mostly based on "Loyalty," and "Orders," "Caution" and "Correctness," and these are the main ideas guiding the fundamental style of management in LTG. Risk taking is avoided in the enterprise as a whole. Mr Chen, Manager of the International Co-operation Department, remarks:

From the Provincial authorities to the top of management in LTG, they all have preference for "No-Mistakes" rather than "High-performance." Because they are more bureaucrats than entrepreneurs; "no-mistakes" secure their positions. Whereas "high-performance" requires both high risk-taking and high capability to handle risks. If they fail to achieve, this will lead to their dismissal from their power positions. The safe way is to sustain the stability and avoid risking their careers, so they can retain a good personal record when they move to the next higher position. What can you expect from this kind of boss in an enterprise? To follow this style and approach is also safe for us. Otherwise they will think we are trouble makers, and sooner or later we will be eliminated from their sight.

(Author interview, 2006)

This common reality deeply affects the style of management in state-owned enterprises and it destroys ambition and entrepreneurial willingness among employees. It also restricts innovation and entrepreneurial development and explains why staff motivation is low in LTG. Mr Ma, Manager of LTIEI, emphasizes:

> Top managers spend most of their time with the higher political authorities. As I know, our general manager has to drive four hours to Shenyang three times a week for meetings and reports. They are not like us; they are more bureaucratic than enterprise managers.
>
> (Author interview, 2006)

Obviously the government authorities and top managers in LTG are favorable to immediate performance in annual profitability rather than to risks in long-term investment. They are more driven by political considerations and the rules of administrative bureaucracy. Future prospects for the development of LTG are more related to political demands than market opportunities. Ms Du, Manager of the Property Management Department, comments on the style of leadership as:

> One of the significant styles of the management we feel is "Authority," which represents absolute ownership in a State-owned enterprise. The other style is about their dual-roles in management. Top managers are guardians for the state assets and they are afraid of losses as this is their responsibility. In decision-making, they are cautious in order to avoid risking state assets. The general manager lacks boldness in business development. But we understand his dual-role, as he is not only the manager of the enterprise, but he also plays the role of being an official bureaucrat. He is at the top and difficult to approach. His office is monitored by CCTV, so he can see who is coming to visit him and won't open the door if it is a person he doesn't want to talk to. We usually report to the relevant vice general manager or Party Secretary, who are more approachable. However, work relations are very formal and we don't have close relations with subordinates and workmates.
>
> (Author interview, 2006)

Work styles differ in the administrative offices and the operational divisions. Both are open style, but the administrative offices are more relaxed and less busy, and work hours are in a routine schedule. But the operational subsidiaries are extremely busy with long working hours, even at weekends. The work tensions are much greater in these operating units. As the Manager, Mr Ma, says:

> We need to learn from western companies in terms of human resource management. We need to have a pragmatic training system as well as an annual vacation system. We work so many extra hours for the company and

with no personal vacation, we are stressed. We are very much pressured by targets.

(Author interview, 2006)

The key spiritual values deeply imbued in the whole enterprise, particularly at the management level, are "Loyalty and Consistency" with the Communist Party. This is an inviolable principle and a prerequisite above the business orientation of LTG. Without this premise, everything is meaningless and irrelevant. Party meetings are held routinely and they are as numerous as business operation meetings. Ad hoc activities assigned from the Central Committee of the Communist Party reinforce the education of "Loyalty and Consistency" on a frequent basis and they constitute a core part of LTG's enterprise activities.

In order to comply with recent Party commands on the reinforcement of a new central spiritual theme, new activities on "Maintaining Progressive Ideas of the Party" are enforced in state-owned enterprises. For example, an Ad Hoc Leading Group on this topic was established in LTG in 2005. Party members were required to spend at least 20 hours reading "Party Statutes", "Reports of the Sixteenth People's Congress" and "the Special Edition for Maintaining Progressive Ideas." Key Party members in leadership groups were required to do twenty-eight hours reading in addition to twelve hours of discussion. The second phase of this political education lasted for five weeks in terms of the analysis of the first phase of study. Sixteen meetings were held on various topics analyzing employees' opinions. This meant that one-and-half days each week was taken up with Party meetings. After this period of intensive political education, there was another twelve months for improving behavior in relation to the routine work of enterprise management. This, of course, is in sharp contrast to management in private- or foreign-owned enterprises. State enterprises spend a great deal of time and effort in such political activities and their senior managers are heavily engaged in Party education; this prevents them from concentrating exclusively on business operations.

Such constantly imposed Party education molds employees' values and this inevitably impacts on management philosophies and behaviors. It further explains the style of management in LTG. The core shared values of "Loyalty and Orders," "Steadiness and Rightness," and "Authority and Hierarchy" are derived from the legitimate authority of the Communist Party as well as the company's bureaucratic culture. Bearing in mind market values that require entrepreneurship and risk, there is an inevitable conflict of cultures within the enterprise as a whole. This is why interviews with senior officials reflect confusion about the future direction of the enterprise. They have no clear idea of what kind of culture the enterprise should have. LTG lacks the necessary construction of a unified organizational culture because of the conflict between Party values and the demands of a market economy.

State-owned enterprise reforms have long been restricted by socialist ideology. Because state ownership is a direct conjunct of state administration and the Communist Party's political systems, it means that economic reforms have to be compatible with existing political systems; i.e. socialist ideals. In order to secure such concordance, key managers are mainly selected from the military and constant education on socialist ideas is enforced among top managers. However, free-market competition requires effective management with "market ideals" other than "socialist ideals," This is the essential contradiction within state-owned enterprises.

The General Manager plays the dual role of entrepreneur and bureaucrat. He has to balance these two roles, as the enterprise requires an entrepreneur to actualize market value and the government administration requires a bureaucrat with whom to communicate. However, as he has been promoted from the operational core, he fully understands how the business should be managed and what managers need. Therefore, two types of culture coexist in LTG to satisfy both market and state needs.

As reforms in China constitute a system change, it is a very complex process. State-owned enterprise reforms play a leading role in this systematic transformation to a market economy. Leadership is an especially vital factor for the successful adjustment of a state-owned enterprise into the market economy. Independent management autonomy in business enterprises is the most significant change compared with the former socialist command model. Involvement in market competition has diluted the old ideology of the planned economy, generating entrepreneurship and institutional innovation in management. This is a demanding task for the leaders of state-owned enterprises. The dual roles they must fill shape a special management pattern that is distinct from that found in private-owned enterprises. In addition, LTG has, particularly as a state-owned enterprise, some special advantages that private companies do not have. For instance, it has privileged access to the essential factors of production—capital, land, and labor. The capital market in China is still not open to foreign investors and the major banks, dominating the capital market, are state-owned banks that favor state-owned enterprises over other types of businesses. As interviewees in LTG mention:

> We have sufficient funds to run the enterprise, and we give increasing profits to the Government each year. We can always get loans at any time from the bank when we need more cash flow. The Bank's managers chase us to lend us money. The availability of sufficient capital is our strength.
>
> (Author interview, 2006)

LTG has never had to worry about a shortage of capital for investment and growth; it is just a matter of whether managers can do it without high risks and mistakes, so that their positions and power can be secured. They also have access to free land to build factories and offices.

Concluding remarks on state-owned enterprises

State-owned enterprises in China are tightly controlled by a "hidden" power—the Communist Party. The Communist Party and administrative authorities are powerful agencies in China that can provide many concessions and favors for state-owned enterprises. Issues associated with government-controlled resources are very demanding for other types of enterprise. Founded in the past, and with economies of scale and cheap access to resources, state-owned enterprises have great competitive advantages. However, their current competences are not enough for long-term sustainability, as businesses in the emerging market economy require a strong entrepreneurial culture and the injection of new human resources for long-term development. State-owned enterprises have to solve the cultural conflicts that operate within their management and building a corporate entrepreneurial culture is one of the future challenges.

The emergence of a private economy with market reforms is challenging communist political control and creating a dilemma for the Party—economy or polity? It endeavours to seek a balance in "market socialism" between socialist ideals and market forces. State-owned enterprises are foremost in the experiment in this ideological transition from a planned to a market-driven economy. This confusion affects motivation and morale as well as the ability of this type of enterprise to develop long-term strategies and visions. Ownership of the enterprise remains state-controlled but without radical change in its political culture and administrative processes, it is unable to adapt flexibility to changing demands from the market. Despite regulatory concessions and access to finance, state-owned enterprises are characterized by ineffective management and a nepotistic culture. Innovation in operating systems and entrepreneurship in managing change are challenges for state-owned enterprises in China. How to reform the administrative system of state control and how to further diversify ownership remain controversial for the Communist Party. The scarcity of guiding theories on creating a *socialist market economy* obstructs the pace of reform in state-owned enterprises and creates uncertainties in the future vision of market socialism. Our case study suggests that there are many issues to be resolved in relation to party control and intervention if state-owned enterprises are to adapt to the changing demands of market forces. The drivers and barriers to state-owned enterprise entrepreneurship are summarized in Table 4.1.

The features of state-owned enterprises do not encourage entrepreneurship. Some top managers and bureaucrats inevitably resist change—even if it is ultimately in their own interest. Structures, systems, rewards, and culture are not aligned with the changes so they inhibit them. Resistance to change and incremental implementation of entrepreneurship are the source of management tensions in state-owned enterprises. To overcome this, the state-owned enterprise will need to address cultural change from the top down and will need to implement entrepreneurial activities in all aspects, from the hardware to the software of the company, integrating every aspect of the organizational process. A shared vision for the future should be clarified and communicated to different levels of employees more effectively to resolve the confusion associated with market transition. Rewards and performance assessments need to be altered to fit the need of entrepreneurs. A learning culture and competent training programs need to be put in place to facilitate staff development and corporate entrepreneurship.

Table 4.1 Drivers and barriers to SOE entrepreneurship

Organization processes	Characteristics	
	Drivers	Barriers
Strategy	Diversification of investment and business growth	Government imposed directives
Structure	Divisionalized and decentralized	Hierarchical and centralized
Systems	Networks and open "informal" decision-making	Formalized and procedure-driven decision-making
Staff	Professional expert qualifications; bonus incentive reward Openness to new idea development	Political and bureaucratic appointments; incompetent performance evaluation and reward mechanism; lack of transparency
Style	Participative leadership and empowerment of employees	Distance leadership and risk-avoidance
Shared values (culture)	Market-oriented values with high customer-focus;	Communist party culture and socialist values
Skills	Resources-based production competence	Absence of human capital development

Governance structure should be designed to minimize government intervention in decision-making processes of state-owned enterprises. The implementation processes need to be reflected in every aspect of management. Unwrapping the process to project an integral understanding of the underpinning drivers and barriers for entrepreneurship is crucial in creating an entrepreneurial enterprise.

Policy implications

The following policy implications are recommended for improving the status quo of state-owned enterprises and building their competitive advantage:

(1) To cut running costs to minimum, it is critical to gain efficiencies in production. SOEs are often burdened by government-assigned obligations and social responsibilities. Operational costs should prioritize market activities and product development. Effective cost control centers are needed to manage this market-driven priority and clarify the focus of investment in core business development.
(2) Selling peripheral non-core assets can enhance productivity and strengthen the core business. Restructuring the premium core asset of SOEs, and stripping off peripheral non-core assets to become public listing companies, has been a trend in the latest reforms. This action has re-energized the efficacy of SOEs; however, it has also placed pressure on effective management and staff competence in post-restructured companies.

80 *Contradictions of state-owned enterprises*

(3) SOEs need to continuously develop their organizational competences through investing in new technologies and skills. These will increase productivity in companies and build up their long-term competitiveness. In the textile industry, Chinese firms are advantaged in their low labor costs, land, and lack of need to pay shareholder dividends, which gives them competitiveness in the price of manufacturing garments. However, this production-based competence positions Chinese firms in the low end of the market value chain that will be vulnerable in the long run. State-owned enterprises should invest in high value-added commodities, while developing new skills of their workforces to gradually foster long-term sustainability in the international marketplace. The competitive advantage in high value-added products requires a holistic approach that encompasses all aspects of management processes and systems. As we discussed in using the 7-S framework, strategy, structure, systems, staff, style, shared values, and skills all interact with each other and cannot exist alone. Understanding the interconnectedness of these organizational factors is the key to addressing a holistic program of management change to build up the competitiveness of SOEs.

(4) SOEs should develop a clear focus in term of strategic direction, objectives, product development, and market opportunities. Investment diversification strategy has echoed among SOEs, as it can diversify the risk of large investments in one field. However, this diversification strategy demands a high capability of the workforce and effective corporate control mechanisms. The absence of effective staff development policies and the lack of systematic training programs for new skills may result in a struggling situation for SOEs operating in this strategic direction. Focusing on new product development and market opportunities may optimize the investment, while investing in new skills development can reduce the risk.

(5) SOEs need strong directive leadership to manage change, and the leaders should be united by a common purpose of shared vision on what needs to be achieved. Leadership is critical in managing change; perhaps this is the key issue in SOEs—a lack of effective leaders. De-personalized leadership in SOEs seems to inhibit the generation and implementation of creative ideas as well as individual development. Autonomy and effective performance assessment mechanisms are crucial to creating strong leadership teams in SOEs.

(6) Excessive over-staffing often holds back the development of SOEs. Laying off uncommitted and unproductive employees, based on appropriate performance assessment systems, can be imperative as the continuous growth of organizations requires the constant injection of fresh and highly-skilled human capital. Inadequate recruitment systems, overwhelming guanxi cultures, and the lack of effective performance evaluation and training schemes are the underlying reasons for over-staffing and incompetence.

(7) Engaging in mergers and acquisitions is an effective way of slimming down the non-core activities of businesses. It can incorporate potential opportunities and strengthen the core competences of firms, resulting in speeding up

growth and forming unique competitive advantages. Removing restraints and setting up effective governance structures can also encourage such engagement, as SOE leaders are often hesitant to initiate mergers or acquisitions due to governance constraints and slow decision-making processes.

(8) SOEs need to encourage the rise of entrepreneurial cultures for innovation and creative thinking by ensuring job security for core staff. Uncertainties can lead to low motivation and can increase the turnover of highly-skilled staff. Transparency of communication and decision-making are crucial in order to convey the understanding of change and reduce staff resistance. SOE management should be more open to new opportunities and proactively encourage individual creativity by introducing flat hierarchical structures and unit autonomy. The change from a bureaucratic culture to an entrepreneurial culture can be a demanding task for SOEs due to their traditions and heritage. It can only take place if SOEs adopt a holistic approach to address change in all aspects of organizational processes, e.g. strategy, structure, systems, style, and staff.

(9) In order to develop a highly-skilled workforce, SOEs need to invest in systematic training programs and staff development mechanisms. Competent human resource management is the vital key to the competitive advantage of organizations in the long run. Lagging systems of human resource management have become a major issue impeding the development of SOEs. Improvement in this aspect demands changes in the whole organizational process. How to win the global talent war will be a key challenge for the Chinese government and its SOEs if they are to survive in the global marketplace.

Note

1 Access to enterprises (particularly to state-owned enterprises) in China is very difficult. In this research, initial contact with the case study companies was established by the researcher through personal connections. These "key" informants—senior directors, or, in the case of the entrepreneurial firm, the owner—then allowed other members of their companies to be interviewed and also approved access to relevant documentary data. These permissions were given on the condition that the companies agreeing to take part in the study should be anonymous. Thus, this case study is presented under a pseudonym—"LTG," throughout the chapter. Likewise, the case study of the privately-owned company is coded as "DAL" in Chapter 5 and the foreign joint venture as "DSF" in Chapter 6.

5 The emergence of privately owned enterprises

Introduction

One of the striking features of China's economic reforms, transforming from a command to a socialist-market economy, is the rise of the entrepreneurial sector. The rapid growth of private-owned enterprise has become a driving force for the Chinese economy as well as a dominant ownership mode in the country. Private enterprises are organized in a very informal way because of how the domestic private sector emerged from its history; in the shadow of the state economy. This informality has given entrepreneurs great flexibility to respond to an uncertain business environment composed of unclear and rapidly changing government policies, taxes, and regulations. But it also hampers their ability to raise capital, and reward managers and employees. Due to lack of management skills and professional managers, private enterprises tend to be stuck in a framework of legal, financial, and governance structures that they have outgrown in terms of the size and complexity of their businesses.

In private enterprises, entrepreneurs are the spirit of the organization as they start up their enterprises and take control of direct and central supervision for management. They make all the decisions and take all the risks for their business ventures. Their success or failure determines the fate of their whole enterprise. As Schlevogt (2001) has suggested, the private Chinese organizational model tends to be very centralized, with an informal structure and strong entrepreneurship, which emphasize enterprise networks and traditional cultural values. These elements distinguish them from state-owned enterprises and foreign joint ventures.

Background of DAL

A privately owned enterprise[1]

DAL is a typical entrepreneurial company; it was founded in 1995 by Mr Zhu with a start-up capital of only RMB 20,000 (US$2,500). In the space of ten years (1995–2005), it has grown to be a company with 200 employees, and total assets of RMB 50 million (US$6million). It manufactures cashmere knitwear and combines all its functions—raw material purchasing, manufacturing, marketing, and retailing on a single site. The company is equipped with advanced computer technology and has 220 production machines. These include auto computing, transverse knitwear machines and 7G–18G manual transverse knitwear machines, manufactured in Japan and Korea. The factory has an annual production capacity of 150 thousand pieces of knitwear and over twenty tons of cashmere yarns.

Mr Zhu, the owner and general manager, is a typical entrepreneur with a self-confident, open-minded and risk-taking approach to the market. In interviews, he tells the story of how he started his business. At the time he had a secure job in a large-scale, state-owned cashmere factory, working as a Deputy Manager. In the early 1990s, a job in a state-owned enterprise was something to be proud of, as it offered guaranteed lifelong security. However, the person who can survive in a state-owned enterprise must be a good listener and follower and must respect seniority, regardless of personal competence. State-owned enterprise culture does not reward performance based on personal ability. Instead, there is an old saying in China that, "The gun will shoot the bird that shows off"; that is, the person who demonstrates personal competence is regarded as a threat to senior management and will be rejected. Mr Zhu was a victim of this. He had to face up to a decision; to either tolerate the situation at work, or leave the security of a state-owned enterprise for a high-risk position. He decided to become an entrepreneur; to take high risks and to make more money. He believed that life should be characterized by personal success and achievement rather than by oppression under the procedures of a state-owned enterprise.

He started his business in 1995–6, using all his savings. He used credit to rent a store to sell his cashmere sweaters and to purchase raw materials. His personal relationships and the business network that he had built in his previous job played a crucial role at this start-up stage. Without the personal trust he enjoyed, he couldn't have obtained credit. His friends gave him loans for his initial capital. Since then, he has always been committed to building up long-term credibility and personal reputation as the basis for his business development. The second stage in the growth of his business was the establishment of manufacturing workshop in 1997. As a technical expert in production, he was knowledgeable about raw materials and knitting technology and this gave him an advantage in setting up his own factory. Through personal contacts in banks and among friends, he obtained loans to extend his retail business to manufacturing. Before 2000, his focus was on the domestic market, and this was the exclusive source of his profit. The period between 1997 and 2000 was particularly important for DAL's domestic market growth, which established his competence in aspects of technology, equipment, skills, and staffing. Following the wider openness of the economic environment and WTO membership, Mr Zhu began to focus on overseas markets as new growth areas for his entrepreneurial company and he invested in new factory facilities and technology to increase its production capacity from 2008. During the period 2008 to 2012, DAL rapidly expanded its sales by between 100 percent and 300 percent per annum.

One of the reasons for DAL's growth is that Mr Zhu always heavily reinvests the company's earnings into the expansion of his company's manufacturing

84 *Emergence of privately owned enterprises*

facilities. Increasing production capability is his strategic focus in business development. When asked for the reason behind his success, he says there are two reasons:

> I should say that the open environment – the free market, provides me with great opportunities to develop my own business. As the market was booming, there were too many opportunities, but it depended on whether you could step out of old ideas. The planned economy and regime had locked people's mind for too long, the economic reform was subversive to most people who were born and brought up under the planned socialist economy. In the late 80s and early 90s, those who started their own private individual businesses were most likely forced into it because of their situation. For example, those with criminal records and the unemployed couldn't find jobs in state-owned enterprises or even in collective-owned enterprises, and so they have to do some individual business or trade to survive. In people's minds, jobs in SOEs were the preferred choice with respectable social status. Private businesses were discriminated by the society. That is why the quality of the first entrepreneurs was poor with low education. There is an old saying in China "The hero grows in the times of disorder." I think the creation of the open market and the high demand for cashmere products were major reasons for my success today. I just did the right things at the right time.
>
> As for me personally, I believe that if you can cope with the hardest of hardships, you can rise in society. Hard work and the ability to endure hardships are important to my success. I reinvest my profits in technology and business expansion, not in pleasure-seeking. As the motto of my company says, "excellence is created from bit by bit", "Ideas determine the path of development and the calibre of people determines the quality of the products."
>
> (Author interview, 2006)

In ten years, Mr Zhu has gradually and constantly reinvested profits and increased his company's technological competence. Despite the fact that he knows little of management theory and has no idea about such terms as "strategy" and "structure," his actions demonstrate unconscious strategic thinking and planning. When Mr Zhu is asked about the business strategy, he is confused. He asks for further explanation of this term. After a few minutes, he says:

> I don't have any strategy or ambitious goals in my business development. I just do what I think is right, following my instinct and rule of thumb, doing work with a down-to-earth style. Firstly I never thought I would have achieved what I have today when I started 10 years ago. Secondly, I have never been satisfied with what I have achieved in each year. I don't have long term objectives like market share, or to build a mansion, or how much profit to make, or to compare myself with others. Maybe it explains my weakness, no planning or explicit goals. I am working step by step. When I saw the opportunity for cashmere products, with my expertise in raw material and cloth making

technology, I decided to become an entrepreneur. But I didn't think anything more than being a retailer. But as my business went well, I thought if I could open a manufacturing facility, it would be more profitable and I would have more control on market supply. Then I borrowed loans and with my profits, I set up a workshop with only 20 hand machines. The market has continually grown and so I have been naturally expanding the scale of production to meet this increasing demand. Actually I have no strategy or plan for my business, but I do look back for what I have done in each year and compare that to the market demand. However, the outcome has never satisfied me, as I always think I can do better. So, I have been trying to improve myself by expanding the level of production and quality control. Our objectives are focused on each customer order, each batch of production, every season of sales, and each step of work. "Excellence is created from bit by bit" is at the core of my guiding principle.

(Author interview, 2006)

Mr Zhu is not pretentious and arrogant in his manner. He talks as a dedicated and focused entrepreneur. He takes risks and he is always looking for new market opportunities. He is committed to steady business growth, constantly investing in technology to improve his volume and quality of production. His strategy is "no strategy!"

As the motto hanging on his wall states, "The idea creates fortune, and the wise person sails the boat with the help of the current." He understands how important it is to use other peoples' resources to achieve his objectives. That is why he was able to set up his business from almost nothing. He gives the impression of honesty and integrity and, through this, he gains other people's trust. Relationships are an important resource for doing business in China, and they are even more important for entrepreneurship. Not only did he rely on personal credit at the start-up stage of his business, but he also drew upon bank loans to expand it. All this required the use of personal relationships and networks, as the bank system in socialist China didn't support private businesses in a formal sense. Without maximizing the use of his personal relationships, he would not have acquired the necessary capital for business growth. But the business was structured on a very informal basis and through his personal integrity he was able to fund his strategies for growth.

In the second stage of business growth, he built up the core competences of his company. Technology and quality were the focus of his thinking, together with the need to identify market needs. Due to the rapid speed of market transition, and political uncertainties in China, it was difficult for him to have an explicit strategy and business plan. He had to respond swiftly to market changes and trends in the business environment.

During the third stage of his growth, he developed a strategic alliance with a Japanese company in 2003. This alliance provides him with market opportunities to expand his business. The business relationship with a foreign company gives him tax advantages. The Japanese partner is responsible for the Japanese market and is signed as an exclusive agent. Japan is a large consumer market for cashmere products, and is therefore vital for DAL's future growth. Following the creation of this strategic alliance in 2003, DAL developed a second line product—women's silk wear—to meet the demand from Japanese customers. Mr Zhu also regards this strategic alliance as a route to international markets. DAL's business strategy is implicit and emergent, responding to market opportunities as they arise.

Business strategy is decided by one person only—the owner. All other employees in middle management have little idea about the company's goals and future development. Five managers from sales, marketing, production, finance, and office administration, respectively, were interviewed and asked about the company's strategy, but no one had any idea about it. They considered it to be the owner's responsibility and they simply focused on their own, present-day objectives. When asked questions that did not relate to their own responsibilities, the five interviewees replied, "don't know" or "it is the owner's responsibility." The ideas and inclinations of Mr Zhu are the sole basis of business decision-making within DAL and these employees do not contribute to the process.

The organizational structure within DAL is almost non-existent. When asked for a chart of the company's structure, Mr Zhu asked his Office Director. But in a later interview with the Office Director, Mr Ding stated they have no such document; neither do they have documents for HR policies, management procedures, or company regulations. As Mr Ding says:

> I have been told to write these papers since last year, but I have been too busy to get it done. This work requires me to sit down but I have been so busy so unfortunately we still don't have it today. I know that formal management structures are important for us and that is what we lack, but it is not easy to set this up because of the nature of this company. You know, it is the way small privately owned companies operate. I would prefer to have a normal structure and procedure in management, which would make things more predictable. However, it is not what we can decide really. Maybe in the future we will formalize our management as the company becomes bigger.
>
> (Author interview, 2006)

During the second interview, Mr Zhu was asked to describe the number of departments the company has, the relationships they have with each other, and the major responsibilities of each of them. According to his description, the organizational chart is shown in Figure 5.1. However, some departments are only a wish for the future (these "supposed" divisions are marked with broken lines in Figure 5.1). An exploration of the relationship between the owner and the functional departments, reveals that Mr Zhu retains total control over all functions of his organization. He is the center and the totality of management. The Vice General Manager and Office Director are like "two hands" of the owner that help him to manage the company, but they report to him for all decisions and are under his direct control. The owner expresses his management style by stating his belief

Emergence of privately owned enterprises 87

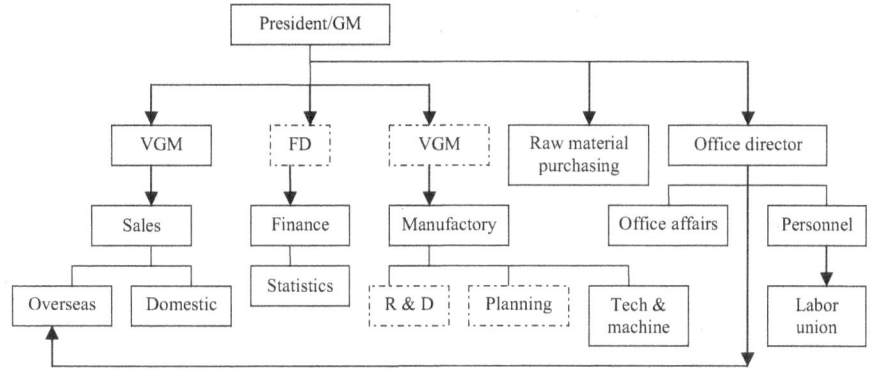

Figure 5.1 The "supposed" structure of the DAL Company.

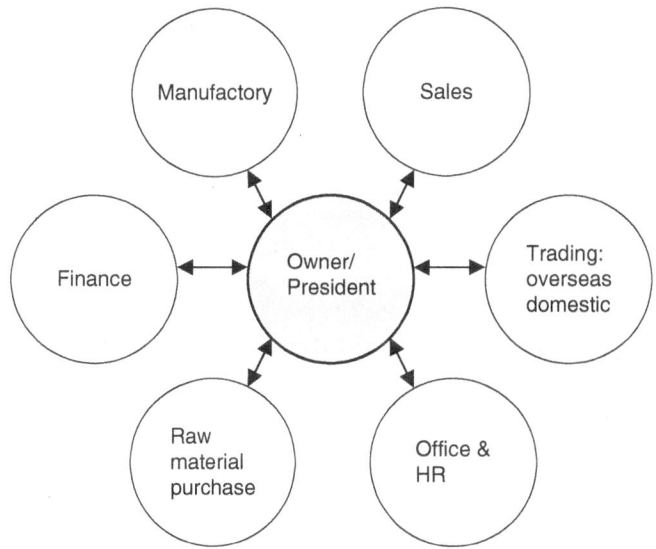

Figure 5.2 The reality of the DAL structure.

that if each process is navigated well, the result will not be wrong. For him, giving autonomy to employees generates risk in the company's management. So, in reality, DAL's organizational structure is as identified in Figure 5.2. Basically it is a non-structure that has a pattern of dependency upon Mr Zhu.

Job specialization in this structure remains very unclear and individual responsibilities are not defined. With the exception of the accountant from the finance department, the other three interviewees, from office administration, marketing, and sales, take on multifunctional duties and have flexible roles in meeting diverse needs as they might arise within the organization. The Vice General Manager, who is in charge of the sales department, is also a manager in manufacturing, but she was transferred to sales when there was a shortage of staff.

Take the designer as an example. During field work in DAL's company, the owner was asked for an interview with the designer. He replied:

> I don't have a professional designer, my technician in tailoring and craftsman in production are doing this job. The professionals are too costly and new graduates are too young and I do not want to spend time training graduates. But I know it is a problem in my company, maybe I will find one in the future.
> (Author interview, 2006)

This is surprising, as the product range is focused upon fashionable women's wear. In fact, as the owner mentioned, being a copycat of other large companies' designs is common for most small- to medium-sized companies operating in the fashion industry.

The Office Director has a more active role in the company structure and deals with requests from the owner and other emergent needs. His responsibilities are very broad—such as government requirements for annual reports and renewals, public relations, personnel issues, and trading affairs (particularly with overseas business). His role is similar to that of a lubricator or a fireman, smoothing and enhancing the flexibility of DAL's entrepreneurial structure so that changes or new situations can be addressed swiftly whenever they arise. This role is a strength in this type of entrepreneurial structure because it releases the proprietor from total management control; at least, to a certain degree. But because it acts as an extension of the proprietor, it has limited autonomy for decision-making. The proprietor is very much at the center of the management web.

Work relations within the structure are carried out in a very informal way. Little paper work is produced—except that required by external agents—and face-to-face communications are the bases for information flows. There are no written rules to guide employees, but, through frequent face-to-face meetings, verbal communications, and mottos, the proprietor passes his unwritten and informal rules to them. By regularly checking on each working process, he "corrects the wrong" and "encourages the right" in line with his criteria to make sure his ideas are being fully implemented.

Despite the owner's total control, informality and high flexibility are still the major characteristics of the DAL entrepreneurial company. In the interview, the proprietor explained why he cannot delegate autonomy to managers. As he said:

> I would be glad to delegate responsibilities to other managers. But the thing is that no one in the business is capable of having these. Their ways of thinking and ways of doing things are not beneficial to this company. They don't treat this company as their own in the way I do. More importantly, no one is competent enough to make important decisions. For example, I had a vice general manager whom I gave full delegation in charge of sales. What I experienced from him was cheating and mistakes. Thus, I keep direct control on

Emergence of privately owned enterprises 89

every procedure to make sure each step is done properly so that the final result meets my expectations. I always believe that if the procedures are right, the outcome will be right. Sometimes I really feel very tired and exhausted, because everything depends upon me. Money is important for an enterprise, but capable staff is the most important asset. I would like to invest an extra RMB 300 thousand (US$36 thousand) every year for recruiting better talent for my company, but the reality is that I cannot find good people. The problem for my company is not a shortage of capital but a shortage of capable talent. When I look back, I realise that I predicted some trends in business development, but unfortunately my good ideas can't be implemented by only my two hands. I don't have enough people to achieve all my plans.

I know reliable statistics are very important for making the right decisions. I cannot always judge everything subjectively. My enterprise needs effective systems and mechanisms to manage these data scientifically. I need to have formal management processes. These are important for the enterprise and we need to gradually build these up in the near future. I am aware of this, but the changes need to take place gradually.

(Author interview, 2006)

Within a minimal skeleton structure, systems of direct control are informal and highly flexible. Communications are carried out in a very informal way, with little paperwork involved. Telephone and face-to-face contact are the means of daily communication. Regular meetings take place on a weekly or fortnightly basis to review the previous week and to plan for the following week. The owner gives a very interesting and visual description of how his organization operates. As he says:

This organisation is like the human body and functions like a transmuted robot. This organism has only one brain which is me, and other employees are the different organs of this body. These organs work together to create the metabolism to be alive. In this sense, every part is important and need to play its own function. They must stay in their own roles and listen to the commands coming from the brain. They cannot be disturbed. For example, the assistants work as my two hands and they have to do what the brain tells them to do. They fulfill the function of being hands and not of being the brains. If they begin to think, they might slap the face when the brain commands them to achieve things. All the organs must be in order and listen to the brain's instructions otherwise the whole organism will breakdown. An enterprise should also act as a transmuted robot. When the different parts are assembled, the transmutable robot can change into different things; for example, an auto car or a gun, or a tank. The people in an enterprise should act like the assembly parts of a robot, in which they can become cars when they are at work and become tanks when they are at home. I can be a car at times and also change to a brain when the situation requires. The enterprise should be able to change into different shapes through combining and reforming these parts, in order to meet the changing demands of the market. Sometimes I feel like a "hemiplegia"; my brain has many ideas but the body cannot move or run as fast as what the brain wants.

(Author interview, 2006)

The Office Director confirmed this:

I worked in a large state-owned enterprise for many years before I came here, so I know the distinct difference in the two types of organisations. In the state-owned enterprise, an approval required many layers of hierarchical processes to pass through, such as from supervisor to manager, and vice general manager to general manager. There was hardly any face-to-face communication, but many boundaries between departments, lack of flexibility and much paperwork. But in this private company, flexibility is supreme, the systems are very flexible. Only one person makes the decisions and there is only one procedure to follow – that stated by the owner. I report everything to him and he decides everything. No written rules or formal processes exist in this company; the systems are open and flexible. Work relationships between employees are very friendly. Harmony is emphasized by the owner in this enterprise.

(Author interview, 2006)

The Labor Union only exists in order to meet a government requirement. It has no powers to represent employees. Its only duty is to arrange (infrequently) some social activities for employees. The company accountant commented on the Labor Union: "It is too far from us. I didn't perceive any benefit from it when I worked in the state own enterprise. It is even more so in this private enterprise."

Mr Ding, the Office Manager, said:

I was appointed by the owner to take charge of the labour union, but it is just a title, no responsibility. The only thing it does is to arrange some social activities, like a dinner or a party for the employees, maybe once a year, which requires the approval and a budget from the proprietor. There are no scheduled activities in the union, and it does not speak for employees rights.

(Author interview, 2006)

When asked about the Labor Union, the Marketing Manager said: "I have no idea about it."

The finance department is controlled directly by Mr Zhu. Weekly and monthly reports are produced for the latter and annual financial plans are prepared. Financial controls are operated by the computing systems and reports are produced for the State Tax Bureau. The accountant, Ms Liang, says:

There are four employees in the finance department, three accountants and one trainee. There is not much lateral coordination with other departments and our planning is made mostly based on the previous year's statistics. Plans for sales and manufacturing are prepared and reported to Mr Zhu. We mediate some financial issues, such as sales targets, production budgets, etc. between sales and manufacturing, or other departments. All final decisions are made by Mr Zhu. The work and management in this department is not very complicated as the principle areas of the business are specialised in two main fields – manufacturing and sales.

(Author interview, 2006)

Between 2000 and 2008, the total number of employees in DAL was about 150–200, with the majority being first-line workers with a low level of education (middle school to high school) and sales and delivery staff. However, by 2012, the number of key personnel had been reduced to seventy-five employees, with approximately twenty managerial staff and eight experienced technicians and engineers in cashmere production and technology maintenance. This significant reduction of employee numbers was the result of the adoption of highly automated computer controlled production systems. Key staff have experience-based qualifications in marketing and manufacturing rather than a formal university education as the owner emphasizes personal reliability and quality traits, together with his own "rule of thumb" as being important elements of the recruitment selection procedure.

The company training program is informal and random, and depends on the requirements of the work process. New workers in production are trained by their supervisors on the factory floor. Training programs are only offered to management staff when the proprietor thinks there is a need, or when special tasks require them; for example, when foreign trading requires an understanding of contract conditions and procedures. However, the proprietor often takes relevant managers to visit other efficient factories or more advanced companies, so they can gain experience from their competitors. The accountant, Ms Liang said:

> I benefited a lot from a visit to an advanced factory in Hong Kong. We saw how the modernised procedures are operating and learnt the techniques of advanced production management. We appreciate and feel excited about such learning experience, which open our eyes to something new and what we have never seen in our lives.
>
> (Author interview, 2010)

Ms Xu, Vice General Manager, also made the same point:

> Mr Zhu often arranges for our key staff to visit other efficient companies on a regular basis. We have learnt about their advanced management philosophy, efficient methods, various new styles in design, production techniques and even how they decorate the outside of retail stores. These field visits have impressed us very much. Particularly, I remember once we visited a big textile spinning factory in Beijing. I have never seen such a large scale

of spinning production. I was shaken up. By learning from these different advanced enterprises, we know where we are and how much difference there is between us and those modern corporations. We are motivated to work harder in the practice.

(Author interview, 2010)

There is no clear or written policy for staff development. The firing policy is simply based on whether or not the owner thinks the employee is doing a good job. Promotion criteria do not exist in either verbal or written forms. Mr Ding, the Office Director stated that:

We don't know promotion criteria and I don't think there is any chance to get promoted. In this private company, the matter is of how much responsibility you can take and how much pay you can get. But the salary depends on the boss's preference, and so does the year-end bonus.

(Author interview, 2010)

Ms Liang, the accountant makes the same point: "we all listen to our boss, and the boss decides everything." It is the same situation with the reward system. The subjective and discretionary judgment exercised by the proprietor is the only criteria for material rewards; there are no written rules or guidelines. The only guaranteed rewards are in the signed contract and are the monthly salary and the social and labor insurance, which are legally required by the government. The year-end bonus is used by the proprietor to keep control over his employees and to retain their commitment to the company; however, it generates insecurity for employees as well.

In addition to the reward system, the owner uses spiritual and moral methods to motivate his employees. Examples of this are the "weekly exemplar" or "monthly paragon" and the "progressive individual." Mr Zhu tends to stress the importance of ethics and morals for his employees in order to create devotion, loyalty, and honesty. This means that less material rewards are required but more commitment and output can be gained.

Mr Zhu emphasizes that he is urgently in need of highly-skilled management talent for his company. To do this he will need to change his present entrepreneurial approach, which does not retain able people because of the absence of an effective human resource management system. A formal system is required and he needs to delegate more responsibilities if he is to retain highly-skilled talent. His insistence on total control over management procedures is against human resource retention. On the one hand, he describes himself as the only brain of the organism and his managers as hands that just to do what he tells them. On the other hand, he feels that he needs highly-skilled and independent talents to share his responsibilities and work, so that he can delegate autonomy to them. This thinking reveals a paradox in his mind. As the company is nearing the limits of his ability to exercise total control, this has caused him to recognize the need to recruit skilled staff to share his responsibilities. His company is reaching a bottleneck in its growth, which is blocking its further potential to expand. He may come to realize that although an entrepreneur requires one brain; a larger business requires a think tank.

Mr Zhu is a typical entrepreneur with charisma. His explicit leadership style is one of managing people by the heart and affection, not by rules. This informal leadership is built on top of his unassailable authority. He demonstrates a hybrid leadership style in his management. He is democratic, amiable, and gracious, he always consults employee's opinions and he is a good listener. He always explains when he rejects a manager's opinions. He is caring to his employees and works as hard as his staff. Nevertheless, he is also an authoritarian with more-or-less arbitrary decision-making processes. He does not allow others to challenge his authority. For instance, he has rejected the idea of a Board of Directors and controls the whole company on his own. In the interview, when asked about the ownership status of his company, which is set up as a limited company, and which should have a Board of Directors involved in decision-making, he says:

> This company is completely mine, and I have sorted them (the board of directors) out by giving them enough money to go away. I am the person who makes all the decisions. I do not like others to be involved in the decisions, and tell me how to do things.
>
> (Author interview, 2006)

Mr Zhu has total control over all strategic decisions; his authority is uncontestable. His professional expertise in cashmere-spinning technology and his knowledge of cashmere raw material makes him venerated among his employees. This also contributes to his successful establishment of his business and its rapid expansion. Raw cashmere is a very rare resource and not every business can have easy access to it. However, his network access to raw material resources and his knowledge in this field guarantee his success. This is the reason why he still directly controls the two areas of raw material purchasing and manufacturing in person, and explains why these processes are not allocated to others.

All his employees share the same perceptions about his style. Besides his authoritarian nature, his leadership is a mixture of supportive, participative, and achievement-oriented approaches. As the Office Director comments:

> He is a democratic leader with affinity, he is amiable and always discussing and consulting with us. He explains the reasons for his decisions and asks you for mutual consent. He has a wise strategic view on things and he is a resolute man when he comes to a decision.
>
> (Author interview, 2006)

His Marketing Manager, Ms Jia says: "His personality is very prompt and decisive. He cares for us and participate with us in our work. He can democratically discuss with us and you can feel his affinity." The Finance Accountant, Ms Liang comments:

> He is a leader who does things with religious care. His style is decent with justice, generosity and patience. He cares for his employees. I still remember that he treated us to a nice dinner as a welcome when we came back from the New Year holiday. He gives us a warm feeling.
>
> (Author interview, 2006)

The Vice General Manager, Ms Xu, comments:

> Mr Zhu knows how to put people to good use; he knows how to develop people's talent. He is an expert in spinning technology. He is good for getting things on hand quickly and he employs the right people for doing things he can't do.
>
> (Author interview, 2006)

The owner manages people with his heart and not by rules. Once, the company had an urgent order from an overseas client. As the delivery time approached, they were still significantly behind schedule. Mr Zhu asked his employees to work at nights and at weekends. He also worked as late as his employees and was the last person to leave the company. He constantly says "thank you" to his employees for their hard work, which normally is very rare for a Chinese boss to do. Although the work makes them exhausted their hearts are happy and content, because what they do is highly appreciated by their boss, who works as hard as they do. Furthermore, he demonstrates his care for his employees, respecting Chinese traditions, such as holidays, and giving small gifts to his employees to keep them happy.

A family atmosphere is successfully cultivated by his leadership style. His emphasis on this type of business culture emphasizes the importance of his authority as the father of this family. He can be an affable father because his authority is secured. Moreover, this family culture also enforces the informality of the business and reinforces his employees' dependency on him.

The significant meaning and guiding concepts that DAL imbues in its employees can be seen in various mottos and creeds that hang on walls in the buildings. Some of these are as follows:

- 'Excellence is created bit by bit'
- 'The idea determines the path of development and the calibre of people determines the quality of product'
- 'The idea creates fortune, the wise man sails the boat with the help of the current'.
- 'Please watch your thinking, it will influence your behavior; please watch your behavior, it will influence your habit; please watch your habit, it will influence your character; please watch your character, it will influence your fate'
- 'FAMILY'—a big Chinese character hanging on the wall in Mr Zhu's office, which demonstrates that he runs the company as a big family.

These statements illustrate the management philosophies that the owner emphasizes as important and valuable for all members of the company. To cultivate the family culture, he shows his democracy, consideration, and respect toward employees. The work climate is friendly and harmonious with little hierarchy, making employees feel psychologically comfortable. He tries to share the attitudes of his employees by educating them to have the right values so they cooperate and comply with his direction and decisions. He is the center of a power culture and imposes total control throughout the whole organization. This is similar to how Handy (1993: 23) describes a power culture, "It depends on a central power source with rays of influence form the central figure throughout the organisation. Control is exercised from centre by the selection of key individuals. There are few rules and procedures, and little bureaucracy."

But additionally, the business prides itself on having a learning culture. This is strongly promoted in the company by Mr Zhu. He frequently arranges field-visits to advanced companies nationwide and actively joins industry associations in order to find ideas for continuous improvement. He constantly educates his employees and stresses the importance of learning and improving their working practices. As Mr Ding, one of the interviewees, says:

> We are in a period of improvement. There are many things in the company that need to be improved, and we are working on that, such as quality, formalization, and advancement in management techniques. We will get it gradually, it takes time, but we are processing.
>
> (Author interview, 2010)

This learning culture has led to innovations in the quality control system and in marketing, but the management structure has not yet been altered.

Leadership is the most important competence in this entrepreneurial business, as everything depends on the proprietor's preference and capability. As a successful entrepreneur, Mr Zhu demonstrates his high capability, charisma, strong leadership, and wisdom. His entrepreneurial qualities definitely account for the strength of the business. His strategic focus and intuitive vision and sensitivity allow him to find opportunities in the market. His flexible and informal structure, with quick decision-making processes, allows him to swiftly respond to market trends. As he describes himself, he can change to any form and be adaptive to any situation when he needs to. He possesses strengths that are lacking in large, formal enterprises. His talents of thinking, decision-making, and charisma of personality enable him to be a successful leader. Equally, this strength could, in turn, become a weakness when his business grows to a certain size and these capabilities cannot be used for total control. His entrepreneurial style will start to limit his potential for further business growth and development.

Business reputation and personal network access to raw resources (raw cashmere is a scarce and expensive resource and there is hardly sufficient supply) are a special strength of the company. In ten years, Mr Zhu has intentionally built up his business reputation by always honoring contracts, and guaranteeing refunds and product returns. As he states:

> Sometime the contract is not for profit purposes but for future strategic alliances. Other businessmen may not do business that creates losses but I will do this for getting market share. It is my long term vision. I am not only a profit-driven person.... I consider the social responsibility of my company, such as donations to the poor and public road maintenance, as I have such capability now. We are part of society and I feel I should do something for others.
>
> (Author interview, 2010)

He says his reputation and personal credibility in the long term are more important to him than short-term profit gain. Thanks to his previous work in the State-owned company, he has established his own resource network, and this has benefited him when he set up his own business. The other competence that helps his company's growth is the technology and mechanization that Mr Zhu has heavily invested in. This strength enables his company to produce 150,000 cashmere sweaters a year. This facilitates his growth not only in the domestic market but also allows him to rapidly expand in overseas markets. His intention is to develop the company from one based on labor-intensive, low technology to one operating with high technology. In view of the core competences DAL possesses, Mr Zhu's entrepreneurial traits play a critical role in its primary success. However, these will limit further business growth unless he delegates and develops management competences among his staff. He needs to shift the company from being dependent on a brain to becoming a think tank.

Entrepreneurial firms suffer restricted access to financial resources because the state-owned banking sector is reluctant to lend to them. Although they share many characteristics of entrepreneurial counterparts in the West, the dynamics of market socialism compels them to occupy "niches" in the market that are not catered for by other types of enterprise. They are regarded by both the state and other market actors as marginal or peripheral to the future development of market socialism. Emirbayer and Mische (1998: 1009) suggest that, "actors who feel blocked in encountering problematic situations can actually be pioneers in exploring and reconstructing contexts of actions." Our case study demonstrates this; DAL utilizes networks of business contacts for overcoming institutional constraints and capitalizing on political connections for securing opportunities. As the owner–entrepreneur in this case study commented:

> In 2008, one day I got a phone call from a friend and noticed that a state-owned enterprise was called for bid of sale in Xiuyuan city. After my investigation in this project, I decided to acquire this company. However, the first difficulty I need to overcome to secure this deal is to obtain the capital required as it demands roughly speaking 50 million RMB (USD $7.4 million) but I only had less than one tenth of this amount in my account at that

time. Many others may have thought it was impossible for me, but I managed to obtain this large amount of capital from a variety of sources – friends, business partners, private venture capital companies and state banks through my business networks and personal contacts. The majority is from private loans with high interest rates and short term as banks can only loan me the small amount with collateral. Despite high risks and financial pressure, I still determined to invest in this new factory because I can see the opportunity of increasing demand in the future. With my expertise and experience in this field, I believe this investment will have profitable return, and it will also give me more control over raw material supply markets and minimize the cost of my finished cashmere goods.

(Author interview, 2011)

Mr Zhu never seems to be satisfied with his achievements and always strives for new opportunities. This quality gives his entrepreneurial firm a competitive edge in the market. Private entrepreneurs in China are now elected to the National People's Congress (NPC) and have gained a legitimacy to participate in government circles. The owner of this private-owned enterprise has been an elected representative to the National People's Congress in the region since 2007. This new identity and status has granted him many benefits, such as easier access to loans, political capital, credibility, and networks for negotiating favorable policies from local and provincial Party officials. As his business partner, as well as a friend, another entrepreneur comments:

> He has good relationship with local government officials and close network connections in this industry. The National People's Congress representative identity has made him a "red-hat" businessman ("hong ding shang ren"), which granted him with the privilege of access to political capital. Having a seat in National People's Congress meetings, meant that he can have his say in policy making for SMEs and be the first to grasp the policy movement. This also gives him credibility among other private businesses. He is very low key as a person but highly influential and capable of almost impossible missions. He has become our access to political guanxi when we need it. We admire his tactic and ability.
>
> (Author interview, 2011)

Despite government policies and the Party's changing attitude towards private entrepreneurs, there are still discrepancies between policies and their actual implementation; for example, suspicions toward entrepreneurs still pertain among some state bank officials (Kshetri 2007; Yang 2002). This requires entrepreneurs to make informal arrangements and negotiations, and sometimes power exchanges—so called "rent-seeking" activities—to achieve their interests (Su and Littlefield 2001; Gao 2011; Chen *et al.* 2011). The emergence of private ownership is a factor of major significance in the development of market socialism in China, since it not only represents a force for contributing to the country's economic growth but also operates as a change agency for restructuring the economy. In a turbulent and changing marketplace, it is not surprising that many such entrepreneurs have emerged as a new class of plutocrats and business magnates. Their entrepreneurial ingenuity has led to their pursuing and securing business opportunities. Their enterprises are in a sharp contrast to state-owned enterprises on every organizational dimension. They are innovative, willing to take calculative risks, and utilize tactics and networks to gain access to resources and achieve results. Their growth has placed demands both on new institutional arrangements and for new laws to legitimate their rights. In June 2002, in accordance with their increasing demands, the National People's Congress passed legislation stipulating that the state should provide positive services for small- and medium-sized enterprises in the areas of financial and fiscal assistance, start-up capital, taxation, technological innovation, the development of markets, and employee welfare services. In March 2003, the government approved constitutional amendments including the recognition of private entrepreneurs as "socialist builders" (Chen *et al.* 2008). It also gave protection of legal rights of private property ownership. These amendments have given entrepreneurs the assurance that the State accepts their legitimate role in the economy.

Entrepreneurial firms are positioned as peripheral actors in Chinese market socialism. However, entrepreneurs act as institutional change agents since they are extremely adaptive and flexible; their pursuit of new opportunities and their collective actions for achieving their own interests have created unintended consequences for the development of market socialism in China. These range from the development of "corrupt" underground economic practices through to their contribution to dynamic economic growth; as such, they are key agents of institutional change and societal transformation (Zheng and Scase 2013).

But this often raises future challenges for the further growth of private-owned enterprises, as an owner-dependent management structure needs to shift to a delegated system with appropriate control mechanism. Through seeking a balance between delegation and control, successful start-ups can grow into large businesses. Supportive government policies for private-owned enterprises to access capital and finance sources will further promote the growth of the non-state, private-owned sector. Non-discriminative treatment should be guaranteed to the non-state sector in terms of prices structures and the availability of goods and services provided by industries, including traffic and transportation costs, energy, basic telecommunications, and other factors for production. Thus, private-owned businesses will continue to grow and enter the fields once monopolized by the state-owned sector.

Note

1 This case study company is illustrated under a pseudonym—"DAL"—throughout the chapter.

6 The impact of foreign joint ventures

Introduction

Foreign joint ventures have been a significant factor in the growth of China's market economy. Through government encouragement, Sino-foreign joint ventures have been a dominant option for companies' entry into the Chinese economy (Yan and Warner 2001). Davidson (1987) pinpoints the factors that determine foreign joint ventures' performance, such as individual personalities, organizational cultures, administrative style, and management philosophy. These factors are often combined in the "One Bed, Different Dreams" symptom (Vanhonacker 1997). Moreover, the "veto-power" of Chinese partners in joint ventures is often a hindrance for foreign partners in their strategic decision-making (China Joint Venturer 1995). All these factors lead foreign joint ventures to adopt "go-it-alone" strategies for running businesses in China.

Nonetheless, Sutter (2000: 15) argues that:

> Wholly foreign-owned enterprise has its disadvantages in several areas. First, in sectors like consumer goods and high-technology hardware, Chinese firms are relatively stronger. In the absence of suitable Chinese partners, a wholly foreign-owned enterprise can be handicapped in the competition by a lack of effective connections to handle governmental work. Having a competent Chinese partner may be useful in developing applications for the local market for the high-tech companies.

Knowledge of local governmental issues, culture, and markets, is critical to both Chinese and foreign investors in China, albeit with different emphases in different areas. Sino-foreign joint ventures overcome economic and political hurdles, and achieve sales volumes more rapidly. Davidson (1987) and Child (1998) point out that wholly foreign-owned enterprises have relatively lower profitability when compared with Sino-foreign joint ventures. However, since China's accession to the World Trade Organization, both types of venture have benefited from market reforms as the business environment has become more market-driven. Many foreign firms' localization programs have been accelerated due to these reforms. The call to transfer management from expatriates to local managers echoes across China (Gamble 2000). More and more studies reveal that the management practices of these joint ventures have adopted a hybrid model in combining characteristics of Western management and Chinese cultural and human resource features. "The rapid localisation has become the mantra of many foreign-invested enterprises in China" (Melvin 1997: 32).

In this case study of a Sino-foreign joint venture, the form of ownership is a joint venture in capital investment rather than management participation. This case is examined as an example of full localization in the management of foreign joint-venture enterprises. As Davidson (1987) mentions, the performance of Sino-foreign joint ventures depends greatly on qualitative factors such as individual personalities, organizational cultures, administrative style, and management philosophy. As disappointments are not unusual with foreign management participation, this case of full localization without foreigners' direct participation may provide a different approach. In this mode of foreign investment venture, an entire "Fit-in Strategy" is maximized through trust-based operational and strategic autonomy. The expatriate managers in this venture, the President and General Manager, are overseas Chinese who were born and brought up in China but who emigrated to the United States. They have adopted advanced Western management approaches through overseas higher education and a deep understanding of foreign culture gained from living in the West. However, they also have a full understanding of Chinese culture and markets, as they have lived and worked in China during their working careers. They have an understanding of both the Western style and Chinese business practices. The characteristics of such joint ventures emerging under market socialism reflect how economic reforms and environmental changes shape management practices and how they find the best way to fit in with local market requirements.

DSF

An American–Chinese joint venture[1]

DSF is an American–Chinese joint venture. In 1997, the US partner invested US$30,000 capital with its Chinese partner, Mr Li, an overseas Chinese businessman who brought US$36,000 capital into the venture in order to set up a joint venture company in the clothing business. The American investment amounted to 45 percent of the total start-up capital and the Chinese party provided 55 percent, with an agreement that full management autonomy was assigned to the President, Mr Li, and that the profit was divided 45:55 on an annual basis. The company's annual report is required to be submitted to the US partner Corporation as a formal method of communicating business performance. The American investment in this company is based on trust, as it had been in the auto parts trading business with Mr Li for many years. Mr Li and his wife, the General Manager of DSF, have both Chinese and Canadian nationality. Prior to this venture, they lived in Canada and America for many years and they engaged in the auto parts trading business and traveled between China and America.

As the President, Mr Li, stated in his interview:

> The American investor injected capital into this ventured business and his interests are guaranteed by a legal treaty in addition to personal trust and confidence in me. We all know that the Chinese market is filled with opportunities; it is just a matter of how you can catch and secure them. You can earn a fortune from the growth of the market economy if you know on which side your bread is buttered. Foreigners see the opportunities but they don't know how to secure them and they don't have know-how in local practices. China has the most complex business environment with a discrete market infrastructure. The legal framework in this market is not the same as in the West and the absence of market laws is a matter of fact. Personal relationships and business networks and nepotism are key values of the business culture. The Americans understand these dynamics and complexity and regard them as the highest risks that can cause failure for their investment in China. I can minimise this risk by offering capital venture with them and taking full responsibility for management practices in China as I know them like the back of my hand. But to do this I need to have full autonomy in management for effective flexibility and control. The opportunity cost is high for exploring the Chinese market. The investment from America is not only important in sharing the high economic cost but also the American venture adds brand value. In addition, a foreign joint venture company can enjoy tax holidays and benefits and gain supportive policies from the government.
>
> (Author interview, 2006)

Foreign joint ventures have a distinctive advantage in advanced management approaches due to direct investment and learning from the West. The foreign joint venture is a form of indigenization that overcomes the shortcomings of foreigners or expatriates directly involved in management, but utilizes the value of foreign capital in resources. This type of localized foreign venture is dependent upon a high degree of trust and tight legal contracts, while access to foreign capital and knowledge is the wherewithal for long-term business growth. In privately-owned companies, there is a deficiency of capital to fund growth while even in state-owned enterprises, with privileged access to financial sources, pressures for short-term profit returns due to performance assessment mechanisms used for managers emphasize immediate profit returns than long-term growth. Foreign joint ventures have competitive advantage in creating high value-added products through their strengths in capital, technology, and advanced Western management techniques.

All the operations and management of the company are focused on the market. The division of work is grouped to meet this objective and tasks are allocated to serve customers' needs. Work relationships in the marketing function are informal and based on teamwork, but sales personnel are given autonomy to achieve their sales targets. In other departments (such as finance, personnel, technology, and manufacturing) hierarchy and authority are enforced by top management. Formal rules and policies are enforced and disseminated from the top to the lower levels.

Total management control is exercised by the top managers, with an emphasis on the formalization of management and systems. Authority is stressed by the General Manager in order to ensure the implementation of commands and strategic plans. However, the marketing division has a flat hierarchy with considerable management autonomy compared with other departments so it can react quickly to external changes and customers' needs. Larry Chen, the Marketing Manager comments:

> Marketing is the main activity of the company. The product has priority in coordination, an absolute priority, and other departments must collaborate with product marketing. We have the most complex structures in other departments; the responsibilities for each job and each unit are clearly defined with given duties to carry out the objectives.
>
> (Author interview, 2006)

Communication systems in DSF are set in hierarchical orders. Employees in each division report to their supervisors and managers. Ignoring orders is regarded as offensive behavior. Middle managers can have direct face-to-face communication with top management. Information flows in a bureaucratic system. Paperwork and formal meetings are the dominant means of communication with top managers. Informal communication processes are pronounced between sales staff. Manufacturing is the department with the strictest bureaucratic rules that standardize routine processes of production. The design department has independent operational autonomy. Creative ideas and design styles are the main output of this department. It has the least number of employees and focuses on fashion culture rather than management issues. Communication and cooperation with manufacturing and technology is close to make sure that designs are developed into products. The marketing department often gives feedback from customers to the designers, so that designing can meet customers' needs. Communication between design and R&D comprises an essential component in this management system in order to meet the objective of brand building.

The DSF Club provides membership and after-sales service for retail customers. Since customers are the key element in brand building, their satisfactory experiences are the main measure for a successful brand. DSF uses "direct-relationship marketing" to forge a close, direct relationship with its customers and offers them free membership of the Club to enjoy experiences and satisfaction from membership services. The DSF brand that represents people's lifestyle, dignity, and quality is delivered and penetrated into customers' perception through membership service. Free events are held for members, such as coffee afternoons and weekend buffets. Such social events give members further experience of the DSF culture and recognition of brand personality. Moreover, as members, they also get access to personal networks, which are regarded as an important social resource in Chinese society. The DSF brand is positioned as a premium price for middle-class, professional female and rich people. They form a valuable resource of social networks when they are organized by the company's club membership.

This is important for word-of-mouth marketing. As the General Manager says:

> The DSF Club is an important communications tool for direct relationships with customers and getting direct feedback from them about their feelings, perceptions and preferences. I always try to attend every event, so that I can listen to what our customers' feel about our brand image and know what they want. Our product targets the segment of luxury goods which mean our customer groups are not in the mass market. They are differentiated from the mass with their own characteristics. They are not easy to satisfy because of their profession, social class, wealth and knowledge. We need to have direct communication with them in order to diffuse our brand values and so that they not only commit their brand loyalty to us but also they can tell others about us through word-of-mouth. More customers are attracted by our Club because they can enjoy a high-class social life and get to know more people who may form a useful social network for their business. In addition, only members of DSF can enjoy privilege discount based on their purchases. In order to guarantee this privilege right of membership, we never have promotion and discount sales in retail stores.
>
> (Author interview, 2006)

The company President exerts direct management control over the finance system, and all budgets and expenditures require his approval. The finance department is directly responsible to the President. Through financial control, the President can then direct and adjust marketing activities at a strategic level. The planning system is an essential mechanism in the company as it has high employee involvement. Employee creativity and participation are high through this planning process. For example, every employee in each department is involved in planning, and they discuss their work with their Departmental Managers on a weekly and monthly basis. The company sets targets (e.g. sales volume and stock rate) for "macro control" and soft targets (e.g. customer satisfaction, work attitude, and creativity) for "micro control" in its planning systems. Cost and quality control are exercised through this system. Responsibilities and division of labor are clearly defined. Personal autonomy is based on level of responsibility and management position. The annual assessment of planning targets is the most important stage in the management process. It is the key element of performance management. Middle management has a high degree of autonomy in deciding how to plan marketing activities with customers and for promoting the brand. However, conflicts between the company strategy and marketing plans are frequent. The Marketing Manager comments that the brand strategy often prohibits discount promotion in order to preserve the value of the brand, whereas the hard targets on sales volume often need to be achieved through discount sales promotions. Coordination and communication between top and middle management are often set in formal and informal meetings to seek solutions when such conflicts emerge. As brand management is a relevantly new concept in the Chinese market, education and training are often required for employees to understand brand strategy and the processes of brand building. Particularly in foreign joint ventures, Western management approaches—the strategic management approach, human resource management, branding management, marketing communications approaches, etc.—are highly adopted and integrated into organizational systems. Local employees need to have a good understanding of these approaches in order to carry out their objectives. The execution of tasks is often unsatisfactory when staff understanding of these concepts is low.

The education level of key personnel in this foreign joint venture is higher than in the other case study companies. The President holds an MBA qualification and the General Manager has a PhD in Management. All other management staff have either postgraduate degrees or undergraduate degrees in relevant marketing, HRM, and technology subjects. Higher education qualifications are an essential requirement for key staff in DSF, as their knowledge is regarded essential for brand building and the company's long-term development. The US partner emphasizes the importance of this. The quality of employees is related to their education and professional background, as the President emphasizes:

> The quality of employees is very important in demonstrating our brand's image, as they represent the company. We try to build up a high quality team with proper courtesy and capability through training and education. The level of knowledge that employees hold determine their degree of creativity and capability. This is crucial for successful marketing communication to our customers.
>
> (Author interview, 2006)

Recruitment policies are based on this strategic vision of brand building. Selection criteria for staff recruitment focus on five elements, "education," "qualification," "ability potential for creativity," "open-mindedness," and "acceptance" of the DSF culture. The selection process includes four procedures: written-format questionnaires; informal interviews; culture workshops; and a final stage of formal interviews. During these procedures, employees' intelligence quotient (IQ) and emotional quotient (EQ) are evaluated. The culture workshop is an important feature in the selection processes, as it is designed as a special observation program. Candidates are invited to this three-day workshop to experience the DSF culture before the final stage of interviews takes place. During these workshops, observations on candidates are recorded to examine their acceptability to the DSF culture. As the General Manager says:

> During workshop activities, some people get excited about the DSF culture and cannot wait to ask questions about it in order to know more. Some are not interested and some are confused. We observe their interests and understanding of the DSF brand philosophies, so that we know whether they can adopt our culture and style, and integrate into this system as a whole.
>
> (Author interview, 2006)

Training programs form an essential part of staff development planning. Written formal assessment of recruits aims to identify specific areas that require training. Tailored training courses are thus designed to meet this need. For example, new sales staff are required to attend one month full-time, off-the-job training courses before they start. The courses include sales techniques, color collections, the art of displaying clothes, retail distribution, etc. in addition to brand management training that is compulsory for all levels of employees. Managerial staff attend training courses that focus on strategy and advanced management approaches. Professors from academic institutions are invited to give lectures. Managers are not only sent to Beijing and Shanghai for learning, but also to France and Italy to learn about brand management, as the DSF brand represents a European style. The design of training in DSF shows that the constant education of employees is focused on their understanding of management knowledge, underpinning the company's brand. Due to the owners' US background and their direct adoption of Western management practices, the strategic vision of the company is based on high value-added product development with rich culture connation, which requires a knowledge-based staff team. Therefore, constant training, including off- and on-the-job training, aims to close the gap between advanced management practices and low-skilled local managers.

Reward and sanction systems, as part of human resource management, generate motivation to drive consistent performance. In a market-focused system, reward based on sales performance is the common approach. The criteria for rewards and sanctions are set in relation to hard and soft targets in the planning system. This is formularized as:

basic wages + performance wages (assessed by hard and soft targets)

+ annual rewards = total employees' pay

Rewards are also increased twice a year, in February and August. The amount of increment is dependent on an individual's performance. The frequency of the latter's faults at work is also recorded. When these are too great, employees may be transferred to other positions or dismissed.

Personnel policies for employees' treatment and welfare are fairly good in this joint venture enterprise. Legal contracts provide employees with cover for five types of insurance, which include housing and pensions. Extra hours at work are paid at the legitimate rate, and holidays and sick-days are also covered by the standard salary. Business travel is compensated by extra subsidiaries. Employees are well treated at DSF in comparison with those in the other case studies; this is a further example of the influence of US ownership participation.

The "soft" means of rewards reflect human relations concerns in DSF; for example, promotion opportunities for every member of staff and opportunities for studying abroad (e.g. France and Italy) are part of the whole reward system. Good working conditions are provided, with personal laptops, company cars, and compensation for travel. These "soft" methods fulfill an important function in motivating staff and developing personal potential. The interviews in DSF suggested that motivation among interviewees is much higher than in the other case companies.

As the Personnel Manager, Mr Liu Ming, comments:

> I feel the company not only meets employees' living needs, but more importantly it gives opportunities for personal development. We have convergent objectives with the company's development. We interact within this organisation as a whole, as the organisation's development depends on us, and our personal actualisation depends on the organisation.
>
> (Author interview, 2006)

The Marketing Manager, Mr Larry Chen, comments:

> This company has very advanced management concepts and philosophies which encourage us to learn management theories that we never looked into before. This is a company with huge potential in development and it can definitely do better as time goes on. However, much has yet to be done and more capable talents need to join us as we grow. A complete motivation system to retain highly skilled talents is in demand, although this company has been very successful in building brand image and culture with precise market position. Further development will put challenges on our human resource management. The motivation incentives are still not enough and rewards systems need to be more improved in order to fully develop personal capabilities. For instance, responsibilities that managers carry out need to relate to specified rewards, and we need to know what we can achieve and what we can do.
>
> (Author interview, 2006)

As the General Manager says:

> We still need to find better solutions to motivate the middle management. Groups of employees at sales level are well motivated by specified sales-related reward mechanisms; whereas other departments, like design, technology and outsourcing that don't have direct links to retail stores and sales, require better incentives. We need a multi-designed motivation mechanism to retain capable talents. Currently this is the most challenging task for our company, as we are struggling with a shortage of capable managers. Our concepts and ideas need to be executed by capable staff, but we don't have enough of them. It is not easy to find skilled managers on the Chinese labour market. Actually we have been trying to train potential employees from internal promotion. However, re-education and training are a tough task for us.
>
> (Author interview, 2006)

Leadership style in DSF is dichotomous. The President represents a democratic and consultative style, whereas the General Manager demonstrates an authoritative and directive role. In the Chinese sense, the President is a Confucian-style leader, who emphasizes intellectual wisdom and courtesy, advocating knowledge education rather than an emphasis on material values. Referring to his overseas education background and expatriate experience, he is open-minded to adopt both Western and Chinese philosophies, showing appreciation of advanced knowledge practices and technology regardless of country boundaries. He is a gracious and approachable person, which makes employees amiable towards him. Communication with him is much easier than with the General Manager.

The General Manager is an authority-based leader, believing in command-and-obey management. Impersonal rules and procedures are her preference, as she emphasizes that discipline to regularize employees' behavior is necessary for effective management. She underlines this in company training programs and stresses that authority plays a key role in reinforcing management and the achievement of company objectives. Brand management is a new concept in the Chinese market, so its enforcement is required to push employees' acceptance of it. Because of her strong preference for authority management, conflicts often occur between the General Manager and the President. In the interview, she complained that the President is too easy with employees. However, although dissension does exist, when it comes to strategic vision, they always reach consensus; if not, she accepts the final decision of the President.

The leadership style in DSF seems to be a good combination of authority and democracy as they compensate each other in order to form a mixed style to serve different needs of management. But, of course, their co-existence creates tensions. The General Manager regards herself as the teacher of the organization, who gives lessons to employees for their training. She has influence over employees. She is not only their manager but also the preacher of the company's culture and brand management concepts. The Personnel Manager comments on her style as:

> The General Manager exerts great influence on the staff in terms of culture, values, management concepts and ways of doing things. She is a perfectionist in everything, so she expects high standards from us and on enterprise development. She is an entrepreneur with strong personal capabilities, which influence everyone around her. She is very authoritative in insisting on her ways of doing things. She is very directive to teach us to do new things. We respect her as she has profound knowledge and experience. She speaks fluent English and always engages in diplomatic affairs with foreigners and different countries. She has a very internationalised style and open mind.
> (Author interview, 2006)

The Manager of Technology comments:

> Leadership in DSF is strong. Our president is a democratic leader, but with very cutting-edge concepts and vision. He represents the American style of management—open and creative. The Chinese general manager is an authoritative leader with a determined mind. She makes sure things get done and she is very good at creating cultural values for the enterprise. Both of them

are very intellectual and knowledgeable. Their leadership is a mixed style in the company.

(Author interview, 2006)

"American companies are often regarded as high profile, and are deemed as the most desirable to work for. Because the Americans are more generous and open, they tell you what to do and let you get on with it." (Gamble 2000: 884) Leadership in this American–Chinese joint venture seems to demonstrate a similar style-high profile, open culture, high management autonomy. DSF emphasizes the importance of end-results from middle managers, while excellent achievements are expected from the top management as the company aims to develop a high profile performance. There are great opportunities to develop personal potential, but the company also challenges the capabilities of managers who take on these responsibilities. As the Marketing manager, Larry Chen comments:

> The company just tell you the objectives, the processes and decisions are left to us to determine. Although the company has taught us so much about new management concept and theories, we have to digest them by time and through practice. We feel the company should provide us with more support in process management, but actually they leave the work completely to us to make decisions, developing the tasks and responsibilities to first-line employees. The president only looks to the results, and the general manager takes a more participative role in daily operations, but she is more likely to be in a supervisory role rather than supportive.
>
> (Author interview, 2006)

The work environment is designed to high professional standards. DSF's headquarters office is located in a prestigious urban area, comprising wealthy people and foreigners, as this matches its brand image and market position. Its location also offers convenience to members of the DSF Club for its social life. The company's physical internal environment is creative and unique in terms of color schemes and space arrangement. The DSF Group's US sign is the biggest logo at the front door, denoting its foreign joint venture status. Coffee-making facilities remind the visitor of this distinction, as a coffee culture is seen as symptomatic of the Western lifestyle. The clothes showroom is arranged in the lobby next to the reception, which customers can walk into. Contrasting colors and designs impress visitors and catch their attention immediately. The workplace plays Mozart and Beethoven music, which reinforces Western values and enhances the work atmosphere as friendly and relaxing. Employees demonstrate proper courtesy and modest manners as befits a well-trained, high-quality team.

The General Manager is the advocator and preacher for creating and enriching the DSF culture. She did primary research to define the DSF brand with both Western and Chinese identification. The creation of cultural connotations forms the orientation of the DSF brand, "...the brand is the symbol that incarnates the feminine style of life, a kind of philosophy, a kind of poetry, a kind of graceful and romantic life style." The company goal is shared by all employees and is described as being "In pursuit of the high and the beyond." "The High," is defined as the highest profile brand in the world; "the beyond" is denoted as the intention to develop DSF into a hundred-year enterprise with a solid foundation. The organizational goal reflects this ambition and long-term development vision, while the spirit of "being the best" inspires employees.

The general manager plays a valuable role in teaching and educating employees to the extent that her values and philosophies have changed their behavior and mentality. She promotes a high profile style of quality of life in relation to the brand, encouraging employees to pursue excellence. Knowledge is highly respected in this company and creativity and innovation in marketing and technology are a key focus in employees' education. The motto being advocated in DSF among employees is "Excel yourself to be creative!" As the General Manager always tells employees; "if you want to change your life, you come to DSF this is the company that can give you the opportunity to be better and can provide you with different cultural experiences." This is the key value in the company's culture that creates an environment in which to develop employees' capabilities and encourage their creativity and innovation. An emphasis on staff autonomy is regarded as an essential philosophy underpinning DSF's management strategy to activate employees' potential, which is a precondition to achieving high performance in the market. The philosophy of performance management is to stress self-oriented, result-driven performance.

The President of DSF, with his MBA background and work experience in the United States, has applied his management knowledge to business practice. In the interview, he demonstrated a full understanding of key management concepts and approaches. An advanced Western style of management is adopted in his company; for instance, "brand building" marketing communications as well as a management pattern, structured as:

marketing + design + manufacturing + outsourcing

This pattern is used by Western brand-focused companies as it prioritizes the marketing and design functions as the main focus, and regards manufacturing as the supply function to serve marketing and design needs. The outsourcing strategy is used in this pattern as supplementary to manufacturing in order to reduce production costs and maintain a focus on high value-added product management:

> Chinese garment factories usually concentrate on labour intensified manufacturing work and low value added products. They lack marketing and branding knowledge to design a strategic management to build up high value added product, thereof they are unable to move up to R&D based industry but cluster in the low technology and labour intensity industries.
>
> (CTIA 2005/2006: 52)

The General Manager, with a PhD qualification, together with a high capability in management, has enhanced the knowledge-based learning and teaching culture in DSF. As she explains, her role is more like a preacher and teacher who directs employees. She converts management concepts and theories into practice and tests them in the Chinese market. This is the strength of the company. However, it is also the cause of problems in management. As they inoculate ideas and theories into their employees, they expect the latter to implement them. However, they don't know precisely what the processes between concepts and results should look like. Management concepts need to be converted into techniques before they can be applied to practices. This is why managers express their confusion about process management, and emphasize the need for more support from top management if they are to refine procedures and processes in terms of how to meet their objectives. They are already aware of the problems in refining process management and one solution offered by the President and his managers is the implementation of an ERP (Enterprise Resource Planning) system. The IT software technology of ERP aims to maximize the use of all the resources in an organization. These resources include: employees and their skills; the business processes, procedures and organizational structure; and IT systems that support the various business areas. ERP promises one database and one user interface across an entire multi-site enterprise. Taking information from every business area, ERP helps managers and employees to plan, monitor, and control the entire business. Improved control of resources means greater efficiency and effectiveness. ERP represents a large investment for DSF, and at the time of the interviews, they were working on the selection, implementation, and optimization of software packages (e.g. BaaN, JBA, JDEdwards, Oracle, PeopleSoft, SAP, SSA), as these must be closely managed to deliver maximum benefits. The investment in ERP also places demands on skills training for staff; it is a challenging learning process for DSF in pursuit of technology innovation and management advancement.

Foreign investment, as a salient constitution of the Chinese economy, plays an increasingly substantial role in market transformation. Foreign joint ventures, as one form of business venture emerging from market socialism, demand the localization and adaptation of foreign investment in China's changing marketplace. DSF, a typical foreign joint venture with expatriate-owned management, is characterized by competitive virtues and a visionary orientation positioned in the high value-added chain of its industry with brand-focused marketing. This case study suggests that a knowledge-based product portfolio and a people-focused management system are the key factors of competitiveness that distinguish foreign joint ventures from domestic enterprises. Building "home brands" is appealing for domestic enterprises, particularly in traditional industries. But in the three case studies outlined here, the foreign joint venture is the only example that is successfully developing brands for the Chinese market. By applying its "learning from the West," it has implemented such practices in the Chinese marketplace through intensive staff training. Its adhocratic and professional structure, in combination with formal and informal management systems, provides openness and the flexibility to promote personal development. The constant dissemination of knowledge through integrated training programs generates a learning orientation to stimulate self-renewal and encourage innovation and creativity. Retaining highly-skilled managers requires an organization to establish an environment that is capable of encompassing relevant supportive systems and processes as a whole. Through this means, this foreign joint venture is able to develop its core competences for its long-term investment strategies.

Foreign-owned joint ventures are major employers in China, and, as a result, their employment policies and practices have a strong bearing on reshaping the pool of human resources and the experience of work for a significant proportion of workers in (Cooke 2004). They are often regarded as a "best practice" benchmark. Furthermore, foreign joint ventures are the dominant force of the non-state economic sector because of their capabilities, based as these are upon a combination of local skills and knowledge with foreign-imported technologies and advanced management practices. This gives them a competitive edge and enables them to position themselves at the high end of the industry chain. They are proactive in responding to market demands because of their creative and deliberative attempts to be at the forefront of market threads. It remains to be seen if this will continue to be the case in the future as the development of indigenous managerial, technological, and scientific skills reduces the need for the Chinese economy to be dependent upon the import of these skills. At present, the state and foreign joint ventures have a symbiotic relationship; they are dependent upon each other for the pursuit of their own separate objectives and agendas. The outcome is market socialism, consisting of dialogue and accommodation between Western capitalist corporations and a growth-oriented Communist Party. Perhaps their key role as agents of change is in the creation of strata of employable knowledge workers constituting an urban, globally integrated middle class, which could, in the future, challenge the legitimacy of the dominant Communist Party.

Note

1 This case study company is illustrated under a pseudonym—"DSF"—throughout the chapter.

7 Case studies: state-owned enterprise LTG, privately owned enterprise DAL and foreign joint-venture DSF

Introduction

This chapter compares and analyzes the distinctive characteristics of three emerging business ventures under market socialism. Case studies on the three most significant types of business venture—state-owned enterprises, private-owned and foreign joint ventures—draw organizational profiles for each form of ownership, to not only examine how the property of ownership is likely to impact on shaping their distinctive characteristics, creating challenges and tensions in each type of venture, but also to draw some conclusions for future trends and policy recommendations for each type of business venture.

The three case studies: some contrasting differences

Using the McKinsey 7-S framework, as used throughout this research, it is possible to identify the major differences between the case studies. The 7-S framework, used by the McKinsey Group for the analysis of organizations, focuses upon (1) strategy, (2) structure, (3) systems, (4) staff, (5) style, (6) shared values, and (7) skills. For a further elaboration of this framework as used in this research, see Appendix pp. 141–7.

Strategy

Even though the three cases operate in the same industry (the textile and garment industry), their strategies vary significantly according to different types of ownership. The motivations that drive companies to develop, the means by which they expand and grow, and the mind-sets of those who built their operations are dissimilar due to diverse ownership. The development strategy of the state-owned enterprise is prominently influenced by state policies and political factors. Thus, its strategy expressly reflects Party policy and political direction to the extent that it may not best suit market needs and the business itself as long as it is responsive to political demands. The state-owned enterprise has the least market-oriented strategy, resulting in the highest tension created by political demands that are inconsistent with market demands.

The state-owned enterprise—LTG—presents its corporate strategy in a very formal fashion, which officially documents its strategic objectives for both the short and the long term. Each stage of development is formulated for specific tasks. This forms a distinct contrast to the private-owned enterprise, where an entrepreneur operates his small and flexible company with "no strategy" and "no paper rules." No formal and explicit strategic planning is stated in this entrepreneurial company; the private owner determines the company's planning and strategy on an ad hoc basis according to how the market changes and what the customers require. Such an informal strategy is never described in documents but only verbally explained by the owner in the direction of tasks for employees. Strategy can randomly change whenever the owner decides. The strategy in the private-owned enterprise is fluid rather than fixed as in the state-owned enterprise, which demonstrates superior flexibility and freedom in planning and operation. The state-owned enterprise has utmost inflexibility and constraints in strategic change.

Due to the tension between political needs and market demands in the state-owned enterprise—LTG—conflict exists at both the operational and corporate levels. The corporate level strategy is a reflection of the state reform objectives, which are politically driven in line with the Party's expectations and ideas of economic development. For instance, the five guidelines for strategy planning at LTG incorporate all the government policies for the reform of state-owned enterprises. These guidelines are sometimes in contradiction with the actual situation of the market in which the enterprise operates. For example, the guideline stipulates that export and import trading is a priority, whereas there is a market demand for own branding. The guideline advocating the establishment of a joint venture with a foreign company, in order to form strategic alliance, is unlikely due to both ownership constraints and political sensitivity. Because the strategic planning of LTG is not fully decided by its own senior management but is mostly driven by the administration agency, AICSA, under the central government, political direction is reinforced. Specifically, strategic planning cannot be constantly adjusted in good time when the market situation changes. Such strategic change in state-owned enterprise requires a long bureaucratic process of approval from AICSA. Lack of flexibility and the absence of entrepreneurship is an evident disadvantage in state-owned enterprise compared with the other types of enterprises, which can adapt quickly to changing market demands. Administration and bureaucratic processes significantly affect the management pattern of the state-owned enterprise (as the main influencing factor) distinguishing the state-owned enterprise from the other types of enterprises that operate in the same market.

The foreign joint venture—DSF—operates a Western approach to high value-added branded goods, with a deep understanding of strategic approaches to brand marketing. The foreign joint venture demonstrates high vision of strategy for long-term planning with management flexibility and knowledge advancement, responding not only to domestic market needs but also to international market standards. In the field of branded clothing, foreign companies have many advantages because of their expertise, advanced knowledge, and long history. Comparatively, indigenous firms are weak in brand building; foreign-invested firms are likely to place brands at the heart of marketing and business strategy. Given the advanced knowledge about brand management, DSF has placed the objective of developing brand equity at the core of the company's strategic management and regarded it as a key determinant of corporate values. However, investments in brand building activities do not have an immediate pay-off. Without an understanding of their future potential value and with no long-term vision of strategic development, many Chinese companies today are unwilling to invest in building product brands. Their reluctance is mainly due to minimal knowledge of know-how in brand building as well as a lack of long-term vision. They tend to be tempted and pressured by short-term profit return. DSF's brand strategy shows a long-term focus that increases its market competitiveness. In relation to ownership, the foreign joint venture has a distinctive advantage in advanced management approaches due to direct investment and learning from the West. The foreign joint venture is a form of indigenization, which overcomes the shortcomings of foreigners or expatriates directly involved in management but utilizes the value of foreign capital resources. This type of localized foreign venture is dependent upon a high degree of trust and tight legal contracts. It is a result of market reforms and adaptation to the regulatory environment. Compared with state-owned enterprises and private-owned enterprises, foreign joint ventures are the only ones positioning themselves at the top of value-added production in the clothing industry. Foreign capital is the wherewithal for the adoption of such a strategy, as brand building requires constant and extensive investment over a long period of time without immediate pay-off. Financial pressure is often the ruthless reason for terminating this type of strategy because investments do not have visible returns in short-term sales and profits. Faced with such elusive, long-term and intangible benefits, it is not surprising that companies and managers always drop this strategy in planning. This is the prevalent situation in China, which has a deficiency of capital to fund growth in private-owned enterprises. Even state-owned enterprises, with privileged access to financial sources, are usually driven by short-term profit returns due to performance assessment mechanisms (used by managers in strategic planning) that emphasise immediate profits. The foreign joint venture shows its competitive advantage in creating high value-added products through its strengths in capital, technology, and advanced Western management techniques.

In general, of the differing types of enterprise in our case studies, the private-owned enterprise holds an aggressive strategy in expansion and growth, which benefits from the entrepreneurial vision of its private owners as well as market demand. By comparison with the foreign joint venture, it is limited by a scarcity of knowledge, technology, and the existence professional teams to achieve its entrepreneurial vision. Private-owned enterprises still have much to learn in order to further develop their competitiveness and capability. Restricted by the property of ownership, the state-owned enterprise is inevitably affected by state administration and governance, resulting in the most conservative strategy for growth and brand building, as it involves long-term investment without instant profit return. This goes against the performance evaluation mechanism stipulated by the government, in spite of having the easiest access to finance resources. The strategy of the state-owned enterprise is subject to state central planning and the political agenda.

Structure

Structure varies according to the size of the enterprise, the nature of work, and the philosophy of the management; it provides the framework of an organization and its pattern of management and it makes possible the application of management processes that create a system of order and command through which the activities of the enterprise can be planned, organised, directed, and controlled (Child 1984; Birkinshaw 2001). Our case studies reveal that the pattern of structure is also determined by the type of ownership and is consistent with the latter's strategy, system, and culture. It reflects the owner's method of control. The state-owned company, LTG, is a typical divisionalized structure with centralized government administration, authority, and bureaucracy. The entrepreneurial firm—DAL—has the most flexible and fluid structure, designed as owner-centered management. The foreign joint venture—DSF—is characterized by a market-focused structure, in order to meet its brand strategy, and by operational flexibility. Such a relatively "open" structure facilitates personal development embedded with a high level of concern to promote intraprenuership.

Compared with two types of ownership—private-owned and foreign joint venture—in our case studies, the structure and systems of the state-owned enterprise are the most sophisticated forms of formally institutionalized bureaucracy. Strategic decision-making in such systems tends to be affected by upper authority rather than by market demands. Despite management autonomy, middle management is tightly controlled through a culture that reflects the continuing dominance of the party and centralized state ownership. Consequently, conventional Communist Party thinking on the planned economy retains a strong impact upon the ideology and behavior of employees in LTG. Whereas structure in the private-owned enterprise is almost non-existent, providing an extreme contrast to the state-owned enterprise. There are not even documents for HR policies, management procedures, or company regulations. Basically, this is *not* a structure, but a pattern of dependency upon the private owner. The proprietor is very much at the center of the management web. Informality and high flexibility are the major characteristics of the DAL entrepreneurial company.

Systems

To be compatible with their different structures, applied systems vary within each form of business venture. The private-owned enterprise possesses the most fluid and informal systems for communication and management. The foreign joint venture organization has an open and knowledge-based mechanism with an emphasis on personal development and intrapreneurship. State ownership requires formal and institutionalized systems for its divisional, large-scale organization.

Institutionalization and formalization of systems are the main features of the large-scale, state-owned enterprise. For instance, LTG is the only case study company that has passed the requirements of QMS and successfully implemented internationally standardized quality-control systems. None of the other companies have implemented such formal standardization of quality control due to the cost of the system and their scale of production. The implementation of QMS is a compulsory command of the State Administration. QMS fits the demand for the institutionalization and corporatization of state-owned enterprises. Moreover, the strong state financial background of LTG gives it the possibility to adopt QMS.

In distinct contrast, in the private-owned enterprise, with a minimal skeleton structure, the systems of direct control are informal and highly flexible. The proprietor is at the center of decision-making. Hierarchy is low, and the proprietor (with direct and total control) is the sole authority for all working procedures. Although this gives flexibility to management, it also gives rise to chaos and muddle when the task becomes more complicated and when the company expands too quickly. In particular, the owner is likely to be saturated with too much information and this results in exhaustion and incapability of exercising total control. It is evident, in the case study of DAL, that formalized structures and systems are required for systematically planning and organizing business activities when a company expands and has over 200 employees.

Nonetheless, by comparison, the foreign joint venture (DSF) has both formal and informal systems in place. It has an open and knowledge-based mechanism in its management structure, which promotes personal development and employee creativity and innovation. DSF emphasizes formal rules for the control of implementation processes and procedures in the production unit, while it gives autonomy to the staff for creativity in the marketing and sales department. A knowledge-based learning system is highly promoted and implemented in the organization, which acts as an incubator for innovation and entrepreneurship. Constant education becomes incumbent upon the employee in DSF. Tension is created between the demand for creativity and the capabilities of employees. However, although more intense education and training is designed to enhance the skills of employees, their capacity to digest such knowledge is still in question. Constant renewal, in order to retain competitiveness, is the major challenge for DSF, as it positions itself at the cutting edge of knowledge and within the high value-added chain of the clothing industry.

Staff

By contrast with the private-owned enterprise and the foreign joint venture, life security and employee benefits are well embodied in the state-owned enterprise. Extra hours at work are paid at a fair rate, annual increments in salary and all round welfare is legitimated and guaranteed for the staff in line with the Labor Law. The state-owned enterprise also offers more benefits, such as stock options, housing, and bonuses, to its key personnel. This is in dramatic contrast with the insecurity of employee benefits and welfare in the private-owned enterprise, where only minimal levels are promised. In the private-owned company, the owner uses financial reward as a control tool; an informal and verbal approach is adopted in order to gain employee commitment and motivation and to create dependency upon his power. This is used at a minimum level whenever the owner feels it is necessary. There is no formal guarantee, or legitimate security, of long-term benefits and welfare. Comparatively, the foreign joint venture (DSF) provides all legally required welfare and benefits to staff together with formal, but short-term, contracts. Furthermore, benefits are presented in order to attract employees. There is also a personal development scheme, offering opportunity and training for ambitious individuals. These distinctive elements—open-minded and high vision, cutting-edge knowledge, and opportunities for personal actualization—are well merged in the staff development system in the foreign joint venture. The "soft" system of rewards reflects HR concerns, such as good working conditions. Employees are provided with personal laptops, company cars, compensation for travel, opportunities to study abroad, promotion, etc., which fulfils the important function of motivating staff and developing personal potential. The education level of key personnel in this foreign joint venture is higher than in the other two case study companies. Higher education qualifications are an essential requirement for key staff in DSF, as their knowledge is regarded as essential for brand building and the company's long-term development. The US partner emphasises the importance of this. Training programs are essential components of staff development planning. Written formal assessments of recruits aim to identify specific areas where they require training. Tailored training courses are thus designed to meet this need. The design of training in DSF shows that the constant education of employees is focused on their understanding of management knowledge, underpinning the company's brand. Due to the owners' US background, and their direct adoption of Western management practices, the strategic vision of the company is based on high value-added product development with a rich culture connation, which requires a knowledge-based staff team. Therefore, constant training, including off- and on-the-job, aims to close the gap between advanced management practices and low-skilled local managers. The interviews in DSF suggested that motivation among interviewees is much higher than in the other three case companies.

In contrast with the foreign joint venture, the state-owned enterprise is disadvantaged and challenged in its personnel management, particularly in the ways it recruits staff. The influence of personal relations culture is more powerful in the state-owned enterprise than in the other types of ownership, "overriding market demands and rules." Such differences between the state-owned enterprise case and the other types of enterprise reveal that political power and hierarchical political authority are much greater in state-owned corporations. This forms the underpinning of cultural norms that direct and guide management behaviors. This common reality shapes the style of management in the state-owned enterprise and destroys ambition and entrepreneurial willingness among employees. It also restricts innovation and entrepreneurial development and explains why staff motivation is low in this type of enterprise. Moreover, the reward system is mainly dependent on the bonus system; the government authorities and managers are driven by profit objectives. This might improve immediate performance in profitability, but does not take into account risks in long-term investment. Future prospects for the development of state-owned enterprises are more related to political demands than market opportunities.

Style

How key managers achieve their organization's goals and manage their employees, creates different patterns of actions. The management philosophy underpinning and directing key managers' behavior is decisive and interactive with other organizational factors, such as structure, systems, culture, and environment etc. The style of managerial behavior, in the three types of business venture highlighted in this book, reflects different patterns according to diverse ownership. The decisive pattern of actions will reflect the attitude of the major stakeholders, and varies depending on how much influence the leaders or senior managers have upon management. For instance, top and middle management all play an influencing role in the state-owned enterprise, due to its divisional structure and decentralized management autonomy in subsidiary business units. On the contrary, in the private-owned enterprise, the owner–entrepreneur accounts for management style, as it is an owner-centered organization. Likewise, the foreign joint venture presents its style through top management, with foreign culture involvement. Western education, life experience in living in America and a US partnership, have formed influencing factors to shape the management style of DSF managers.

The style and principles of state administration shape the management practice of the state-owned enterprise, whereas the other types of enterprise reflect their owners' interests. Leadership in relation to ownership function is vital in shaping management structures, as it is crucial to directing enterprises towards either success or failure. The major difference in leadership between the state-owned enterprise and other types is that the leaders in the former do not represent independent individualism but the embodiment of the Party and government as a whole. In practice, if not in theory, they cannot make decisions on their own, but must be consistent with political direction and Party principles. This is in contrast with the leaders of the private-owned enterprise and foreign joint venture, who freely present their own ideas, identities, and styles. Leadership styles vary to a large extent according to ownership. For example, in line with Maslows' need hierarchy (1987), the foreign joint venture demonstrates a delegating approach to leadership, providing both high supportive behavior and guidance so that employees are expected to carry out tasks by themselves. Managers work for their own interests, achievements, and advancements. An open culture and delegating style of management gives the highest motivation to employees in DSF. Likewise, the owner of the private-owned enterprise has a participating and consultative style, providing a high degree of supportive behavior and developing a close interdependent relationship with his employees. However, the level of guidance is relatively low in terms of detail, as employees are expected to accept a level of independence in their own work, despite final decisions needing to be passed to the owner. The owner–entrepreneur works for himself as a self-motivated leader, but his followers do not have the same high level of motivation due to unstable and lower rewards in this small entrepreneurial firm.

Comparatively, the state-owned enterprise presents a "selling" style of leadership, providing both a high level of supportive behavior and specialized guidance for administrative control and governance (Hersey *et al.* 2001). Good working conditions, life security, a high standard of welfare, and bonus rewards satisfy employee requirements in terms of physical needs, safety, and social support; but there is a lack self-actualization for workers. This is mainly caused by the absence of opportunities for personal creativity and inflexibility for entrepreneurship or intrapreneurship, which engenders tensions and hinders management development. The style of the state-owned LTG reflects the contrasting approaches of "state-planning" and "market-orientation" that will become sources of greater internal inconsistency as further market reforms are introduced within state-owned enterprises. State-owned enterprise reforms have long been restricted by socialist ideology. Because state ownership is directly linked to the state administration and the Communist Party's political systems, economic reforms need to be compatible with existing political systems, i.e. socialist ideals. In order to secure such concordance, key managers are mainly selected from the military and constant education of socialist ideas is enforced among top managers. This strong political and socialist culture significantly distinguishes state-owned enterprises from the other two types of ownership enterprises. However, free-market competition requires effective management with "market ideals" other than "socialist ideals." This is the essential contradiction within state-owned enterprises, which reflects the tensions in China's integrated dual-track economy.

The owner–entrepreneur is the determining factor for the success of the DAL company. His explicit leadership and charismatic style influences people's hearts and wins affection; he does not influence them by imposing rules. This informal leadership is built on top of his unassailable authority. He demonstrates a hybrid leadership style in his management. Besides his authoritarian nature for control of his own business, his leadership is a mixture of supportive, participative, and achievement-oriented approaches. This owner participates in all activities and decision-making in this business. He prefers to share ideas and consult with his managers before final decisions are made. He expects his employees to take independence for task implementation. However, his employees' readiness sometimes seems to be lower than what he expects. Insecurity and low rewards may also affect the commitment and motivation of his employees.

Leadership within the foreign joint venture—DSF—is dichotomous. The President and General Manager represent different preferences of management style; one has a democratic and consultative style and the other uses an authoritative and directive approach. They form a strategic combination to provide both styles in an open system, despite the ongoing tensions between the two leaders. DSF provides opportunities for personal development and promotes a learning culture throughout the whole system. Delegation is often authorized to middle management and managers are expected to make their own decisions and determine implementation procedures to achieve their final objectives. Leadership in this American–Chinese joint venture seems to demonstrate a similar style—high profile, open culture, and high management autonomy. DSF emphasizes end results from middle managers, while excellent levels of achievement are expected by top managers as the company aims to develop a high profile performance. There are great opportunities to develop personal potential, but the company also challenges the capabilities of managers who take these responsibilities.

Shared values

The guiding concepts, values, and beliefs underpinning each type of business venture are in significant contrast. Such dissimilarity seems to be a corollary of different types of ownership as the orientation and interests of ownership property vary. The foreign joint venture adopts more Western cultural values with its absorption of Western management philosophy and knowledge. This explains why the foreign joint venture leads the cutting edge of brand development. The private-owned enterprise is a purely entrepreneurial-driven business with intrinsic motivation and total market-orientation as the guiding belief, thus it has a fluid, flexible, loose, and owner-dependent management structure. The owner's philosophy and behavior determines the organizational processes and cultural norms. To the extreme extent, the state-owned enterprise is significantly influenced by state administrative norms and political bureaucracy culture, which creates a dramatic difference in comparison with the other two types of business venture.

The key spiritual values that drive the state-owned enterprise, particularly at the management level, are *Loyalty and Consistency* with the Communist Party—the central authority. This is an inviolable principle and a prerequisite above the market orientation of LTG. Without this premise, everything is meaningless and irrespective. Party meetings are held routinely and are as numerous as business operation meetings. Ad hoc activities assigned from the Central Committee of the Communist Party reinforce the education of "Loyalty and Consistency" on a frequent basis and they constitute a core part of LTG's enterprise activities. This special character predominantly distinguishes the state-owned enterprise from the other types of business venture. Such driving belief is decisive in how managers prioritize their time and work; it also unravels an important reason why the state-owned enterprise is slow to react to market changes. Such constantly imposed Party education moulds employees' values and this inevitably has an impact on management philosophies and behaviors. The top managers strive for an infallible performance and short-term returns rather than long-term investment. This kind of management philosophy is deeply embedded in both the state administration mechanism and performance assessment systems. It is not surprising that prudent and myopic behavior is predominant amongst managers in the state-owned enterprise. Too many constraints and interventions from the state administration give little versatility to the operation and practice of state-owned enterprises in the market. This further explains the style of management in LTG. Bearing in mind market values that require entrepreneurship and risk, there is an inevitable conflict of cultures within the enterprise as a whole. Take the recruitment system as an example: the state-owned enterprise has no choice but to opt for a closed, internal allocation of recruitment because of its deeply embedded political hierarchy culture. Anyone who wants to survive in the state-owned enterprise must make a compromise in political matters. Such an inexorable underpinning of culture and values will inevitably restrict further reforms in market-driven management. Although reshuffle reforms instantly ameliorate the status quo of the state-owned enterprise, it is likely to encounter a plateau afterwards.

The management philosophies of the owner–entrepreneur in DAL, the private-owned enterprise, focus on the importance of family culture and on showing democracy, consideration, and respect to all employees. The work climate is friendly and harmonious with little hierarchy, making employees feel psychologically comfortable. The owner–entrepreneur tries to share the attitudes of his employees by educating them to have the right values so that they cooperate and comply with his direction and decisions. The proprietor is at the center of a power culture and imposes total control throughout the whole organization. This is similar to how Handy (1993) describes a power culture, "It depends on a central power source with rays of influence form the central figure throughout the organisation. Control is exercised from centre by the selection of key individuals. There are few rules and procedures, and little bureaucracy."

But the business also prides itself on having a strong learning culture, which is strongly promoted by the owner–entrepreneur. Peter Senge (1999) observes that learning organizations can only be built by leaders who possess both fire and passion. Timmons (1999) says that successful entrepreneurs are "patient leaders, capable of instilling tangible visions and managing for the long haul. The entrepreneur is at once a learner and a teacher, a doer and a visionary." Being a learner and a teacher are two of the prime tasks for a leader in a learning organization (Burns 2005). The owner of the DAL entrepreneurial firm frequently arranges field visits to advanced companies nationwide and actively joins industry associations, in order to find ideas for continuous improvement. His approach is more pragmatic and direct compared with the traditional training courses. He constantly educates his employees and stresses the importance of learning and improving their working practices. Such a learning culture has led to innovations in the quality control system and marketing. Burgoyne (1995) says that a learning organization facilitates the learning of all its members and continuously transforms itself. Garratt (1994) views learning organizations as essentially liberating and energizing, and as crucial for organizational survival and growth.

In like manner, the organizational culture in the foreign joint venture (DSF) is distinctively educational and knowledge-based; it is keen on constant renewal of itself. Learning is reinforced through constant training programs. The willingness and urgency to learn new things have become both formal and informal norms for staff. The manager entrepreneurs of DSF are also the advocates and preachers of the dissemination of brand connation and the promotion of a learning culture. The goal of the company is shared by all employees, and is described as "In pursuit of the high and the beyond." "The High" is defined as the highest profile brand in the world; "the beyond" is denoted to develop Sunfed to be a hundred-year-old enterprise with a solid foundation. This organizational goal reflects the company's ambition and long-term development vision, while the spirit of "being the best" inspires employees. Rich cultural connotations and the "legend" behind the brand, express a prolific brand personality and value, which gives customers an emotional experience that builds the company's competitiveness in a way that competitors find hard to imitate. The top managers play a valuable role in teaching and educating employees to the extent that their values and philosophies have changed employees' behavior and mentality. They promote a high profile style of quality of life, encouraging employees to pursue excellence. Knowledge is highly respected in this company and creativity and innovation in marketing and technology are an important aspect of employee education. This is a key value in the company's culture. An emphasis on staff autonomy is regarded as an essential philosophy underpinning DSF's management style. This enables the organization to activate employees' potential, which is a precondition to achieving high performance in the market. The philosophy of performance management is to stress self-oriented, result-driven performance.

To sum up, the private-owned and foreign joint venture enterprises are the organizations in possession of strong learning cultures, which are in sharp contrast with the administrative culture in the state-owned enterprises. As Hofstede and colleagues (1990) suggest, the different dimensions of organizational cultural discriminate between entrepreneurial and administrative organizations. Such contrasts are summarized in Table 7.1.

Table 7.1 Entrepreneurial vs. administrative cultures

Entrepreneurial (private-owned enterprise & foreign joint venture)	Administrative (state-owned enterprise)
Results driven	Process orientation
Job orientation	Employee orientation
Small and fluid	Inflexible and institutional
Open system	Closed system
Loose control	Tight control
Pragmatic	Normative orientation
Market driven	Political driven
Capitalist with market ideal	Socialist ideal
Low power distance	High power distance
Low uncertainty avoidance	High uncertainty avoidance
High risk taking	Low risk taking

Skills

"Skills" refers to the distinctive capabilities of key personnel and the firm as a whole, which form the core of competitive advantage that firms are keen to sustain. In line with resource-based theory (Grant 2005) a firm's strategic capability is underpinned by the resources available to it. From a strategic perspective, an organization's resources include both those that it owns and those that can be accessed to support its strategies. These can be classified as physical resources (e.g. machines, buildings, or production capacity), human resources (e.g. knowledge, skills of people, and adaptability), financial resources (e.g. capital, cash, shareholders, and bankers) and intellectual capital (e.g. patents, brand, customer database, and partner relationship). Amongst these, human, intellectual, and reputational assets are more often difficult to imitate, and can, therefore, be the source of competitive advantage (Haberberg and Rieple 2001).

Management autonomy is now demanded in state-owned enterprises and is the most significant change compared with the former socialist command model. Ownership diversity and involvement in market competition have diluted the old ideology of the planned economy, requiring entrepreneurship and institutional innovation in management. This is a demanding task for the managers of state-owned enterprises. LTG, as a state-owned enterprise, has some special advantages that the other types of ownership enterprise do not have. Benefiting from its long history of development, state-owned enterprises have trained a large number of professional teams and experienced specialists in core businesses, which form the elite of the organization, with expertize and loyalty. Moreover, state-owned enterprises also have privileged access to other types of resources, such as capital, land, and labor. In particular, access to the capital market in China is still limited; the major banks dominating the capital market are state-owned banks that favor state-owned enterprises over other types of enterprise. Furthermore, the Communist Party and administrative authorities are powerful agencies that can provide many concessions and favors for state-owned enterprises. Such issues associated with government-controlled resources are very demanding for other types of enterprise. For instance, free access to capital and loans is a common problem for all private-owned enterprises, and policy discrimination creates higher entry barriers for private ownership, such as the restricted permission of export and import licenses and the large capital requirement for industry sector entry.

Following the rapid pace of economic growth, state-owned enterprises have attempted to become more market-focused. In order to build up its competitiveness, LTG has adopted a diversification strategy in an attempt to utilize its resources as a defence response to external changes. LTG had purchased and merged with other dyeing companies and further invested in state-of-the-art dyeing technology and equipment. This buy-out had a dual purpose, as not only did it help another state-owned enterprise avoid bankruptcy but it also gained greater control of wider industry chains. Guided by its diversification strategy, LTG has also invested in other areas, such as real estate and logistics transport, in order to increase its competency. It is clearly evident that the state has centrally ordered mergers and acquisitions across major state-owned enterprises in different sectors and industries in order to form large corporate groups. This political attempt not only aims to scale up the dominance of the state sector but also to leverage the competitiveness of state-owned enterprises by developing economies of scale of production. In theory, this is a solution to external changes, as companies under market competition pressure need to define their served market broadly rather than narrowly (Levitt 1968). However, the organizational conditions for this strategy should be made obvious, as such broadening of the target market is of little value if the company cannot easily develop the capabilities required for serving customer requirements across a wide front. Grant (2002) suggests that serving broadly-defined customer needs is a difficult task, which creates serious management problems.

As its businesses scope has widened, the top management of LTG has experienced a shortage of capable talent to run its divisional businesses, which suffer from a lack of skills in human resource management. Due to constraints in rewards and the performance assessment system, LTG is unable to retain its core competences—those highly skilled talents. Some employees have left the state-owned enterprise and become competitors in the same industry. The current imperative task for the state-owned enterprise is to build an entrepreneurial culture throughout the corporation that can facilitate the growth of "intrapreneurs." As Burns (2005: 134) defines it, "the term 'intrapreneur' is used to describe the individual charged with pushing through innovations within a larger organisation, in an entrepreneurial fashion. They are entrepreneurs in larger organisations." The emerging market economy requires a strong entrepreneurial culture and the injection of new human resources is necessary for the healthy development of state-owned enterprise in the long run. Transformation from conventional personnel management to a system of market-driven human resource management is a tough challenge for state-owned enterprises under the ideology of socialism. Their intrinsic recruitment systems are certainly in need of a change toward free-market mechanisms. However, for traditional reasons and the authority and relationship culture, the transition to an open recruitment mechanism will inevitably engender greater tensions and conflicts in the power structures of state-owned enterprises. The current status quo of the latter does not encourage either entrepreneurship or intrapreneurship. Some top managers and bureaucrats inevitably resist change—even if it is ultimately in their own interest. They will even resist it to the point of trying to sabotage it. As Kirby (2003: 148) argues, this could because:

- they think it will have a negative impact on them;
- it affects their social relationships within the organization;
- it means long-standing habits have to be changed;
- the reasons for, and benefits of, change have not been properly communicated;
- structures, systems, and rewards are not aligned with the changes and inhibit them;
- they feel coerced, not in control.

These reasons for resistance to change seem to be prevalent in the state-owned enterprise case study, and they are also the source of management tensions. To overcome this, the state-owned enterprise will need to develop a shared vision for the future and communicate with different levels of employees more effectively. Rewards and performance assessment need to be altered to fit the need of intrapreneurs. A learning culture needs to be put in place to facilitate innovation and corporate entrepreneurship (Lambing and Kuehl 2007). Although the state-owned enterprise may experience a "control crisis", this change is a necessary growth process that cannot be avoided (Haberberg and Rieple 2001).

The private-owned enterprise, as a typical entrepreneurial firm, has successfully exploited opportunities in the cashmere fashion market. Within ten years, it has developed its own featured capabilities and skills in the market. These core competences in DAL enterprise are analyzed in terms of: leadership, business reputation and networked resources, and technology in mechanization. The leadership is the most important area of competence in this entrepreneurial business, as everything depends on the proprietor's vision and capabilities. As a successful entrepreneur, the owner demonstrates his high capability, charisma, and wisdom. He is the determining factor for the fate of the organization and his strong leadership is a facet of uncontrollable competitiveness. His entrepreneurial qualities definitely account for the strength of the business. The strategic focus and intuitive vision and sensitivity allow him to find opportunities in the market. His flexible and informal structure, with quick decision-making processes, allows him to swiftly respond to market trends. He leads an adaptive and organic firm and cultivates a strong learning culture to facilitate innovation and constant breakthrough. However, as their businesses grow, and the natures of their organizations change, entrepreneurs face challenges and problems. The faster the growth, the greater the difficulty is. Entrepreneurs have to change the way they operate—recruit reliable managers, delegate to them and control and monitor their performance. The organization must become more formal and to a certain extent some formal rules and processes need to be applied and built into the structure and systems so that the implementation of complex tasks can be predicted and monitored. The entrepreneur of the private-owned business is likely to face the next growth phase of his company—"autonomy crisis" and "control crisis"—as Greiner (1972) suggests in his growth model for the entrepreneurial firm. In particular, entrepreneurs generally have a strong internal locus of control, which means that there is a danger they will be unable or unwilling to delegate responsibility to their management team. The entrepreneur needs to shift the company's dependence from a brain to a think tank. The leader then faces a crisis of autonomy that will only be addressed by putting a management team in place and delegating work to it. Growth in this phase comes because the team is in place and effective delegation is taking place. The business is no longer a one-man-brain. However, there is always the danger that delegation becomes abdication of responsibility and, as the firm continues to grow, there is a loss of proper control. Entrepreneurs will then encounter the next control crisis.

In the foreign joint venture, core competences are gained by developing people and providing opportunities for self-actualization. Elements such as key staff in marketing, brand design, technology, and the R&D center mold inimitable skills in DSF. The open and learning culture facilitates its formation of distinctive capabilities as constant training and knowledge education help to overcome "personal failure." Western culture, together with advanced knowledge in marketing and branding, widens the staff's viewpoint and raises their desire for learning. The use of foreign capital and joint ownership gives the company a competitive strength. Lack of skills and advanced management and technical knowledge are common problems for most domestic firms. As The China Development Report on the Textile Industry reveals:

> Chinese garment factories usually concentrate on labour intensive manufacturing work and low value-added products. They lack marketing and branding knowledge to build high value-added products, therefore, they are unable to become a R&D based industry but cluster in the low technology and labour intensity industries.
>
> (CTIA 2004/2005: 52)

Foreign joint ventures are effective and offer ways of strategic learning for Chinese firms, allowing them to shift their locus from low value to high value knowledge advancement. Compared with the other two case studies—the private-owned enterprise and even the state-owned enterprise that place their focus on manufacturing and outsourcing with low value-added products—the foreign joint venture has a high profile in producing value-added branded goods. It reflects how this foreign joint venture operates on the basis of very different principles (derived from its US co-ownership) compared with other types of indigenous-owned case studies.

In view of the case study findings, the comparisons between the four types of ownership, as analyzed by the McKinsey 7-S framework, may be summarized in Table 7.2.

Concluding remarks

Evidence from the three case studies suggests that different types of ownership present distinct dissimilarities in their organizational characteristics and management patterns. Environmental influencing forces, such as economic reforms, WTO accession, globalization, and competitors, are likely to impact upon organizational change and ownership evolution of each type of business venture (see Chapter one). These form the social and economic conditions for a changing system of market socialism in which these three types of business venture have emerged.

The textile industry, in which three types of enterprise operate, is a traditional industry with a long history. It is a major contributor to China's export revenue. Since 1995, China has become the largest supplier of textile goods, taking approximately one-sixth of the global share, and competing with other three major players: the US, the European Union and Japan. Following WTO accession,

Table 7.2 Organizational profiles of each of the three case studies according to the McKinsey 7-S framework

	State-owned enterprise	Privately-owned enterprise	Foreign joint venture
Strategy	Cautious, diversification	Growth in capability	Brand focus (market penetration)
Structure	Multi-divisionalized business units	Organic and entrepreneurial	Adhocratic and professional
Systems	Closed formal; institutional; personal connections	Informal and open	Combination of formal and informal; open
Staff	Professional and specialist; and political	Multiple roles; opportunities for individual development	Highly-skilled; high vision of personal development
Style	Administrative and bureaucratic	Adaptive and fluid	Open and entrepreneurial; knowledge-centered
Shared values	Political culture, socialist ideals	Market-driven; family-type management	Learning orientation; belief of knowledge power; self-actualization
Skills	Expertise competence; technology and production capacity; access to finance	Production capacity; expertise of team; capabilities of owner	Highly-skilled managers; knowledge advancement; brand; foreign capital

world markets have opened up for China as quotas on textile goods are nullified. As a result, export quantities to WTO member countries have significantly increased. On the other hand, non-tariff and non-quota barriers have been raised against China's textile goods. These have often taken the form of technical barriers, anti-dumping action, labor standards issues, specific permission requirements, and administrative delays. As global competition becomes more severe, trade friction with other countries producing textile goods is increasing. During the first half-year of 2005, there was a total of 16 cases of this nature, when WTO member countries imposed specific requirements and administrative delays against China's textile trade. In responding to this, the Chinese government nullified export tariffs on 81 types of textile goods on June 1, 2005. Nevertheless, as a result of trade friction, exports to the United States and the European Union have fallen by 60 percent and 35 percent respectively in 2006 (EU 2006). According to the agreements signed in 2005 between China and the EU, and China and the US, annual growth rates for the export of certain textile products is restricted to between 8 to 12.5 percent and 10 to 17 percent, respectively, until 2008.[1] "Trade difficulties are going to be diversified and complicated with some frictions more difficult to cope with such as anti-dumping, social responsibility and technical barriers" Zhang Li (2006). These comments were made by officials from the Bureau of Economic Operations under the National Development and Reform Commission (NDRU).

These influencing factors from international markets will inevitably have an impact on the strategy and organizational process of those enterprises involved in foreign trade. Furthermore, in 2007, the depreciation of the RMB has become a major issue for garment manufacturing companies in exports, as the trade requires a turnaround time of two to three months; a 1–2 percent fluctuation in profit margins is already factored in from the beginning (*Xinhua* February 8, 2007). The revaluation of the RMB, and the likelihood that it will continue to appreciate in time to come, has raised concerns for the continued competitiveness of China's textile industry, which has until now been riding on its one market advantage: its low price. The appreciation of the RMB will have a long-term effect on those companies with a focus of international trade business; the state-owned enterprise (LTG) being an example. It will see its lucrative profit margin decline if the RMB appreciation continues by 5 percent. The average gross profit of the textile sector is approximately 5 to 10 percent. Since the majority of Chinese products are low-end and easily replaced, it would be difficult to expect foreign customers to absorb any extra costs. Evidence suggests that "diversified investment" and "specific high-technology development" have been the emerging shift-strategies for Chinese textile enterprises responding to these external threats. "Home brand building," however, as a long-run strategy with a more advantageous level of competitiveness, is not widely adopted by domestic firms, despite the Chinese government's appeals to domestic firms to do so. The recognition of brands is scanty among the majority of domestic firms and this is mainly a result of poverty in knowledge and management theory. The literature on Chinese management still remains meagre, which raises the demand for rich theory development to guide and direct practices. Moreover, the financing of the private sector and knowledge dissemination system is not well developed and industry infrastructure and government advocacy to promote "home brands" still has a long way to go. It will be a challenge for the Chinese government to change its administrative role from that of "support" to effective policies that will re-adjust the infrastructure of China's industries and its regulatory environment.

Note

1 On June 11, 2005, China and the EU reached an agreement on the annual growth of exports to the European market for the ten lines of Chinese textile products, from June 11, 2005, to the end of 2007. With an agreed base quantity, annual growth limits are set between 8 and 12.5 percent during this period.
In November 8, 2005, the US and China signed a three-year agreement. A total of 21 types of clothing and textiles were placed under import restrictions, and the agreement provides for progressive annual increases in imports of major textile and apparel products from China by 10 to 15 percent in 2006, 12.5 to 16 percent in 2007, and 15 to 17 percent in 2008.

8 Emerging trends in Chinese market socialism

Over the last two decades, China has been transformed from a socialist planned economy to a market-oriented economy. Confronted with ever-intensifying international competition, enterprises in China (whether state-owned or not) have to make constant adjustments in order to keep abreast with these changing conditions. The Chinese government has deepened economic reforms in the state sector and made further melioration of the regulatory conditions for foreign investment in the 2000s. For instance, barriers in the financial service and banking sectors are being lifted for foreign capital entry and an amendment in the Foreign Enterprise Law allows wholly-owned foreign enterprises to set up in China. The new Foreign Trade Laws that were implemented on July 1, 2004, allow for the full entry of collective-owned enterprises and private-owned enterprises to engage in foreign trade. During 2001 to 2005 domestic firms with licenses for foreign trading have dramatically increased from 45,000 to over 200,000 (CITPC 2005: 269). Following the sixteenth National Congress of the Communist Party, convened in November 2002, some laws and regulations that are consistent with international practice and beneficial to the development of the national economy were put forward to ensure compliance with international arrangements. Policies and regulations that discriminate against the development of the private sector will gradually be abolished and replaced by amended versions, which have been improved in order to support and encourage the development of private enterprises.

After thirty years of reforms, many world-renowned transnational companies (e.g. Motorola, Siemens, Alcatel, Nokia, Philips, Apple, and General Motors) have established joint ventures and wholly-owned enterprises in China. They have achieved success in the Chinese market, as market-oriented reforms are a powerful statutory support to their efforts in developing world markets. These companies are witness to the development of Chinese market socialism, significantly influencing China's economic development and facilitating "learning from best practice" for domestic firms. The Chinese government will continue to facilitate continuous promotion and attraction for foreign direct investment and this will lead to increasingly fierce competition between Chinese enterprises and large foreign-owned enterprises in the domestic marketplace. It is expected that the role of the non-state-owned private sector in China's economic development will

130 *Emerging trends in Chinese market socialism*

be continuously reinforced and will make further contribution to the growth of the national economy. It is likely that market socialism is changing to market capitalism; the "socialist ideal" will be diluted and eventually replaced by "market ideals," although there may still be a long way to go.

Future trends of the four types of business venture

The current status of the Chinese economy is clearly divided into two major dominant sectors—the state-owned and the private sectors. The state-owned sector includes state-owned and state-controlled enterprises, while the non-state-owned sector comprises private-owned and foreign-invested enterprises. Comparing the emerging forms of private business venture, the foreign joint venture and the private-owned enterprise appear to have the greatest growth potential. Both types have strong entrepreneurial learning cultures and a high market orientation. Foreign joint ventures benefit from access to advanced knowledge, capital, and technology to facilitate their growth and competitiveness. These influences also shape the "behavior model" of managers in these organisations, which increasingly mould the formulation of organizational processes in terms of their strategies, systems, structures, cultures, human resources, and product portfolios. As a consequence, innovation and entrepreneurship are becoming the foundation of their competitive advantage. The two types of enterprises all reflect innovation in the following areas:

- constant introduction of new or improved goods or service(s);
- constant introduction of new processes in service delivery systems – new production, marketing, sales, distribution, and supply chain management systems;
- opening up new markets in either overseas or domestic segments;
- identification of new sources of supply of raw materials;
- continuing adoption of new technologies.

While foreign joint ventures are built on knowledge-based processes, which allows them to develop higher value-added products, private-owned enterprises are comparatively disadvantaged in this respect. However, they can overcome this flaw by attracting highly-skilled talents to develop more knowledge-centered product profiles. This trend increases the demand for a supply of graduates and skilled capable managers. The problem is, that at this present juncture in its development, there is a scarcity of such talent in the Chinese labor market (Tung 2007).

The trend of marketization of state-owned enterprises is towards corporatization and diversification. A new management system for state property was established in 2003, together with the issuance of relevant laws. In the days to come, except in some special fields (of national security and vital economic significance), large- and medium-sized state-owned enterprises will be largely transformed into non-state-owned but state-controlled enterprises. State-owned enterprises are now more market-orientated in respect of price setting. However, there are still some significant non-market elements in corporate governance and internal management. For instance, "closed" recruitment mechanisms, leading not only to senior management being subject to government appointment or removal, but also staff who are often selected by "who-they-know" internally through a political hierarchy. Moreover, inconsistent performance assessment systems, with government stipulated reward standards, demonstrate the non-separation of government from enterprise management. As state-owned enterprises face severe competition from both domestic entrepreneurial firms and foreign firms, their inflexibility and constraints from the administrative culture will ultimately hinder their growth and competitiveness. They will decline if future reforms in innovation and entrepreneurship cannot provide significant remedies. Undeniably, further reforms in corporate entrepreneurship will be a huge challenge in order to change the behavior model of the "socialist ideals" of state-owned enterprises. Collective-owned business ventures (cooperatives) are likely to fail in the future. The contradiction between the interests of different owners in this type of business venture is irreconcilable. The collective-owned enterprise is a special historical legacy that will gradually decline under market socialism, to be replaced by private ownership. As competitive conditions continue to change the international and domestic markets the impact will be addressed by this type of enterprise, which relies on overseas orders and on producing low-cost, value-added goods at a low-cost advantage. Evidence provided by the case studies shows that labor unions play a dependent and weak role in the power structure in the state-owned sector, while their function in the non-state-owned sector is almost non-existent. The growth of the Chinese market economy has given rapid rise to a private sector that has yet to develop a code of business ethics and corporate social responsibility (McEwan 2001; Ying 2002; Snell and Tseng 2002). This lies ahead as a challenge to the further development of a rule-based market economy.

China's "going global" strategy

It is evident that the state has made deliberate attempts at sponsoring and creating powerful Chinese "multiple national corporations" (MNCs) as global market players, (particularly in the state sector) in order to compete in the international marketplace; take Huawei Telecom in the UK, Hairer Electronics in Europe, Lenovo in the US, and China State Grid in Australia for example. In fact, the Chinese government is pushing for more outward foreign direct investment as part of its "going global" policy, which was launched in 2000. According to the McKinsey Global Institute analysis, in 2010, China's total capital cross-border outflows totalled US$405 billion, the highest among emerging markets, while its inflows remained at US$84 billion (Roxburgh *et al.* 2011: 30). Firms that meet government investment aims in support of China's economic development are offered financial help with using the country's foreign exchange reserves. This is made possible because the country controls capital movements and resources. It is a Chinese global strategy that creates conglomerate companies through mergers and acquisitions of global brands and key technologies. For example, in 2005, the Chinese Lenovo Group purchased the IBM personal computer business at the cost of

US$1.25 billion. This acquisition made Lenovo the third largest computer maker in the world by volume. In 2013, the Chinese company, Shuanghui International, announced that it paid a cash sum of US$7.1 billion for the Virginia-based Smithfield Foods Company, which included the latter's debt.[1] This strategy facilitates the transformation and quick catch-up of Chinese firms in improving their competitiveness by investing in product quality, technology, and world-class brands. In the years to come, there will be more overseas investment deals made by Chinese firms as a substantial part of China's future growth strategy.

The role of the Communist Party in China

Compared with the governments of Western countries, the Chinese Communist Party plays a different role in developing the market economy. China's market socialism is the result of government policy shifts from the traditional socialist planned regime. It is also a process leading the Communist Party to gradually change its functions; to decentralize its administrative control; to reduce the size of government; to reform the economic administrative system; and to create a dynamic market economy. China has a deep national political interest in becoming a respected global power to reduce poverty and to sustain economic growth. This goes to the heart of its reform direction and foreign policy and perhaps pushes China's participation in the reshuffle of the global order. In the past three decades, China has dedicated its efforts towards developing a market economy and focusing on economic and GDP growth. The political intention is to continue this modernization, while maintaining the social stability of society domestically, and promoting strategic international stability in East Asia.

The new leader of Chinese Communist Party in 2013, Xi Jinping, has announced that the reform direction is one of moving forward on the path of socialism with a "China Model" rather than changing to the universal values of the West and the Western political system (Chai and Song 2013). This seems to imply that political and democracy reform is unlikely to happen in the short run. The Chinese Communist Party firmly believes that a richer and wealthier country will strengthen and stabilize its rule. Continuous economic growth and the building of a highly efficient government will be the top priority on the political agenda of Chinese market socialism development in the coming decades.

The state-owned sector will continue to have a major share of the economy and this reflects the government's political will. Tensions between "state" and "market" socialism become prominent when market reforms go so deep, they touch the political and cultural underpinnings of the political regime. One major challenge that lies ahead on the long road of reforms for the Chinese Communist Party is to balance these competing values with the need for institutional capabilities to provide resolutions to conflicts and tensions (Zheng and Scase 2013). Market socialism comprises both opportunities and problems, which generate complexity and diversity in its unique market structures. Understanding these dynamics of market socialism is important for understanding business practices, as we have illustrated and discussed in this book.

The crisis of legitimacy

By permitting the growth of the private economy, the Chinese Communist Party has inevitably created market forces that challenge the centralized political control system. The coexistence of "dictatorial" socialism and "free" capitalism is a challenge as well as a puzzle to be resolved by China, with its single party rule. However, the Party has justified the "China Model" as a "market economy with Chinese characteristics," which adopts a dual-track economic system and a gradualist experimental approach for its economic reforms. But the emergence of market forces in the private sector is creating tensions and incompatibilities within the socialist institutional fabric (see Zheng and Scase 2013). Despite the rapid growth of the private economy, an authoritarian political regime remains intact in China. The private economy challenges the legitimacy of the dominant role of the Chinese Communist Party, since a free market increasingly demands political democracy and individual freedoms in political and social institutions. Public anger at corrupt Party officials and their abuse of power and growing pressure from Western countries have raised the bar on the urgency of political reform of the single party system and its concentrated decision-making administration structure (Chai and Song 2013). This becomes a major challenge for "when" and "how" political reforms will be initiated during the next decade.

The literature on former socialist systems concludes that any effort to reform their economies without drastic political change is doomed to fail because authoritarian political control and non-market coordination mechanisms are intertwined with each other (Kornai 1992; Li and Wang 2006). However, it seems that the Communist Party does not believe this is the only way to develop a market economy. China adopts a different approach to responding to political change in relation to the market economy. Instead of permitting a multiple-party political and legal system like the West, it develops and modernizes a "political elite" system, which incorporates a variety of representatives of business entrepreneurs and social forces into the decision-making process—namely to grant them legitimate membership of the Party and engage their participation. This gives both private entrepreneurs and owners access to political capital and allows them to play a key role in policy-making. For instance, the Communist Party has gradually developed policies and regulations for the private sector. In the 2000s state policies toward private businesses were further liberalized. On July 1, 2001, the President (Jiang Zeming) stipulated that the Communist Party should be representative of all social productive forces, including entrepreneurs (Xinhua 2001). This marked a milestone in the Party's political policies toward private companies. In June 2002, the National People's Congress passed legislation stipulating that the state should provide positive services for small- and medium-sized enterprises in financial and fiscal assistance, start-up capital, taxation, technological innovation, the development of markets, and employee welfare services. In March 2003, the government approved constitutional amendments, including the recognition of private entrepreneurs as "socialist builders" (Chen *et al.* 2008). Empirical evidence from our case studies also reveals that entrepreneurs can submit their initiatives for new policy-making and oppose unfair decisions through the People Congress. They can represent entrepreneurs to lobby local and central governments for policies favouring their interests. Economic conflicts are reflected in two forms: communism versus the free market and central planning versus laissez-faire (Manin 1997; Hardin 2013). In China, state-owned corporations want regulation, subsidiaries, and tariff policies that can benefit them against a fully-liberated market economy. Private entrepreneurs want licensing, financial support, and protection against imports. The "China Model" works because of its political stability and the level of efficiency of political control (Li and Wang 2006). These two conditions have ensured the Party's implementation of reforms through central planning. Owing to direct state control over the actions of state sectors that dominate large segments of the economy, especially in banking and major industrial sectors, the Chinese Communist Party can quickly order them to ramp up investments and lending to leverage economic growth. To balance the opposing forces in an integrated economy, the Party has incorporated different groups into its political elite governance structure to justify the coexistence of socialism and a market economy. In this way, it can strengthen its own legitimacy and dominance.

The major task ahead for the Party is to tackle corruption and to develop a "cleaner" and more "efficient" government in a culture where Guanxi is still very significant. Political reform is not on the Party's agenda, despite the public desire for such reform. Thus, any drastic political change is unlikely to happen in China, owing to the logic of the political economy, which is deeply rooted in its ideological beliefs and historical heritage. The ruling Party can afford to moderately loosen its political control in order to integrate the economic dual-track systems and to create market forces, with the aim of reaping subsequent economic benefits. The founder of economic reform, Deng Xiaoping, emphasized that one fundamental principle of reforms was that the Party must maintain its absolute leadership role in China (Li and Wang 2006). Following this principle, the Party has been extremely sensitive to any organized protest, whether about economic or political issues. The government has been carefully monitoring and controlling any risk of political instability. It strongly pursues the guiding principle for reform: the so-called creation of a "harmony-oriented" society (Jing and Zhu 2012).

Despite the Party's capability to constrain outright conflicts, there is growing public distrust of the government. The power exchange phenomena and rent-seeking corruptions (see Chapter 3 for the discussion of "Guanxi" and corruption), extending to food safety and pollution issues, show a weak and incompatible facet of the legal and political infrastructure of China's integrated economy. Hardin's (2013) study argues that public distrust in government does not matter very much, as a declining trust in government is an inevitable result (in the age of globalization) of the global economic system becoming so advanced that it has become independent from traditional state governmental control and regulation. The Chinese Communist Party's proven ability to plan and manage the market economy with a dual-track system has won public support and seems to further enhance its belief that economic growth will satisfy its people, thereby strengthening its legitimacy and international influence, regardless of ideological differences with the West.

China's focus on economic growth has resulted in significant gains, such as reducing poverty dramatically and becoming an emerging giant in the world economy. Will China's GDP decline in the next ten years? Can China continue to keep its growth by replying on exports and FDI? In fact, China still has enormous potential for economic growth. Its high foreign reserves, large savings bank deposits and under-developed credit domestic market (see Roxburgh *et al.* 2011 for detail) all indicate that it does not have to depend on other countries and exports for further growth. Unlike Western countries, such as Greece, the US, and the UK for example—whose economies are based on borrowing and fiscal-driven policies (Burger 2012)—China has a domestic consumer market of around 1.3 billion people, whose purchasing power is currently underestimated. According to a research report from the McKinsey Global Institute in mid-2011, the US total debt-to-GDP ratio was approximately 279 percent and the UK reached 507 percent, the second highest among the top ten countries on the list (Roxburgh *et al.* 2012: 13). By contrast, China ran a much lower debt-to-GDP ratio of 184 percent in 2011 (Roxburgh *et al.* 2012: 14). The Chinese economy is driven by exports, FDI, and production outputs. Both government fiscal policy and social culture encourage saving instead of borrowing. Thus Chinese consumers are most likely to spend on their debit/cash cards instead of their "credit cards." This means that there is huge domestic market consumption potential to boost further economy growth. With the continuous rise of China's economic power, perhaps one day we will start to pursue the "China Dream" instead of the "US Dream." But, can money buy everything we want? This is the question for the future.

From "copycat" to "innovator"

China has undoubtedly accomplished much over the past few decades. It is transforming its image, from that of "copycat" to that of world leading "innovator," by heavily investing in technology and innovation. According to OECD (2012), China's spending on R&D has increased steadily, from about 0.69 percent of GDP in 1995 to about 1.6 percent in 2011. By comparison, the US has remained steady at 2.7 percent and Japan at 3.2 percent. The technology profile of China's patent portfolio is similar to that of other major patenting countries, such as Japan, the US, Europe, and Korea. However, in terms of chemical engineering, China is number two, while the US remains at number one in world rankings. It is estimated that China's double-digit growth in R&D spending is expected to match and surpass that of the US by about 2023, as R&D growth over the past 15 years has consistently exceeded 10 percent (*R&D Magazine* 2011: 2). In June 2013, China's supercomputer—Tianhe-2 (developed by the National University of Defence Technology)—became the world's most powerful system, replacing the US at the top spot in this area of expertise. This is part of the Chinese government's effort to make the country's hi-tech industries more competitive and less dependent on overseas rivals. It is evident that China is making significant gains in intellectual capital and technology innovation. Nevertheless, despite rapid advances in technology, without reform in the education system and a culture tolerant of failure, it will be difficult to keep the momentum of innovation progress in the long run. China's censorship is arguably the inhibitor of individual creativity and free competition. It reinforces a compliance culture and suppresses the freedom of diversified views. There will be growing pressure and a desire for improvements in the rule of law and greater transparency in the near future. Our case study evidence also reveals that the lack of highly-skilled talent is becoming a major barrier to business growth in both private-owned and foreign joint ventures (see Chapters 5 and 6). Without this pool of human talent, China's economic growth will slow down and its ambitious policy of outward foreign direct investment will suffer. China's ability to meet this human resource challenge remains to be seen, as further reforms would touch the fundamental value of the communist political system.

Note

1 Examples of mergers and acquisitions information can be accessed at Lenovo and Shuanghui International's company websites under "company history" and "news" categories.

Appendix

The research investigation and the selection of case studies

Introduction

In this appendix, the methodology used for the empirical research is outlined. We discuss four aspects of research design: (1) the theoretical ground and what questions to study; (2) what research strategy to employ; (3) what data are relevant and how to collect them; and (4) how to analyze the results. Following the qualitative research philosophy of Philliber and colleagues (1980), we aim to seek explanations and to answer the fundamental question of this research: "What are the management characteristics of emerging forms of business venture under market socialism in China?"

A contingency theoretical perspective

The underpinning theory of this research is the "Contingency Approach," as applied to explaining organizational forms emerging under market socialism in China. This approach provides theoretical principles for understanding how a changing business environment and different ownership forms can impact on management practices. In contingency theory, there is no one best design of organization. The most appropriate patterns of management are therefore dependent upon the contingencies of the situation and the environment in which the organization operates. It suggests that organization theory should provide insights into the situational and contextual factors that influence management decisions. Our research design follows this approach. The contingency approach focuses attention on the relationships between the effects of uncertainty in a changing external environment and the impact upon organizational change and management practices. It is concerned with understanding the interdependent relations between the internal characteristics of an organization and its external environment.

The proponents of this perspective differ in the ways in which they have conceptualized and/or measured internal organizational characteristics and the work of the organization. For example, Woodward (1970) focused on a variety of types of technology as the key variable. Lawrence and Lorsch (1967) conceptualized the organization's work as dealing with its external environment and viewed the important internal organizational parameters as differentiation, integration, and conflict resolution. Thompson (1967) has been concerned with both technology and environment, as well as with a different set of organizational variables (e.g. structure, discretion, and control). Lorsch and Morse (1974) suggested how the personal characteristics of organization members are related to organizational factors and how these shape organizational effectiveness. At the centre of contingency theory, there is a focus on the interdependency between the internal characteristics of an organization and its external environment (Lawrence and Lorsch 1967; Snow et al. 1992; Blosch and Preece 2000; Wiklund et al. 2009; Daniels and Radebaugh 2001; Watson 2002;). This highlights the relationships between strategy, structure, methods of operations, and the nature of environmental influences, and provides a further possible means of differentiation between alternative forms of organization and management (Waterman et al. 1980; Peters and Waterman 1980; Woodward 1970). The proponents of this perspective differ in the ways in which they have conceptually measured internal organizational factors and the activities of the organization (Gartner and Shane 1995). The cultural and institutional contexts shape the perception and interpretation of organizational change and influence choice and the strategy governing its management (Triandis 1994; Holt 1997; Kshetri 2007; Faucheux et al. 1982).

Change may be seen as linear, rational, and the result of planned actions, or as the circular, continuous, and spontaneous interplay between interdependent forces. Those who engage in cross-cultural, change-related practices often ignore the surrounding cultural context. Furthermore, Budhwar and Debrah (2001) propose that an analytical distinction should be made between different levels of context, including the national cultural context, the industrial context, and the organizational strategy-level context. These "context-specific" and "culture-bound" factors influence the nature of HR practices (Dessler 1976).

Contingency theory seems to provide a suitable approach for understanding the evolution of management in contemporary China, as it addresses interrelations of organizational change within the context of a changing business environment. Managerial practices cannot be independent of the environment within which organizations operate. This approach better explains the complexity and dynamics within such rapidly changing environments—"socialist" to "market socialist"; "closed" to "open" political paradigm; and "planned" to "free" economy. The sole focus on an organization's internal environment is not valid in view of the fundamental political and economic changes that are occurring in China. It is important to address the evolution of ownership in market socialism, as it has evolved from the past planned economy. Market socialism is the context for the growth of emerging business ventures, while economic reforms are the activator of such emergence. Unlike Western enterprises, which were born in a free capitalist market, Chinese enterprises grew out of socialist market transformations. Their management practices are significantly affected by this ownership paradigm and political economy. This research explores these issues on the basis of detailed case studies of three different types of business ownership.

The utility of case studies

Case studies were conducted to collect data in order to explain the nature of management and organizational behavior in emerging business ventures, as these are related to different forms of ownership properties under market socialism. Through case investigation, we aimed to demonstrate some connections between theory and practice. The development of management theory is based on summarizing and analyzing management practices (Eisenhardt and Graebaner 2007; Stake 1995). As McGregor (1987: 6) puts it:

> Every managerial act rests on assumptions, generalizations, and hypotheses – that is to say, on theory. Our assumptions are frequently implicit, sometimes quite unconscious, often conflicting; nevertheless, they determine our predictions that we do a, b will occur. Theory and practice are inseparable.

In each of the four case studies, open-ended interviews were conducted with key informants in each organization's management team. Noaks and Wincup (2004: 80) suggest that, "in order to achieve 'rich data', the key note is 'active listening' in which the interviewer allows the interviewee the freedom to talk and ascribe meanings while bearing in mind the broader aims of the project." These aims have been described as "understanding the language and culture of the respondents" (Fontana and Frey 2004: 654). In order to achieve such understanding, the open-ended interviewer must resolve several main issues:

- Deciding how to present yourself, e.g. as a student, as a researcher, etc.
- Gaining and maintaining trust, especially where one has to ask sensitive questions.
- Establishing rapport with respondents, e.g. attempting to see the world from their viewpoint without going native.

As Byrne (2004: 182) suggests:

> Qualitative interviewing is particularly useful as a research method for accessing individuals' attitudes and values – things that cannot necessarily be observed or accommodated in a formal questionnaires. Open-ended and flexible questions are likely to get a more considered response than closed questions and therefore provide better access to interviewees' views, interpretation of events, understandings, experiences and opinions. Qualitative interviewing when done well is able to achieve a level of depth and complexity that is not available to other methods of data collection.

The key purpose of our case studies is to explore evidence in relation to the following questions: (1) What are the distinctive managerial and behavioural characteristics of emerging forms of enterprise under market socialism? (2) How do rapid environmental and institutional changes in economic reforms impact

140 *Appendix: the research investigation*

upon them, particularly in reshaping their management models and fostering their entrepreneurial growth? (3) What are some of the general patterns in the development of business ventures under the dynamic conditions of the Chinese economy?

Three cases were selected, so that each represents a particular type of ownership of business venture. All the selected case companies operate within the textile industry. They are selected for comparison in order to explore the casual links between ownership and organizational development and performance. The literature review suggests that transitional re-deployments in economic configuration have changed the nature of business relations and deepened institutional restructuring in the state sector. Equally, the rapid growth of the private sector has led to continuous ownership diversification and increased market competition. The selected case studies cut across both state and private sectors in order to highlight the casual links between organizational change and emergence of management models within the context of the unique features of Chinese market socialism.

Operational measures used in the research

General logic in setting operational measures

Emerging forms of business ventures under market socialism in China are examined according to the following scheme (Figure 8.1):

Government economic policies and legal reforms are the "push" factors causing a changing business environment to be characterized by increasing market competition, globalization, technology advancement, and institutional

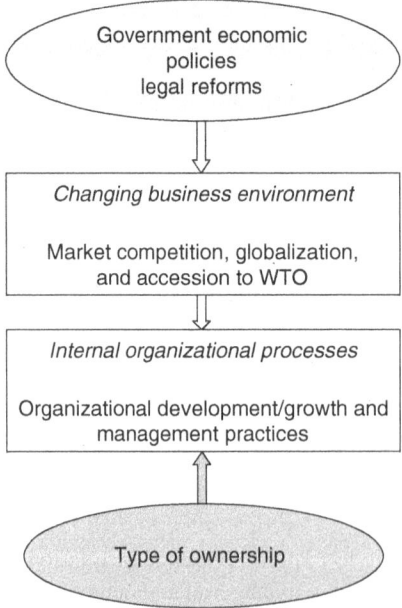

Figure 8.1 The analytical framework.

restructuring. China's WTO accession further opened up the domestic market to world markets and gradually changed the regulatory environment in which businesses operate to more international standards. These "push" factors change and shape enterprise management and development. Data are collected from the case study enterprises to explore these issues. The main features of management practices under different types of ownership are conveyed by reference to the emergence of different business ventures as derived from economic reforms and institutional transformations. The links between situational factors and organizational characteristics are corroborated by empirical data (Yin 1994).

Using the McKinsey 7-S framework

For the purposes of collecting data and undertaking the case studies, the McKinsey 7-S framework was adopted. This was used for "organizing" and "pinpointing" the main characteristics of each of the case study organizations. This framework was originally designed by Peters and Waterman for their study of 62 American companies with so-called "excellence traits." From their research, Peters and Waterman (1980: 9) report that:

> Any intelligent approach to organising had to encompass, and treat as interdependent, at least seven variables: structure, strategy, people, management style, systems and procedures, guiding concepts and shared value (e.g. culture), and the present and hoped-for corporate strengths or skills. We defined this idea more precisely and elaborated what came to be known as the McKinsey 7-S framework. With a bit of stretching, cutting and fitting, we made all seven variables start with the letter S and invented a logo to go with it.

This 7-S-model can be used as an analytical tool and as an organizing framework for collecting data and for obtaining insights into organizations.

Richard Pascale and Anthony Athos' book, *The Art of Japanese Management*, was an exemplary case study for further developing the 7-S-model in examining management practices. It successfully explored Japanese management practices in a case study of Matsushita by comparison with a US company. As Pascale and Athos (1986: 80) claim,

> the 7-S framework has been approved as an effective way of perceiving and cutting through the complexity of the organisation. These 7 variables selected are of crucial importance. More would be hard to grasp systematically; fewer would leave something central out.

Three elements in the 7-S model: structure, strategy, and system are seen as "hard S's", and the other four are regarded as "soft S's." Figure 8.2 visualizes the seven elements for describing and understanding an organization as a whole. The 7-S framework is not merely an analytical tool; it also serves as a conceptual underpinning to indicate what range of information needs to be collected. Each

142 *Appendix: the research investigation*

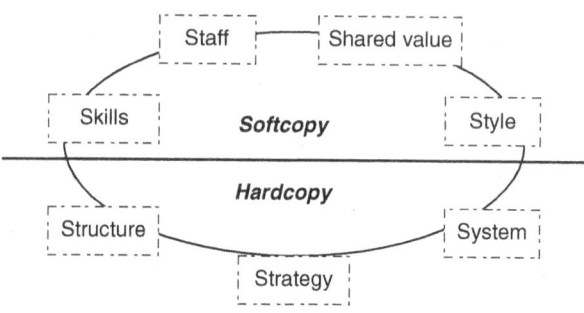

Figure 8.2 The McKinsey 7-S framework.

S-factor can be operationally stipulated and used for measuring key organizational variables. However, these factors interact and explain each other; they cannot exist alone. For example, structure shapes strategy and vice versa; the characterization of structure can be revealed by the ways staff work; the style of managers' behaviour reflects the culture and beliefs of the organization. The interconnectedness of these seven variables is the key feature of this framework. By examining variables within the 7-S framework, "a profile of organizational characteristics" can be established. Accordingly, it is a framework that allows us to compare and contrast organizational features by performance and types of ownership. At this point, it is useful to describe in more detail each of the components of the McKinsey 7-S framework.

Structure is the characteristics of the organization chart. As Mintzeberg (1983: 2) states: "the structure of an organization can be simply defined as the sum total of the ways in which its labor is divided into distinct tasks and then its coordination is achieved among these tasks." Peters and Waterman (1980: 273) also suggest that "the structure is how the organization divides up tasks, is one of emphasis and coordination – how to make the whole thing work." The structure can be classified in several ways such as, for example, organic-open or closed-mechanic bureaucracy, flat or tall hierarchical, functional or divisional, and centralized or decentralized. In contingency theory, how the structure is designed in an organization depends on both internal variables and external situational factors. The structure of an organization usually incorporates a division of work; hierarchy of authority; formal lines of command and authority; and the degree to which authority is centralized or decentralized.

Systems are about those operating procedures and mechanisms designed within the skeleton of the structure that determine how work is done and tasks are undertaken. Peters and Waterman (1980: 273) define this concept as: "by systems, we mean all the procedures, formal and informal, that make the organization go, day by day and year by year." Systems also refer to how decisions are made and include such factors as financial systems, planning procedures, hiring practices, marketing systems etc. These systems are seen as "management's most powerful tool for expressing how it wants an organization to work and what they want to accomplish" (ibid.). This provides the key to understanding how an organization really does (or doesn't) get things done. Therefore, systems include communication channels/procedures and routine processes (paperwork, information flow, meetings, in a formal or informal manner); control systems (e.g. financial control); planning systems (how managers plan to achieve for objectives); reward and sanction systems (principle criteria for management efficiency and performance in each division as well as evaluation for individual); and marketing systems (product, sales, marketing communications).

Strategy is about planning in relation to the allocation of a firm's scarce resources, over time, to reach identified goals. According to Peters and Waterman (1980: 273):

> By strategy, we mean those actions that a company plans in response to or anticipation of changes in its external environment – its customers, its competitors. Strategy is the way a company aims to improve its position vis-à-vis competition – perhaps through low-cost production or delivery, perhaps by providing better value to the customer, perhaps by achieving sales and service dominance.

This element can be viewed as consisting of two aspects: the corporate and the tactical. Corporate strategy refers to the long-term planning in relation to organizational development and making decisions in relation to the external environment in order to achieve goals. "Tactical" strategy is about short-term planning in guiding the operations of those major functions of an organization, such as production, marketing, and finance.

Johnson and Scholes (2002) suggest that the absence of an explicit strategy may result in members of an organization working at cross-purposes. The intentions of top management may not be communicated clearly to those at lower levels in the hierarchy who are expected to implement them. Change comes about from either subjective or intuitive assessment, which becomes increasingly unreliable as the rate of change increases. Developing a corporate strategy demands explicit creative effort. If strategic planning is to be successful, it requires effective communication flows within the total organization.

Staff refers to the "demographic" description of an organization, that is, its human resource capabilities. Peters and Waterman (1980: 274) define "staff" in two ways: "at the hard end of the spectrum, we talk of appraisal systems, pay scales, formal training programs, and the like. At the soft end, we talk about moral, attitude, motivation and behaviour." Lynch emphasizes the importance of people as a vital resource for sustaining competitive advantage. And for some industries, people are not just important but the key factor for successful performance. HR policies and practices have an important role to play in facilitating the effective implementation of management processes, such as "total quality management." Research by West and Patterson (1998), in an intensive examination of more than 100 medium-sized manufacturing firms in the UK over seven years, confirmed the strong link between effective people management and business performance. Their results draw attention to appropriate HR practices including: (1) effective recruitment and selection; (2) strategic training and appraisals; (3) jobs designed to promote autonomy, flexibility and problem-solving; and (4) favorable reward systems, harmonization and involvement.

Style involves the characterization of how key managers behave in achieving the organization's goals as well as managing their employees. However, Peters and Waterman (1980: 275) stress that:

> We think it is important to distinguish between the basic personality of a top-management team and the way that team comes across to the organization. Not words, but patterns of actions are decisive. The power of style, then, is essentially manageable. One element of a manager's style is how he or she chooses to spend time. Anther aspect of style is symbolic behaviour.

According to Mullins (2005), the essential part of management is coordinating the activities of others and guiding their efforts towards goals and objectives of the organization. Leadership is a central feature of any organization and can vary from very democratic to directive approaches.

Shared values refers to the significant meanings or guiding concepts that an organization imbues in its members, such as belief in the value and ways of doing business, and the social as well as economic purpose of the business. Peters and Waterman (1980: 275) define this as follows:

> By super-ordinate goals (shared values), we mean guiding concepts – as set of values and aspirations, often unwritten, that goes beyond the conventional formal statement of corporate objective. They are the fundamental ideas around which a business is built. They are its main values. They are the broad notions of future direction that the top management team wants to infuse throughout the organization. They are the way in which the team wants to express itself, to leave its own mark.

Handy (1993) has contributed to the discussion of shared values and organizational culture by outlining four culture types: power culture, role culture, task culture, and person culture. *Power culture* depends on a central power source with rays of influence radiating from the central figure throughout the organization. It is frequently found in small entrepreneurial organizations and relies on trust, empathy, and personal communications for its effectiveness. Control is exercised from the centre by the selection of key individuals. There are few rules and procedures, and little bureaucracy. *Role culture* is often stereotyped as a bureaucracy and works by logic and rationality. It rests on the strength of strong organizational "pillars"— the functions of specialists in, for example, finance, purchasing, and production. The work of, and interaction between, the pillars is controlled by procedures and rules, and coordinated by the pediment of a small band of senior managers. Role or job description is often more important than the individual and positional power is the main source of power. *Task culture* is job-oriented or project-oriented. An example is the matrix organization. Task culture seeks to bring together the right resources and people, and utilizes the unifying power of the group. Influence is widely spread and based more on expert power than on position or personal power. *Person culture* is where the individual is the central focus and any structure exists to serve the individuals within it. When a group of people decide that it is in their own interests to band together to do their own thing and share office space, equipment, or clerical assistance, then the resulting organization would have a person culture. Management hierarchies and control mechanisms are possible only by mutual consent. Individuals have almost complete autonomy and any influence over them is likely to be on the basis of personal power.

Hofstede (1980) has extended the work on organizational cultures by discussing the impact of national cultures. Arguing that culture is, in a memorable phrase, "collective programing" or "software of the mind," Hofstede initially identified four dimensions of culture: *power distance, uncertainty avoidance, individualism and masculinity*. A fifth dimension of culture, long-term/short-term orientation, was originally labeled as "Confucian work dynamism." This dimension was developed from the work of Bond in an attempt to assess the impact of Chinese cultural values on the workplace (Hofstede and Bond 2005). Hofstede's four dimensions can be used to explore organizational values and culture from a cross- national comparative analysis:

- *Power distance* is essentially used to categorize levels of inequality in organizations, which, Hofstede claims, will depend upon management style, willingness of subordinates to disagree with supervisors, and the educational level and status accruing to particular roles. China is thought to display a high level of power distance. In contrast, the US is characterized as a low-power distance society.
- *Uncertainty avoidance* refers to the extent to which members of a society feel threatened by unusual situations and risk. China is estimated as displaying a medium level of uncertainty avoidance, and the USA is said to have a low-to-medium level.
- *Individualism* refers to the relatively individualistic or collectivist values and ethics evident in a particular society. Thus, according to Hofstede, the US displays high level of individualism in contrast with Hong Kong and China, which are collectivist societies.
- *Masculinity* refers to a continuum between "masculine" characteristics, such as assertiveness and competitiveness, and "feminine" traits, such as caring, a stress upon quality of life and concern with the environment. High masculinity societies included the US and Hong Kong, whereas China is estimated as "medium" in this dimension.

Every organization will have its own unique culture and core values and most large businesses are likely to be a mix of cultures in various areas of their organization. However, the type of culture built within an organization should facilitate management effectiveness and unify the organization as a whole. Nowadays, attention is given to the importance of culture construction in organizational development and performance. It is recognized that a "strong" culture can provide the norms and guidance for solving conflicts and releasing tensions. An organization will benefit from a shared value belief in its long-term strategic development and growth.

Skills refers to the distinctive capabilities of key personnel and the firm as a whole. As defined by Peters and Waterman (1980: 276), "these dominating attributes or capabilities are what we mean by skills." This also refers to the core competences the firm possesses. In a rapidly changing environment, particularly in a market with institutional transition, Chinese organizations are facing challenges in building management capacity. Management skills are practically lacking and inhibit organizational development. Technological skills are also vital for innovation and competitive advantage.

These are the factors that make up the McKinsey 7-S framework. Each interacts with the other to create an organizational profile. As Peters and Waterman state, the 7-S framework is an analytical tool for exploring the dynamics of organizational life. They stress that it is for the research investigator to construct organizational dimensions for each of the "S's" that are relevant for the enquiry being undertaken. For the purposes of this research, the dimensions created for each "S," as the basis for data collection were as follows:

Strategy

(1) business long-term strategies and goals for the next five to ten years
(2) implementation planning processes
(3) short-term strategies at the operational level
(4) strategic development and changes in relation to influencing factors of the external business environment
(5) strategy decision-making participants—top teams and key influencers.

Structure

(1) organizational charts and their specification of roles, responsibilities, and authorities
(2) key decision-making processes
(3) operational management systems
(4) performance targets and management objectives
(5) departmental functions, job specialization, relations, and coordination between departments
(6) departmental goals and performance measuring mechanisms; budgeting and planning control processes.

Systems

(1) financial systems and methods of account management
(2) communication channels—formal and informal
(3) planning systems for achieving management objectives

(4) reward and sanction systems
(5) marketing and production processes
(6) mechanisms for innovation, R&D, and technological development.

Style

(1) leadership and senior management styles
(2) approaches to problem- and conflict-solving
(3) work climate—strategies for employee motivation and morale
(4) communications mechanisms (e.g. paper, face-to-face, formal, or informal meetings)
(5) Influence of Western management theory (e.g. learning and practice).

Staff

(1) professional and expert competences of key personnel
(2) recruitment policies of HR (e.g. selection criteria, training, and mentoring processes for new recruits)
(3) training program and policies
(4) staff development policies
(5) performance evaluation systems
(6) impact of Western HR management ideas in working practices.

Shared values

(1) management philosophies (indicators including consideration, respect, and trust, recognition and credit, involvement and availability, fair and equitable treatment, positive action on individual basis, and emphasis on end-results)
(2) organizational culture (indicators including routines, rituals, stories, symbols, power structures, and control methods)
(3) key values driving employees' beliefs and understanding of business development.

Skills

(1) capabilities and expertise of key personnel
(2) technologies employed (including office, manufacturing, and R&D)
(3) competitive advantages in relation to "core" competences.

As a complementary addition to the 7-S dimensions, *Situational Factors* are also examined to further explain how the external environment shapes management practices. These situational factors include:

(1) opportunities and threats in the evolving market
(2) the impact of legal reforms and government policies
(3) history and background of the enterprises and the "legacy effect" on business development.

The selection of case studies

As outlined in the first two chapters, state and collective ownerships were the only forms of enterprise in China under the earlier socialist regime (before 1978). After two decades of reform, the economy has evolved into a state sector and a private sector, with diversified forms of ownership. Three distinctive case study companies were chosen to represent these two sectors. These are (1) a state-owned enterprise—LTG; (2) an entrepreneurial enterprise—DAL; and (3) a foreign joint venture—DSF.

The three cases representing different types of ownership are selected from the textile industry. The three case companies are located in Liaoning province, one of most internationalized regions in North-east China, which has a population of over six million. Its annual Fashion Festival is a major international event and the clothing industry is a major economic component of its industrial structure. In 1997, the central government decided to use the textile industry as an experiment for restructuring state sector enterprises. Therefore, as both a traditional and competitive industry, the textile sector is a pioneer for the implementation of government reform experiments. It offers a perfect case for assessing the impact of legal reforms and organizational change for management practices. This is why the three case studies were chosen in this sector.

As a consequence of the prior planned economy, the textile industry was overstaffed, over-indebted, and had heavy social responsibilities. The textile industry had always suffered losses; in 1997, this amounted to RMB 1060 billion (US$ 128 billion), and accounted for the highest percentage of state enterprise losses. A total of 54 percent of state-owned enterprises in the textile industry were in debt at a rate far higher than the average for state industries (CTIA 2000/2001: 139). Following reforms in the textile industry since 1997, some significant improvements have been achieved. Losses have been reduced and new technologies installed as a result of capital investment programs. Enterprises are more market-focused and management skills have been improved (Wang 2001). The textile industry plays a pioneering role in economic reforms and demonstrates significant management restructuring. Following China's accession to the WTO, the textile industry has access to international markets. This has given the sector opportunities for rapid business growth. The textile industry also provides a useful context to study economic reforms, the emergence of new forms of ownership, and re-structured management practices. In this sector, the number of state-owned enterprises now makes up only 6 percent of all enterprises; collectively-owned enterprises constitute 4.7 percent of the sector; foreign joint ventures account for 43.5 percent; and entrepreneurial enterprises for 45.8 percent (CTIA 2002/2003: 128). This sector therefore offers an appropriate industry context for a comparative study of case companies characterized by different ownership forms. In the market transition process, it is witnessed that collective ownership has gradually shifted from the state sector to the private sector alongside the progress of economic reforms in China (Li *et al.* 2004; Chao 1998; Shirley 1999; Chiu 2006; Wen 2004). By 2005, collective-owned enterprises only accounted for 4 percent of investment in fixed assets in urban areas, compared with 65 percent for state-owned enterprises, 17 percent for private-owned enterprises and 14 percent for foreign-investment enterprises (CYS 2007). Owing to their insignificant influence, three types of business ownership are chosen in this research, namely the state-owned enterprise, the private-owned business, and the foreign joint venture.

The collection of data

Multiple sources of evidence were used; that is, data were collected from the different types of organization, but focused on the same set of facts/findings through one organizational framework, the McKinsey 7-S framework. The case study databases, as a formal assembly of evidence, are in both paper and computerized forms and comprise questionnaires and interviews (in paper format archives); documents and company archives, which are categorized in case unit files; financial data; digital recordings of all interviews; and photographs of each case company.

A chain of evidence is maintained as a source of explicit links between the questions asked, the data collected, and the conclusions drawn; it is characterized with clear cross-referencing of methodological procedures and illustrations of interrelations of the resulting evidence (Yin 2003). The incorporation of these principles into a case study investigation can increase its quality substantially. In order to ensure quality control in the data collection process, the fieldwork investigation was well designed and organized in a scientific manner and certain formally required procedures were rigorously followed in the process of fieldwork. For instance, a protocol of fieldwork research was designed before the investigation started, which included the field procedures to be followed; criteria of case selection; timetable for interviews' arrangement; dimensions of questionnaires and criteria for data analysis.

Fieldwork investigation

Gaining full access to the case study companies was very difficult. The state-owned enterprise (LTG) was accessed through personal contacts. This is virtually the only way a researcher can gain entry into Chinese state-owned enterprises. The pilot fieldwork in the three case companies took one year in total to complete, starting from May 2005 to May 2006. Second revisits were arranged in 2009 to track down organizational changes. Following the second revisits, investigative fieldwork was undertaken consecutively in 2010, 2011, and 2012 to keep up longitudinal data renewal of the companies. All the interviews were tape-recorded and then filed in computerized format. Duplicated paper copies of all interviews were also taken and documented. Relevant photos to demonstrate the product, office, and work climate were taken at each case site. The interviews were structured according to the McKinsey 7-S framework, and each required two to three hours with respondents. All case companies also provided relevant documents and financial data for the research. A letter of introduction was sent to all the case companies involved in the investigation explaining the academic purpose of the research and guaranteeing confidentiality of company information.

Sources of data collection

There were four sources of data that provided the evidence for each of the case study companies: (1) Formal and informal interviews: These were conducted with the key managers and owners of each case company in an open-ended and conversational manner. In addition, informants interviewed also included government officials responsible for policy issues in relation to business and the regulatory environment, together with solicitors, accountants, and a focus group of industry experts. Interviews were recorded in the Mandarin language and then translated into English in the form of transcripts. (2) The use of company documents: Documents were inspected in relation to management procedures, personnel policies, contracts, and other issues relevant for exploring the 7-S framework topics. These were also used to compare with data offered by the key informants in the interviews. (3) The use of archival records: Organizational records, such as organizational charts and budgets/finance, were analyzed. These provided quantitative data about financial performance. (4) Non-participant observation: While conducting the interviews, the researcher also observed formal and informal patterns of behavior as indicators of culture, style, and management practices. Examples included meetings, supervisory styles, and office lay-out. (5) Direct participation observation: During the fieldwork, the researcher was invited to participate in the case study company's business activities; for example, new factory inspection tours, negotiations, meetings with overseas clients etc. In this way, the investigator could obtain a good depth of data by exploring how research participants operated and behaved (thus understanding the values, meanings, motivations, and logics that governed their actions (Curran and Blackburn 2001: 113)) and by seeking close-up details of the underlying reality (Gummesson 2000) through naturalist modes of inquiry (Silverman 2000: 37) within a predominantly inductive framework.

Analyzing the data

Throughout the fieldwork, more than 50 interviews were conducted with 30 interviewees (including revisits) and all relevant data were gathered. These form the completed archives for each case study. The next goal after the initial data collection was to analyze this data to discover key information and cross check evidence. De facto, the data analysis stage started during the interview process and this information was added to later interviews with other respondents. More interviews and questions were put to informants, while the questionnaires were also modified to suit emergent and contingent situations in the field research (Rubin and Rubin 1995).

The data, over 50 digital recordings along with six boxes of documents, were then categorized in relevant subjects in accordance with operational measures in relation to the McKinsey 7-S framework. By reading and listening to the data, each theme was referenced according to the structured topics of the McKinsey 7-S framework. These responses were then grouped together describing the same idea or process. In other words, the data were organized to describe the structure, strategy, system, staff, style, skills, and shared values (7-S) for each of these four case study organizations.

Some considerations and limitations on the present research

The use of case studies is still controversial in management research. The measurement problem, "a small number of cases and big conclusions," often raises questions of generalization of findings (Lieberson 2000). This is the case with the present research and is, indeed, a factor that has to be taken into account when interpreting the findings. Since case studies allow for the analysis of complex issues and are able to probe into the insight of the organization processes, they can gather a "richness and depth" of information to build up explanations of emergent phenomena for which no established theory yet exists (Eisenhardt and Graebaner 2007; Yin 2003). In this sense, quantitative surveys and questionnaires are not appropriate approaches for this purpose. The complexity of these in the case studies was managed by using the McKinsey 7-S framework, providing an analytical framework for understanding qualitative data. Owing to the fact that the vague nature of qualitative information is a major problem of the case study approach, this can be overcome by structured data collection. Furthermore, multiple sources of evidence can be utilized to minimize the risk of researcher bias. By comparative analysis across contrasting cases, differences and similarities can be analyzed in order to examine the impact of ownership. The cases were selected as typical representatives of emerging forms of ownership ("typicality" of cases is a fundamental criterion for the selection of a small number of cases.) This may not cover all the variety of ownership forms, but as typical representations, the likelihood of generality can be obtained to a certain extent. For instance, the common characteristics of state-owned enterprises distinguish them from private-owned enterprises; and foreign joint ventures also demonstrate critical contrasts. Each type of business venture represents distinctive behavioral patterns and organizational profiles due to its different ownership form. These are generalizable and applicable to other enterprises with similar ownership forms. Nonetheless, the limitations of a small number of cases are inevitable, as they cannot cover the whole variety of management practices under market socialism. We are aware of the complexity and diversity of ownership restructuring accompanying rapid enterprise development in these changing market conditions. Therefore, we have taken a longitudinal approach to keep track of organizational changes and performance outcomes over a prolonged period of time from 2005 to 2012. As is common in qualitative analysis, purposive sampling, rather than statistical sampling is used, thus the propositions only suggest some insights on new variables or relationships to provoke further research questions and direction. The authors' hope is that this work has served to cast some new light on how small firms grow in a systematic manner and that it will act as a signpost for further research, including other, and possibly larger, longitudinal studies of this topic.

Furthermore, the use of the McKinsey 7-S framework played a key role in the study of our cases. It comprises seven elements for describing and understanding an organization as a whole. The 7-S framework is not merely an analytical tool; it also operates as a conceptual underpinning to indicate what range of information needs to be collected. Each "S-factor" can be operationally stipulated and used for measuring key organizational variables. However, these factors interact and explain each other; they cannot exist alone. This feature facilitates the analysis of management processes for an "interaction effect" of all the variables that make up a comprehensive explanation. The McKinsey 7-S framework can be useful when applied to the understanding of an organization as a whole. It covers almost every aspect of management, providing a systematic method of analysis to cut through the complexity of an organization. However, it demands full access to organizations and high "time-energy cost" in fieldwork. The enterprise must be open to this research, which often raises issues of confidentiality. Moreover, it requires access to a wide range of information from informants, and sufficient time and energy to devote to interviews and observation. In our fieldwork, we benefited from both the patience and time needed to conduct case studies. We revisited our key informants more than three times to complete our questionnaires and on every revisit, we spent more than one hour in each interview. This places a high demand on the co-operation of case study companies. It would not be realistic to conduct such research without the commitment of CEOs and managers. Our research benefited from this advantage.

This present research is entirely focused on qualitative analysis. It needed to explore how organizational processes work and how owners and managers behave in each type of business venture. It needed to analyze the "interaction effect" among seven elements (strategy, structure, systems, staff, style, shared value, and skills) of our case study organizations. People's perceptions and points of view needed to be examined; strategies and systems needed to be described; decision-making processes and leadership style had to be portrayed. All of these required a quality approach. How these management processes operate demands a qualitative case study approach. Quantitative research is unable to explore these organizational processes in depth.

The last, but not the least, factor to address, is the challenge of conducting research in the Chinese context. It is necessary to mention that the access to case study companies can be a very crucial issue as well as a major barrier for researchers collecting data. Companies may be willing to answer survey questionnaires, but managers and owners may not commit their time for interviews and the disclosure of their internal processes and decision-making styles. This is particularly the case in China, and especially in state-owned enterprises, because of the state's direct administrative control and political confidentiality. The Administration and Inspection Committee of State Assets (AICSA) as a powerful government agency centralizes the administration of all state-owned enterprise in China. It explicitly stipulates that state-owned enterprises are forbidden to expose any internal information to external bodies. Managers in state-owned enterprises will rarely risk their careers by breaking such political rules. Gaining full access to a state-owned enterprise has been a major achievement in the present research. Full access to case study companies is a key factor in determining the success of qualitative management research, besides factors such as limited budgets and time-energy costs over a prolonged period of years. In fact, despite the need for more research in Chinese market socialism, access to companies is one of the major challenges facing those who wish to do management research in China. In this, we succeeded when many others have failed.

Future research

The agenda for further research should focus on the relationship between innovation and entrepreneurship and ownership forms. Our present work has studied some emerging trends of ownership formation and the impact of these for organizational profiles on entrepreneurial growth and organizational performance. Further research should explore the competitive effect of ownership diversification, addressing the importance of innovation and entrepreneurship in both state and private sectors. The impact of ownership on organizational development and decision-making can be tested in different growth contexts and, possibly, through a quantitative approach to verify its specific causal relationship with different growth factors (Zahra *et al.* 2000). Furthermore, the area of knowledge management in entrepreneurship research has been a growing field with increasing attention being paid to the role of new competency development. Resource-based competency is increasingly seen as a knowledge-based view of a firm, with knowledge emerging as the most valuable of resources; how to access, manage, and apply knowledge is a major research issue (Lockett *et al.* 2009). Additionally, it is useful to draw on the nascent strategic entrepreneurship literature to better understand how Chinese enterprises can maximize the value of entrepreneurial opportunity by developing their strategic dynamic capability to meet the demand of technological, economic, and global changes. One possible means is through effective leadership. Through ownership diversification practices, enterprises are expected to develop their competitiveness and create a system of market-oriented management to fit in with changing market conditions. In China, deregulation, privatization, internationalization, and technology advancement demand that all types of enterprise should build their competitiveness in order to survive in the new market environment. The generation of new ideas, and the development of new products and services, is crucial for the constant renewal of organizations. Linking the effects of ownership diversification, this future research needs to explore how innovative and entrepreneurial activities in different types of organization result in entrepreneurial spin-offs, new products, and services. Such research needs to develop concepts and methods for creating organizational cultures that facilitate the development of innovation and entrepreneurship.

Indeed, more research is required to explore the changing dynamics of management practices as government reforms continue to change the conditions of market socialism in China. The literature on Chinese management and organizational behavior generated by empirical case study research is meagre. Our intention in this research was to explore (if only by reference to a small number of case study enterprises) some emerging trends. If this stimulates more detailed studies of evolving ownership forms and the effects of these for management practices under Chinese market socialism, this research will have served its purpose.

Bibliography

ACFIC (2007) "An Analysis Report on the Seventh Sampling Survey of All-China Private Enterprises in 2006," *China Business Times*, February 15, 2007.
Alexashin, Y. and Blenkinsopp, J. (2005) "Changes in Russian Managerial Values," *International Journal of Human Resources Management*, 16 (3), 427–44.
America (2007) "The Next Bill Gates," 196 (2), 4.
Anderson, A. R. and Lee, E. Y.-C. (2008) "From Tradition to Modern: Attitudes and Applications of Guanxi in Chinese Entrepreneurship," *Journal of Small Business and Enterprise Development*, 15 (4), 775–87.
Antoncic, B. and Hisrich, R. D. (2003) "Privatization, Corporate Entrepreneurship, and Performance: Testing a Normative Model," *Journal of Developmental Entrepreneurship*, 8 (3), 197–218.
Aoki, M. and Jin, Y. (1997) *The Functions of Government in Asian Crisis*, Beijing: China Economics Press.
Ashton, B., Hill, K., Piazza, A. and Zeitz, R. (1984) "Famine in China, 1958–1961," *Population and Development Review*, 10 (4), 122–78.
Baark, E. (2001) "Technology and Entrepreneurship in China: Commercialisation Reforms in the Science and Technology Sector," *Policy Studies Review*, 18 (1), 112–29.
Bailey, W. J. and Spicer, A. (2007) "When does National Identity Matter? Convergence and Divergence in International Business Ethics," *Academy of Management Journal*, 50 (6), 1462–80.
Barney, J. B. (1986) "Strategic Factor Markets: Expectations, Luck and Business Strategy," *Management Science*, 32 (10), 1231–41.
Barringer, B. R. and Bluedorn, A. C. (1999) "The Relationship between Corporate Entrepreneurship and Strategic Management," *Strategic Management Journal*, 20, 421–44.
Bas, M. and Causa, O. (2012) "Trade and Product Market Policies in Upstream Sectors and Productivity in Downstream Sectors: Firm-level Evidence from China," OECD Economics Department Working Papers, No. 990, OECD Publishing.
Basu, B. and Yao, J. F. (2009) "FDI and Skill Formation in China," *International Economic Journal*, 23 (2), 163–79.
Baumol, W. J., Litan, R. E. and Schramm, C. J. (2007) *Good Capitalism, Bad Capitalism, and the Economics of Growth and Prosperity*, New Haven, CT: Yale University Press.
Baverman, H. (1974) *Labour and Monopoly Capital*, London: Monthly Review Press.
Behave, M. P. (1994) "A Process Model of Entrepreneurial Venture Creation," *Journal of Business Venturing*, 9, 223–42.

Bergmann-Lichtenstein, B. M. and Brush, C. G. (2002) "How Do 'Resource Bundles' Develop and Change in New Ventures? A Dynamic Model and Longitudinal Exploration," *Entrepreneurship Theory and Practice*, 25 (3), 37–58.

Bian, Y. and Ang, S. (1997) "Guanxi Networks and Job Mobility in China and Singapore," *Social Forces*, 75 (3), 981–1005.

Birkinshaw, J. (2001) "The Structure Behind Global Companies" in Pickford, J. (ed.) *Financial Times Mastering Management*, London: Financial Times Prentice Hall, p. 75.

Bjorkman, I. and Fan, X. C. (2002) "Human Resource Management and the Performance of Western Firms in China," *International Journal of Human Resource Management*, 13 (6), 853–64.

Blosch, M. and Preece, D. (2000) "Framing Work through a Socio-technical Ensemble: The Case of Butler Co.," *Technology Analysis and Strategic Management*, 12 (1), 91–102.

Bo, Yi-bo (1993) *The Retrospect of Several Important Decisions and Events*, Beijing: CPC, Central Party School Publisher, pp. 679–702.

Boisot, M. H. (1987) "Industrial Feudalism and Enterprise Reform: Could the Chinese Use Some more Bureaucracy?" in Malcolm Warner (ed.) *Management Reforms in China*, London: Francis Pinter.

Boisot, M. H. and Child, J. (1988) "The Iron Law of Fiefs: Bureaucratic Failure and the Problem of Governance in the Chinese Economic Reforms," *Administrative Science Quarterly*, 33 (4), 507–27.

Boisot, M. H. and Child, J. (1996) "From Fiefs to Clans: Explaining China's Emerging Economic Order," *Administrative Science Quarterly*, 41 (4), 600–28.

Boisot, M. H. and Liang, X. G. (1992) "The Nature of Managerial Work in the Chinese Enterprise Reforms, a Study of Six Directors," *Organization Studies*, 13 (2), 161–84.

Boli, J. and Thomas, G. (1997) "World Culture with World Polity: A Century of International Non-government Organisation," *American Sociological Review*, 62 (2), 171–90.

Brand, V. and Slater, A. (2003) "Using a Qualitative Approach to Gain Insights into the Business Ethics: Experience of Australian Managers in China," *Journal of Business Ethics*, 45, 167–82.

Branstetter, L. G. and Feenstra, R. C. (2002) "Trade and Foreign Direct Investment in China: A Political Economy Approach," *Journal of International Economics*, 58 (2), 335–58.

Bruton, G. D., Ahlstrom, D. and Obloj, K. (2008) "Entrepreneurship in Emerging Economies: Where are they Today and Where Should the Research Go in the Future?," *Entrepreneurship Theory and Practice*, 32, 1–14.

Budhwar, P. and Debrah, Y. (2001) "Introduction" in Budhwar, P. (ed.) *Human Resource Management in Developing Countries*, London: Routledge, pp. 1–15.

Burger, P. (2012) "Fiscal Sustainability and Fiscal Reaction Functions in the US and UK," *International Business & Economics Research Journal*, 11 (8), 935–42.

Burgoyne, J. (1995) "Feeding Minds to Grow Business," *People Management*, 1 (22), 7–15.

Burns, P. (2005) *Corporate Entrepreneurship: Building an Entrepreneurial Organisation*, Hampshire: Palgrave Macmillan, p. 134.

Buttery, E. A. and Wong, Y. H. (1999) "The Development of a Guanxi Framework," *Marketing Intelligence and Planning*, 17, 147–54.

Byrd, W. A. and Lin, Q. S. (1990) *China's Rural Industry, Structure, Development, and Reform*, Oxford: Oxford University Press.

Byrne, B. (2004) "Qualitative Interviewing" in Seale, C. (ed.) *Researching Society and Culture*, second edition, London: Sage, p. 182.

Campbell, A. (1995) "Vertical Integration Synergy or Seduction?" *Long Range Planning*, 28 (2), 126–8.
Chai, H. and Song, X. (2013) "The Adaptive State—Understanding Political Reform in China," *Policy Studies*, 34 (1), 73–8.
Chan, A. (1993) "Revolution or Corporatism? Workers and Trade Unions in Post-Mao China," *The Australian Journal of Chinese Affairs*, 29, 31–61.
Chan, A. (2001) China's Workers under Assault: The Exploitation of Labour in a Globalising Economy, New York: M. E. Sharpe.
Chao, J. (1998) "Factors Affecting the Competitiveness of China-based Companies," *Competitive Intelligence Review*, 9 (3), 39.
Chatterjee, S., Lubatkin, M. and Schoenecker, T. (1992) "Vertical Strategies and Market Structure: A Systematic Risk Analysis," *Organisation Science*, 3 (1), 138–56.
Che, J. H. and Qian, Y. (1998) "Institutional Environment, Community Government and Corporate Governance: Understanding China's Township-Village Enterprises," *Journal of Law, Economics and Organization*, 14 (1), 1–23.
Chen, C. C. and Chen, X.-P. (2009) "Negative Externalities of Close Guanxi within Organisations," *Asia Pacific Journal of Management*, 26, 37–53.
Chen, J. J. (2004) "Corporatisation of China's State-owned Enterprises and Corporate Governance," *Journal of Corporate Ownership & Control*, 1 (2), 82–93.
Chen, J., Chen, Y. and Vanhaverbeke, W. (2011) "The Influence of Scope, Depth, and Orientation of External Technology Sources on the Innovative Performance of Chinese Firms," *Technovation*, 31, 362–73.
Chen, J. C. H., Lin, Bin-shan, Li, Ling-li and Chen, P. S. (2004) "Logistics Management in China: A Case Study of Haier," *Human Systems Management*, 23 (1), 15–27.
Chen, J.-G., Liu, Y.-Q., Liu, X.-H. and Ge, L.-C. (2008) *Research on the 30 Years of China's Non-State-Owned Units Reform and Development*, Beijing: Economy & Management Publishing House.
Chen, J. Y. (1998) *Township and Village Enterprises Model Studies*, Beijing: China Social Science Press.
Chen, N. X. (1994) *The Study on Direction of Policy for Township-village Enterprises in China*, Beijing: Economic Management Press, p. 262.
Cheng, L. and Rosett, A. (1991) "Contract with a Chinese Face: Socially Embedded Factors in the Transformation form Hierarchy to Market 1978–1989," *Journal of Chinese Law*, 5, 143–244.
Child, J. (1984) *A Guide to Problem and Practice*, London: Harper & Row.
Child, J. (1994) *Management in China during the Age of Reform*, Cambridge: Cambridge University Press.
Child, J. (1995) "Change in the Structure and Prediction of Earnings in Chinese State Enterprises during the Economic Reforms," *International Journal of Human Resource Management*, 6 (1).
Child, J. (1998) "PRC investment control: exploring the myths," *China Direct Investor*, August, 10–15.
Child, J. and McGrath, R. G. (2001) "Organizations Unfettered: Organisational Form in an Information Intensive Economy," *Academy of Management Journal*, 44 (6), 1135–48.
Child, J. and Tse, D. K. (2001) "China's Transition and Its Implications for International Business," *Journal of International Business Studies*, 32, 5–21.
China Daily (1999) "Deng Xiaoping's Inspection Tour to South China," 16th Party Congress, available online at: http://app1.chinadaily.com.cn/highlights/party16/leaders/dengtour.htm (last accessed on August 27, 2013).

China Daily (2004) "The Determinations on Key Issues of the State-owned Enterprise Reform and Development (1999)," CPC 15th National Congress of Central Committee, September 30, 2004.

China Economy and Trade Yearbook (2005) Compiled by Committee of Inspection and Administration of State Assets, State Council, Beijing: China Economy Press, p. 64.

China Foreign Economy and Trade Yearbook (2005) Compiled by the Committee of Inspection and Administration of State Assets, State Council, Beijing: China Economy Press, p. 64.

China Joint Venturer (1995) "Do You Need a Partner in China?" *China Joint Venturer*, 2 (2), 3–5.

China Textile Industry Associate (CTIA) (2000/2001) *China Development Report of Textile Industry*, Beijing: China Textile Press, p. 139.

China Textile Industry Associate (CTIA) (2002/2003) *China Development Report of Textile Industry*, Beijing: China Textile Press, p. 52.

China Textile Industry Associate (CTIA) (2004/2005) *China Development Report of Textile Industry*, Beijing: China Textile Press.

China Textile Industry Associate (CTIA) (2005/2006) *China Development Report of Textile Industry*, Beijing: China Textile Press, p. 52.

Chinese Trade Unions Statistical Yearbook (1994) Beijing: ZGGTN, pp. 399–400.

Chiu, C. (2006) "Changing Experience of Work in Reformed State-owned Enterprises in China," *Organisation Studies*, 27 (5), 677–97.

Chung, M. L. and Bruton, G. D. (2008) "FDI in China: What We Know and What We Need to Study Next," *Academy of Management Perspectives*, 22 (4), 30–44.

CITPC (2005) *China Foreign Economy, Trade, Co-operation and Enterprise Yearbook (2005)* Compiled by China International Trade Promotion Committee (CITPC), Beijing: China Commercial Press.

Claro, S. (2002) "What to Expect from China's Entry into WTO," *Journal Article of Tariff and FDI Liberation*, 27 (1), 35–60.

Cooke, F. L. (2002) "Ownership Change and Reshaping of Employment Relations in China: A Study of Two Manufacturing Companies," *Journal of Industrial Relations*, 44 (1), 19–39.

Cooke, F. L. (2004) "Foreign Firms in China: Modelling HRM in a Toy Manufacturing Corporation," *Human Resource Management Journal*, 14 (3), 31–53.

Cooke, F. L. and Rubery, J. (2002) "Minimum Wage Policies, Gender and the Urban/Rural Divide in China," Consultancy Report, Geneva: International Labour Organization (ILO).

Curran, J. and Blackburn, R. A. (2001) *Researching the Small Enterprise*, London: Sage.

CYS (China Statistical Yearbook) (2005) Compiled by National Bureau of Statistics of China, Beijing: China Statistics Press, pp. 526–49.

CYS (China Statistical Yearbook) (2007) Compiled by National Bureau of Statistics of China, Beijing: China Statistics Press.

CYS (China Statistical Yearbook) (2011) Compiled by National Bureau of Statistics of China, Beijing: China Statistics Press.

Daniels, J. D. and Radebaugh, L. H. (2001) *International Business: Environments and Operations*, ninth edition, New Jersey: Prentice Hall.

Davis, H. and Scase, R. (1985) *Western Capitalism and State Socialism: An Introduction*, London: Basil Blackwell.

Davison, W. H. (1987) "Creating and Managing Joint Ventures in China: Motivation and Management of Political Risk," *California Management Review*, XXVII (4), 44–58.

Deakins, D. and Freel, M. (2006) *Entrepreneurship and Small Firms*, fourth edition, Maidenhead: McGraw-Hill.

Dessler, G. (1976) *Organisation and Management: A Contingency Approach*, London: Prentice-Hall.

Diamante, T. and London, M. (2001) "Expansive Leadership in the Age of Digital Technology," *Journal of Management Development*, 21 (6), 404–16.

Ding, D. Z., Ge, G. and Warner, M. (2004) "Evolution of Organizational Governance and Human Resource Management in China's Township and Village Enterprises," *International Journal of Human Resource Management*, 15 (4), 836–52.

Djankov, S., Qian, Y.-Y., Roland, G. and Zhuravskaya, E. (2006) "Who Are China's Entrepreneurs?," *American Economic Review*, 96 (2), 348–52.

Dorn, J. A. (2001) "Creating Real Capital Markets in China," *CATO Journal*, 21 (1).

Dunfee, T. W. and Warren, D. E. (2001) "Is Guanxi Ethical? A Normative Analysis of Doing Business in China," *Journal of Business Ethics*, 32, 191–204.

Eisenhardt, K. M. and Graebaner, M. E. (2007) "Theory Building from Cases: Opportunities and Challenges," *Academy of Management Journal*, 50 (25), 25–32.

EIU (2004) "The Economy, Country Profile of China," New York: Economic Intelligence Unit, p. 32.

Emirbayer, M. and Mische, A. (1998) "What is Agency?," *American Journal of Sociology*, 103 (4), 962–1023.

"EU China Trade Brief" (2006) *Oxford Analytica*, November 2006.

Fan, C.-Y. (2002) "Government Support for Small and Medium-sized Enterprises in China," *Problems of Economic Transition*, 45 (11), 51–8.

Fan, J. P. H., Wong, T. J. and Zhang, T.-Y. (2007) "Politically Connected CEOs, Corporate Governance, and Post-IPO Performance of China's Newly Partially Privatized Firms," *Journal of Financial Economics*, 84 (2), 330–7.

Fang, Z.-W. (Officer of the State Finance Ministry) (2004) "The Role of CASISA and Target Models of State Assets Administrational Institution," *The State Asset Management*, 160 (7), 8–10.

Faucheux, C., Amado, G. and Laurent, A. (1982) "Organization Development and Change," *Annual Review of Psychology*, 33 (3), 343–70.

Financial Times (2004) August 26, 2004, p. 20.

Financial Times (1998) November 25, 1998, p. 22.

Fontana, A. and Frey, J. (2004) "The Interview: From Structured Questions to Negotiated Text" in Nenzin, N. and Lincoln, Y. (eds) *Handbook of Qualitative Research*, second edition, Thousand Oaks, CA: Sage.

Fontana, A. and Frey, J. (2004) "The Interview: From Structured Questions to Negotiated Text" in Nenzin, N. and Lincoln, Y. (eds) *Handbook of Qualitative Research*, second edition, Thousand Oaks, CA: Sage, pp. 654–5.

Foss, N. J. (1996) "Knowledge-based Approaches to the Theory of the Firm: Some Critical Comments," *Organisation Science*, 7 (5), 470–6.

Freeman, C. (1991) "Networks of Innovators: A Synthesis of Research Issues," *Research Policy*, 20, 499–514.

Fu, X. (2012) "How Does Openness Affect the Importance of Incentives for Innovation?," *Research Policy*, 41, 512–23.

Gabriel, S. J. (1998) "Technological Determinism and Socialism with Chinese Characteristics: Pulling the Cart without Watching the Road?," Satya Gabriel's Online Papers: China's Essay Series, available online at: https://www.mtholyoke.edu/courses/sgabriel/economics/china-essays/8.html (last accessed on August 28, 2013).

Gamble, J. (2000) "Localizing Management in Foreign-invested Enterprises in China: Practical, Cultural, and Strategic Perspectives," *International Journal of Human Resource Management*, 11 (5), 883–903.

Gangemi, J. (2007) "Study: U.S. Start-up Activity Down Slightly in '06," *Business Week Online*, November 1, 2007, p. 2.

Gao, Y. and Tian, Z. (2006) "How Firms Influence the Government Policy Decision-making in China," *Singapore Management Review*, 28 (1), 74–85.

Garnaut, R., Li, G. S., Yang, Y. and Wang, X. (2001) *Private Enterprise in China*, Canberra: Asia Pacific Press.

Garratt, B. (1994) *The Learning Organisation*, London: Harper Collins.

Gartner, W. B. and Shane, S. (1995) "Measuring Entrepreneurship Over Time," *Journal of Business Venturing*, 10, 283–301.

Gartner, W. B., Mitchell, T. R. and Vesper, K. H. (1989) "A Taxonomy of New Business Ventures," *Journal of Business Venturing*, 4, 169–86.

Ge, Y., Lai, H. and Zhu, S. C. (2011) "Intermediates Import and Gains from Trade Liberalization," Mimeo.

Ghobadian, A. and O'Regan, N. (2006) "The Impact of Ownership on Small Firm Behaviour and Performance," *International Small Business Journal*, 24 (6), 555–86.

Giddens, A. (1971) *Capitalism and Modem Social Theory*, Cambridge: Cambridge University Press.

Goodall, K. and Burgers, W. (1998) "Frequent Fliers," *The China Business Review*, 17 (2), 50–2.

Goodall, K. and Warner, M. (1997) "Human Resources in Sino-foreign Joint Ventures: Selected Case Studies in Shanghai and Beijing," *International Journal of Human Resource Management*, 8 (5), 569–94.

Gordon, R. H. and Lienesch, W. (1991) "Chinese Enterprise Behaviour Under the Reforms," *American Economic Review*, 81 (2), 202–7.

Gospel, H. F. and Littler, C. R. (1983) (eds) *Managerial Strategies and Industrial Relations*, London: Heinemann Educational Books.

Grant, R. M. (1991) "Resource-based Theory of Competitive Advantage: Implications for Strategy Formulation," *California Management Review*, 33 (3), 114–36.

Grant, R. M. (1996) "Knowledge, Strategy, and the Theory of the Firm," *Strategic Management Journal*, 17, 102–22.

Grant, R. M. (2005) *Contemporary Strategy Analysis*, fifth edition, Oxford: Blackwell Publishing, pp. 152–9.

Gregory, N. and Tenev, S. (2001) "Special Report: China's Private Sector—China's Home-Grown Entrepreneurs," *The China Business Review*, 28 (1), 14–18.

Greiner, L. E. (1972) "Evolution and Revolution as Organisations Grow," *Harvard Business Review*, 50 (4), 37–46.

Grieves, J. (2000) "Introduction: The Origins of Organisation Development," *Journal of Management Development*, 19 (5), 345.

Guadamillas, F., Donate, M. and Sanchez de Pablo, J. D. (2008) "Knowledge Management for Corporate Entrepreneurship and Growth: A Case Study," *Knowledge and Process Management*, 15 (1), 32–44.

Gummesson, E. (2000) *Qualitative Methods in Management Research*, Thousand Oaks, CA: Sage.

Guo, B. and Guo, J.-J. (2011) "Patterns of Technological Learning within the Knowledge Systems of Industrial Clusters in Emerging Economies: Evidence from China," *Technovation*, 31, 87–104.

Guo, C. and Miller, J. K. (2010) "Guanxi Dynamics and Entrepreneurial Firm Creation and Development in China," *Management and Organisation Review*, 6 (2), 267–91.

Gupta, V., MacMillan, I. C. and Surie, G. (2004) "Entrepreneurial Leadership: Developing and Measuring a Cross-Cultural Construct," *Journal of Business Venturing*, 19, 241–60.

Guth, W. D. and Ginsberg, A. (1990) "Guest editor's introduction: 'corporate entrepreneurship'," *Strategic Management Journal*, 11, 5–15.

Guthrie, D. (1998) "The Declining Significance of Guanxi in China's Economic Transition," *The China Quarterly*, 154, 254–82.

Haberberg, A. and Rieple, A. (2001) *The Strategic Management of Organisations*, London: Financial Times Prentice Hall, pp. 248–52.

Haier Group information is available at: www.haier.com (last accessed on December 6, 2004).

Hamel, G. and Prahalad, C. K. (1993) "Strategy as Stretch and Leverage," *Harvard Business Review*, 71, 75–84.

Handy, C. B. (1993) *Understanding Organisation*, fourth edition, London: Penguin.

Hardin, R. (2013) "Government Without Trust," *Journal of Trust Research*, 3 (1), 32–52.

Hassard, J., Morris, J., Sheehan, J. and Xiao, Y. (2010) "China's State-Owned Enterprises: Economic Reform and Organisational Restructuring," *Journal of Organisational Change Management*, 23 (5), 500–16.

Hay, D., Morris, D., Liu, G. and Yao, S. (1994) *Economic Reform and Chinese State-Owned Manufacturing Enterprises 1980–87*, Oxford: Clarendon Press.

He, X.-H. (2009) "The Development of Entrepreneurship and Private Enterprise in the People's Republic of China and Its Relevance to Transitional Economies," *Journal of Developmental Entrepreneurship*, 14 (1), 39–58.

Held, D., McGrew, A. G., Goldblatt, D. and Perranton, J. (1999) *Global Transformations: Politics, Economics and Culture*, California: Standford University Press.

Hersey, P., Blanchard, K. H. and Johnson, D. E. (2001) *Management of Organizational Behaviour: Leading Human Resources*, eighth edition, New Jersey: Prentice Hall.

Hitt, M. A., Ireland, R. D., Camp, S. M. and Sexton, D. L. (2001) "Integrating Entrepreneurship and Strategic Management Actions to Create Firm Wealth," *Strategic Management Journal* (Special Issue), 22 (6), 479–92.

Ho, S. (1994) *Rural China in Transition: Non-Agricultural Development in Rural Jiangsu, 1978–1990*, Oxford: Oxford University Press.

Hofstede, G. (1980) *Culture's Consequences*, London: Sage.

Hofstede, G. and Bond, M. H. (2005) "The Confucius Connection: From Cultural Roots to Economic Growth," *Organisational Dynamics*, Spring, 4–21.

Hofstede, G., Neuijen, B., Ohayv, D. D. and Sanders, G. (1990) "Measuring Organisational Cultures: A Qualitative and Quantitative Study across Twenty Cases," *Administrative Science Quarterly*, 35 (2), 285–316.

Holden, N. J. (2002) *Cultural Management: A Knowledge Management Perspective*, London: Financial Times Prentice Hall.

Holt, D. G. (1997) "A Comparative Study of Values Among Chinese and US Entrepreneurs: Pragmatic Convergence between Contrasting Cultures," *Journal of Business Venturing*, 12 (6).

Huang, Jr.-T., Kuo, C.-C. and Kao, A.-P. (2003) "The Inequality of Regional Economic Development in China Between 1991 and 2001," *Journal of Chinese Economic and Business Studies*, 1 (3), 273–85.

Huang, Y.-S. (1996) "Central-local Relations in China During the Reform Era: The Economic and Institutional Dimensions," *World Development*, 24 (4), 655–72.

Ireland, R. D., Hitt, M. A., Camp, S. M. and Sexton, D. L. (2001) "Integrating Entrepreneurship and Strategic Management Actions to Create Firm Wealth," *Academy of Management Executive*, 15 (1), 49–63.

Jefferson, G. H. (1999) "Are China's Rural Enterprises Outperforming State Enterprises? Estimating the Pure Ownership Effect" in Jefferson, G. H. and Singh, I. (eds) *Enterprise Reform in China: Ownership, Transition, and Performance*, New York: Oxford University Press, pp. 153–70.

Jenkins, W. (2000) "Talking Your Way into the Dragon's Lair," *Reactions*, 20 (7), 23–6.

Jiang, Fu-ming (2006) "The Determinants of the Effectiveness of Foreign Direct Investment in China: An Empirical Study of Joint and Sole Ventures," *International Journal of Management*, 23 (4), 891–908.

Jiang, Xufeng (2010) "China's FDI Policies Aim to Boost Industry Upgrading," *Xinahua News*, February 1, 2010, available online at: http://news.xinhuanet.com/english/2010-01/02/content_12742852.htm (last accessed on August 28, 2013).

Jin, H. and Qian, Y.-Y. (1998) "Public versus Private Ownership of Firms: Evidence from Rural China," *The Quarterly Journal of Economics*, 113 (4), 773–809.

Jing, Y. and Zhu, Q. (2012) "Civil Service Reform in China: An Unfinished Task of Value Balancing," *Review of Public Personnel Administration*, 32 (2), 134–48.

Johnson, G. and Scholes, K. (2002) *Exploring Corporate Strategy*, sixth edition, London: Financial Times Prentice Hall, pp. 320–2.

Jonathan, U. and Chan, A. (1995) "China, Corporatism, and the East Asian Model," *The Australian Journal of Chinese Affairs*, 33, 29–53.

Kennedy, S. (2005) *The Business of Lobbying in China*, Cambridge, MA: Harvard University Press.

Kirby, D. (2003) *Entrepreneurship*, Berkshire: McGraw-Hill Education, p. 148.

Kodithuwakku, S. S. and Rosa, P. (2002) "The Entrepreneurial Process and Economic Success in a Constrained Environment," *Journal of Business Venturing*, 17, 431–65.

Kogut, B. and Zander, U. (1996) "What do Firms do? Coordination, Identity and Learning," *Organisation Science*, 7, 502–18.

Kornai, J. (1992) *The Socialist System*, Oxford: Princeton University Press and Oxford University Press.

Krug, B. (2004) *China's Rational Entrepreneurs: The Development of the New Private Business Sector*, London: Routledge.

Kshetri, N. (2007) "Institutional Changes Affecting Entrepreneurship in China," *Journal of Developmental Entrepreneurship*, 12 (4), 415–32.

Laaksonen, O. (1988) *Management in China During and After Mao*, Berlin: De Gruyter.

Lai, H.-Y. (2006) *Reform and the Non-State Economy in China: The Political Economy of Liberalization Strategies*, Gordonsville, VA: Palgrave Macmillan.

Lai, Y.-B. (2010) "The Political Economy of Capital Market Integration and Tax Competition," *European Journal of Political Economy*, 26 (4), 475–87.

Lall, S. (1992) "Technological Capabilities and Industrialisation," *World Development*, 20 (2), 165–86.

Lambing, P. and Kuehl, C. (2007) *Entrepreneurship*, fourth edition, New Jersey: Pearson Prentice Hall.

Langlois, J. D. (2004) "Party and Government and China's Financial System" in Yesheng, Huang, Anton, Saich, and Steinfeld, Edward *Financial Sector Reform in China*, Cambridge, MA: Harvard East Asian Press.

Lardy, N. R. (1999) *China's Unfinished Economic Revolution*, Beijing: China Development Press.

Lardy, N. R. (2003) "Trade Liberalization and Its Role in Chinese Economic Growth," Proceedings of International Monetary Fund and National Council of Applied Economic Research Conference "A Tale of Two Giants: India's and China's Experience with Reform and Growth," November 14–16, New Delhi, India. (available online at: http://www.imf.org/external/np/apd/seminars/2003/newdelhi/lardy.pdf (last accessed on August 27, 2013).

Lawrence, P. R. and Lorsch, J. W. (1967) *Organization and Environment: Managing Differentiation and Integration*, Boston: Harvard University Press.

Lee, L. T. (1986) *Trade Unions in China, 1949 to the Present*, Singapore: Singapore University Press, p. 26.

Legge, K. (2000) "The Ethical Context of HRM: The Ethical Organization in the Boundaryless World" in *Ethical Issues in Contemporary Human Resource Management*, Winstanley, D. and Woodall, J. (eds) London: Macmillan, pp. 23–40.

Leitch, C., Frances, H. and Neergaard, H. (2010) "Entrepreneurial and Business Growth and the Quest for a 'Comprehensive Theory': Tilting at Windmills?," *Entrepreneurship Theory and Practice*, 3, 249–60.

Levitt, T. (1968) *Innovation in Marketing: New Perspectives for Profit and Growth*, London: Pan Books.

Lewegie, J. (2002) "Control and Co-ordination of Japanese Subsidiaries in China: Problems of an Expatriate-based Management System," *International Journal of Human Resource Management*, 13 (6), 901–19.

Li, D. D. and Wang, Y. (2006) "Political Conditions for Reform: China vs. Eastern Europe Revisited," *Journal of the European Economic Association*, 4 (2–3), 342–51.

Li, Fu-chun (2004) "The Report of the First Five Year Plan about Developing National Economy," cited from Peng, G., Huang, W. P. and Guo, Y. S. (2004), *Studies on Theory and Practice of Economic Development in China*, Beijing: China People University Press, p. 6.

Li, Shao-min, Ian, V. and Zhou, Dong-shen (2004) "The Emergence of Private Ownership in China," *Journal of Business Research*, 57 (10), 1145–52.

Li, W. W., Yang, J. L., Chen, Y. and Wang, S. Q. (1993) "The Relationship between the Government and State Enterprises in China—A Study of the Contract Responsibility System," Institute of national Economy, Shanghai Academy of Social Science, Working Paper, No. 12, January 1993.

Li, X.-J. (2003) *The Essentials of Management: Structure and Integration*, Beijing: China Economy Press, p. 154.

Li, X.-X. (2004) "Improving Administrative Mechanism of State Assets," *The State Assets Management*, (by The Finance Ministry, The State Council, and The Administration and Inspection Committee of State Assets), 160 (7), 4–7.

Li, Y. (2010) "Analysis on the Disparity in Economic Growth and Consumption between Urban Sector and Rural Sector of China: 1978–2008," *Frontier of Economics in China*, r, 5 (4), 559–81.

Liang, Yuan (2007) "China's Textile Factories Earn Less than National Industrial Average," *Xinhua News*, February 8, 2007.

Lichtenstein, P. M. (1992) "The Political Economy of Left and Right During China's Decade of Reform," *International Journal of Social Economics*, 19 (10), 164–80.

Lieberson, S. (2000) "Small N's and Big Conclusions: An Examination of the Reasoning in Comparative Studies Based on a Small Number of Cases" in Gomm, R., Hammersley, M. and Foster, P. (eds) *Case Study Method*, London: Sage Publications.

Lin, Justin, Yi, Fu, Cai, Fang and Li, Zhou (1996) *The China Miracle: Development Strategy and Economic Reform*, Hong Kong: Chinese University Press.
Lin, C. (2001) "Coporatization and Corporate Governance in China's Economic Transition," *Economics of Planning*, 34 (1), 5–35.
Lin, J., Yi, F., Cai, F. and Li, Z. (1998) "Competition, Policy Burdens, and State-owned Enterprise Reform," *American Economic Review*, 88 (2).
Lin, K. Z. (1999) "Income Taxation and Foreign Direct Investment in China," *International Tax Journal*, 25 (2), 72–92.
Liu, G. S. and Garino, G. (2001) "Privatization or Competition," *Economics of Planning*, 34, 35–51.
Liu, G. S. and Woo, W. T. (2001) "How Will Ownership in China's Industrial Sector Evolve with WTO Accession?," *China Economic Review* 12 (1), 137–61.
Liu, K. C. (1995) "State Control and Performance Evaluation—The Case of State Owned Enterprise in China," *International Journal of Public Sector Management*, 8 (6), 39–50.
LNCIQ (2011) *Liaoning Entry-Exit Inspection and Quarantine Bureau*, available online at: http://www.lnciq.gov.cn/zwpd/jgjs (accessed on July 31, 2011).
Lockett, M. (1988) "Culture and the Problem of Chinese Management," *Organization Studies*, 9 (4), 475–96.
Long, N. and Long, A. (1992) *Battlefields of Knowledge: Interlocking Theory and Practice in Social Research and Development*, London: Routledge.
Lorsch, J. W. and Morse, J. J. (1974) *Organisations and Their Members: A Contingency Approach*, New York: Harper & Row Publishers.
Lu, Q. (2006) *WTO Outline*, Shanghai: Shanghai Fudan University Press, p. 217.
Lu, Y. and Bjorkman, I. (1997) "MNCs Standardization versus Localization: MNC Practices in China-Western Joint Ventures," *International Journal of Human Resource Management*, 8 (4), 614–28.
Luo, Y. and O'Connor, N. (1998) "Structural Changes to Foreign Direct Investment in China: An Evolutionary Perspective," *Journal of Applied Management Studies*, 7 (1), pp. 95–109.
Luo, Ya-dong;, Tan, J. J. and Shenkar, O. (1998) "Strategic Responses to Competitive Pressure: The Case of Township and Village Enterprises in China," *Asia Pacific Journal of Management*, 15 (1), 33–50.
Luo, X., Zhou, L. and Liu, S. S. (2005) "Entrepreneurial Firms in the Context of China's Transition Economy: An Integrative Framework and Empirical Examination," *Journal of Business Research*, 58 (3), 277–84.
Lyles, M. A., Baird, I. S., Orris, J. B. and Kuratko, D. F. (1993) "Formalize Planning in Small Business: Increasing Strategic Choices," *Journal of Small Business Management*, 38–50.
Lynch, R. (2003) *Corporate Strategy*, third edition, London: Financial Times Prentice Hall.
Ma, H. (2003) "China Market Development Report, compiled by Development and Research Centre of State Council, Beijing: China Development Press.
McEwan, T. (2001) *Managing Values and Beliefs in Organisations*, London: Financial Times Prentice Hall.
McGregor, D. (1987) *The Human Side of Enterprise*, London: Penguin.
McGregor, R. (2004) "Chinese Growth Bound Tightly to Private Sector," *Financial Times*, Friday, August 27, 2004.
McKelvie, A. and Wiklund, J. (2010) "Advancing Firm Growth Research: A Focus on Growth Mode Instead of Growth Rate," *Entrepreneurship Theory and Practice*, 34, 261–88.

McNeely, C. L. (1995) *Constructing the Nation State: International Organisation and Prescriptive Action*, Westport: Greenwood Press.

Malerba, F. (1992) "Learning by Firms and Incremental Technical Change," *The Economic Journal*, 102, 845–59.

Man, T. W. Y., Lau, T. and Chan, K. F. (2002) "The Competitiveness of Small and Medium Enterprises: A Conceptualization with Focus on Entrepreneurial Competencies," *Journal of Business Venturing*, 17, 123–42.

Manin, B. (1997) *The Principles of Representative Government*, Cambridge: Cambridge University Press.

Mao, Ze-dong (1953a) *The Anthology of Mao Zedong: The General Route of the Communist Party in the Transition of Socialism*, Vol. 5, Beijing: The People Press, p. 89.

Mao, Ze-dong (1953b) *The Anthology of Mao Zedong: Two Talks about the Agriculture Communal Corporation*, Vol. 6, Beijing: The People Press, p. 298.

Marcussen, M. and Kaspersen, L. B. (2007) "Globalization and Institutional Competitiveness," *Regulation and Governance*, 1, 183–96.

Martinsons, M. G. (2008) "Relationship-based E-commerce: Theory and Evidence from China," *Information Systems Journal*, 18 (4), 331–56.

Marx, K. (1969) *Capital: A Critical Analysis of Capitalist Production*, translated from the third German edition by Samuel Moore and Edward Aveling and edited by Frederick Engels, London: George Allen & Unwin.

Masahiko, Aoki and Hyung-Ki, Kim (eds) (1995) "Corporate Governance in Transitional Economies: Insider Control and the Role of Banks," Washington DC, World Bank.

Maslow, A. H. (1987) *Motivation and Personality*, third edition, London: Harper & Row.

Melvin, S. (1997) "Passing the Torch," *The China Business Review*, 23 (3), 32.

Milana, C. and Wu, H. X. (2012) "Growth, Institutions, and Entrepreneurial Finance in China: A Survey," *Strategic Change*, 21, 83–106.

Millington, A., Eberhardt, M. and Wilkinson, B. (2005) "Gift Giving, Guanxi and Illicit Payments in Buyer-Supplier Relationships in China: Analysing the Experience of UK Companies," *Journal of Business Ethics*, 57, 255–68.

Miner, J. B., Chen, C.-C. and Yu, K. C. (1991) "Theory Testing under Adverse Conditions: Motivation to Manage in the People's Republic of China," *Journal of Applied Psychology*, 76 (3), 343–9.

Minzberg, H. (1983) *Structure in Fives: Designing Effective Organisations*, New Jersey: Prentice Hall Inc., p. 2.

Montagu-Pollock, M. (1991) "All the Right Connections," *Asian Business*, 27 (1), 20–4.

Morphy, K., Shelfer, A. and Vishny, R. (1992) "The Transition to a Market Economy: Pitfalls of Partial Reform," *Quarterly Journal of Economics*, 107 (3), 889–906.

Morrison, W. M. (2012) "China's Economic Conditions," *Congressional Research Service* (CRS), June 26, 2012.

Mullins, J. L. (2005) *Management and Organizational Behaviour*, seventh edition, London: Financial Times Prentice Hall.

Nair, S. R. (1996) "Doing Business in China: It's Far from Easy," *USA Today*, 124 (2608), 27–9.

Naughton, B. (1994) "Chinese Institutional Innovation and Privatization from Below," *American Economic Review*, 84 (2), 266–70.

Naughton, B. (1995) *Growing out of the Plan: Chinese Economic Reform 1978–93*, Cambridge: Cambridge University Press.

Nee, V. and Opper, S. (2010) "Political Capital in a Market Economy," *Social Forces*, 88 (5), 2105–32.

Ng, S. H. and Warner, M. (1998) *China's Trade Union Management*, London: Macmillan.

Ng, W. and Thorpe, R. (2010) "Not Another Study of Great Leaders: Entrepreneurial Leadership in a Mid-sized Family Firm for its Further Growth and Development," *International Journal of Entrepreneurial Behaviour and Research*, 16 (5), 457–76.

Noaks, L. and Wincup, E. (2004) *Criminological Research: Understanding Qualitative Methods*, London: Sage, p. 80.

Nonaka, I. and Takeuchi, H. (1995) *The Knowledge Creating Company*, Oxford: Oxford University Press.

North, D. C. (1990) *Institutions, Institutional Change and Economic Performance*, Cambridge: Cambridge University Press.

OECD (Organisation for Economic Co-operation and Development) (2002) "An OECD Perspective on Regulatory Reform in China," published as "Chapter 11" in *China in the World Economy: The Domestic Policy Challenges*, by Scott Jacobs, Managing Partner, Jacobs and Associates.

OECD (Organisation for Economic Co-operation and Development) (2005a) "Improving the Productivity of the Business Sector," Economic Survey of China 2005, Chapter 2, OECD, September 16, 2005.

OECD (Organisation for Economic Co-operation and Development) (2005b) "Key Challenges for the Chinese Economy," Economic Survey of China 2005, Chapter 1, OECD.

OECD (Organisation for Economic Co-operation and Development) (2005c) "Economic Survey of China 2005: Policy Briefs," *Economic Outlook*, 77, June 2005.

OECD (2010) (Organisation for Economic Co-operation and Development) "Product Market Regulation and Competition," OECD Economic Surveys of China, Paris: OECD Publishing, pp. 1–236.

OECD (Organisation for Economic Co-operation and Development) (2012), "Active with the People's Republic of China," pp. 1–61.

Opper, S. (2001) "Dual-track Ownership Reforms: Lessons from Structural Change in China, 1978-1997," *Post-communist Economies*, 13 (2), 205–27.

Otsuka, K., Liu, D. and Murakami, N. (1998) *Industrial Reform in China—Past Performances and Future Prospects*, Oxford: Clarendon.

Park, S. H. and Luo, Y.-D. (2001) "Guanxi and Organizational Dynamics: Organizational Networking in Chinese Firms," *Strategic Management Journal*, 22 (5), 455–78.

Pascale, R. T. and Athos, A. G. (1986) *The Art of Japanese Management*, London: Penguin, pp. 80–1.

Peng, M. W. (1997) "Firm Growth in Transition Economies: Three Longitudinal Cases from China," *Strategic Management Journal*, 18, 247–54.

Peng, M. W. (2001) "How Entrepreneurs Create Wealth in Transition Economies," *Academy of Management Executive*, 15 (1), 95–108.

Peng, G., Huang, W. P. and Guo, Y. S. (2004) *Studies on Theory and Practice of Economic Development in China*, Beijing: China People University Press.

Peng, Y., Zuck, L. G. and Darby, M. R. (1997) "Chinese Rural Industrial Productivity and Urban Spillovers," NBER Working Paper, No. 6202, Cambridge: National Bureau of Economic Research.

Penrose, E. (1960) "The Growth of the Firm—A Case Study: Hercules Powder Corporation," *The Business History Review*, 34, 1–23.

Peters, T. J. and Waterman, R. H. (1980) *In Search of Excellence*, New York: Harper & Row, p. 9.

Phan, P., Jing W. and Abrahamson, E. (2008) "Special Issue on Creativity, Innovation and Entrepreneurship in China," *Management and Organisation Review*, 4 (1), 151–2.

Philliber, S. G., Schwab, M. R. and Samsloss, G. (1980) *Social Research: Guides to a Decision-making Process*, Itsaca: Peacock.
Pierson, C. (1995) *Socialism after Communism: The New Market Socialism*, Pennsylvania: The Pennsylvania State University Press, pp. 84–5.
Porter, M. E. (1980) *Competitive Strategy: Techniques for Analyzing Industries and Competitors*, London: The Free Press, p. 35.
Porter, M. E. (1990) *The Competitive Advantage of Nations*, London: Macmillan.
Putterman, L. and Dong, X. Y. (2000) "China's State-owned Enterprises," *Modern China*, 26 (4), 36–48.
Qian, Y.-Y. (2000) "The Process of China's Market Transition (1978–1998): The Evolutionary, Historical, and Comparative Perspectives," *Journal of Institutional and Theoretical Economics*, 156 (1), 151–71.
Qian, Y.-Y. (2003), *Contemporary Economics and China Economic Reforms*, Beijing: China People's University Press.
Qian, Y.-Y., Roland, G. and Xu, Cheng-gang (2006), "Coordination and experimentation in M-form and U-form organisations," *Journal of Political Economy*, 114 (2), April 2006, pp. 366–402.
R&D Magazine (2011) "China's R&D Momentum: 2012 Global R&D Funding Forecast," *R&D Magazine*, 53 (7), 60–1.
Ravasi, D. and Turati, C. (2005) "Exploring Entrepreneurial Learning: A Comparative Study of Technology Development Projects," *Journal of Business Venturing*, 20, 137–64.
Reeder, J. A. (1984) "Entrepreneurship in the People's Republic of China," *Columbia Journal of World Business*, 19 (3), 43–52.
Ren, Da-fang and Ren, An-tai (1993) *Century Ups and Downs—The Evolutionary Path of Modern China National Commerce and Industry*, Beijing: China Broadcast and Television Publication Co., pp. 335–6.
Richter, F. J. (2000) "China's Entry into the WTO and the Impact on Western Firms," *China Economic Review*, 11 (2), 423–6.
Rollinson D. and Broadfield A. (2005) *Organisational Behaviour and Analysis: An Integrated Approach*, third edition, Harlow: Financial Times Prentice Hall.
Romijn, H. and Albaladejo, M. (2002) "Determinants of Innovation Capability in Small Electronics and Software Firms in Southeast England," *Research Policy*, 31, 1053–67.
Rommer, A. G. L. (1990) "Vertical Integration as Organisational Strategy Formation," *Organisation Studies*, 11 (2), 239–60.
Roxburgh, C., Lund, S., Daruvala, T., Manyika, J., Dobbs, R., Forn, R. and Croxson, K. (2012) "Debt and Deleveraging: Uneven Progress on the Path to Growth," *McKinsey Global Institute (MGI)*, January 2012.
Roxburgh, C., Lund, S. and Piotrowski, J. (2011) "Mapping Capital Markets 2011," *McKinsey Global Institute (MGI)*, August 2011.
Rubin, H. J. and Rubin, I. S. (1995) *Qualitative Interviewing: The Art of Hearing Data*, London: Sage, p. 226.
Salancik, G. R. and Pfeffer, J. (1980) "Effects of Ownership and Performance on Executive Tenure in U.S. Corporations," *Academy of Management Journal*, 23 (4), 653–64.
Sanders, R. and Chen, Y. (2005) "On Privatization and Property Rights: Should China Go Down the Road of Outright Privatization?," *Journal of Chinese Economic and Business Studies*, 3 (3), 231–45.
Scase, R. (2007) *Global Remix: The Fight for Competitive Advantage*, London: Kogan Page.

Schlevogt, K. A. (2000) "Doing Business in China, Part II: Investing and Managing in China—How to Dance with the Dragon," *Thunderbird International Business Review*, 42 (2), 201–26.

Schlevogt, K. A. (2001) "The Distinctive Structure of Chinese Private Enterprises: State versus Private Sector," *Asia Pacific Business Review*, 7 (3), 1–33.

Schumpeter, J. A. (1996) *The Theory of Economic Development*, New Jersey: Transaction Publishers.

Scott, M., Fadahunsi, A. and Kodithuwakku, S. (1997) "Tackling Adversity with Diversity" in Birley, S. and Muzyka, D. F. (eds) *Mastering Enterprise: Your Single-Source Guide to Becoming an Entrepreneur*, London: Financial Times Mastering Series, Pitman.

Senge, P. (1999) "It's the Learning: The Real Lesson of the Quality Movement," *Journal for Quality & Participation*, 22 (6) 34–40.

Seung, W. B. (2000) "The Changing Trade Unions in China," *Journal of Contemporary Asia*, 30 (1), 46–66.

Shepherd, D. and Wiklund, J. (2009) "Are We Comparing Apples with Apples or Apples with Oranges? Appropriateness of Knowledge Accumulation Across Growth Studies," *Entrepreneurship Theory & Practice*, 33 (1), 105–23.

Sheehan, J., Morris, J. and Hassard, J. (2000) "Redundancies in Chinese State Enterprises: A Research Report," *Journal of Industrial Relations*, 39 (3), 486–501.

Shen, T. Y. (1994) "An Institution for Entrepreneurship in Chinese Economic Reform," *Journal of Socio-economics*, 23 (3), 303–21.

Shirley, M. (1999) "Bureaucrats in Business: The Role of Privatization versus Corporatization in State-owned Enterprise," *World Development*, 27 (1), 115.

Simmons, L. C. and Munch, J. M. (1996) "Is Relationship Marketing Culturally Bound: A Look at Guanxi in China," *Advances in Consumer Research*, 23, 93–6.

Silverman, D. (2000) *Doing Qualitative Research*, London: Sage.

Smallbone, D., Leigh, R. and North, D. (1995) "The Characteristics and Strategies of High Growth SMEs," *International Journal of Entrepreneurial Behaviour and Research*, 1 (3), 44–62.

Snell, R. and Tseng, C. S. (2002) "Moral Atmosphere and Moral Influence under China's Network Capitalism," *Organisation Studies*, 23 (3), 449–78.

Snow, C., Miles, R. and Coleman, H. (1992) "Managing 21st Century Network Organizations," *Organizational Dynamics*, 20 (3), 5–21.

Spender, J. C. and Grant, R. M. (1996) "Knowledge and the Firm: Overview," *Strategic Management Journal*, 17, 5–9.

Steinfeld, E. S. (1998) *Forging Reform in China: The Fate of State-owned Industry*, Cambridge: Cambridge University Press.

Stake, R. E. (1995) *The Art of Case Study Research*, London: Sage, p. 24.

Standifird, S. S. and Marshall, R. S. (2000) "The Transaction Cost Advantage of Guanxi-based Business Practices," *Journal of World Business*, 35 (1), 21–42.

Starkey, K., Tempest, S. and McKinlay, A. (2004) *How Organizations Learn: Managing the Search for Knowledge*, second edition, London: Thomson.

Stiglitz, J. E. (1994) *Whither Socialism?*, London: The MIT Press.

Storey, D. (1994) *Understanding the Small Business Sector*, London: Routledge.

Su, C. and Littlefield, J. E. (2001) "Entering Guanxi: A Business Ethical Dilemma in Mainland China?," *Journal of Business Ethics*, 33 (3), 199–210.

Sun, Li. and Duan, Ya-bing (2003) *The Development Path to the Small and Medium-sized Enterprise: The Rise of the Small Giant*, Beijing: China Times and Economies Press.

Sun, Yu-chin (2005) *The Effect of Economic Reforms on the Foreign Trade Systems*, Beijing: University Press of Foreign Economy and Trade, pp. 153–4.
Sutter, K. M. (2000) "Investors' Growing Pains," *The China Business Review*, 27 (6), 14–21.
Tan, J. (2002a) "Culture, Nation, and Entrepreneurial Strategic Orientations: Implications for an Emerging Economy," *Entrepreneurship Theory and Practice*, 2 (4), 95–111.
Tan, J. (2002b) "Impact of Ownership Type on Environment-Strategy Linkage and Performance: Evidence from a Transitional Economy," *Journal of Management Studies*, 39 (3), 333–54.
Tang, Y. W., Chow, L. and Cooper, B. J. (1994) *Accounting and Finance in China: A Review of Current Practice*, Hong Kong: Longman.
Tang, Z., Zhang, Y. L. and Li, Q. W. (2007) "The Impact of Entrepreneurial Orientation and Ownership Type on Firm Performance in the Emerging Region of China," *Journal of Developmental Entrepreneurship*, 12 (4), 383–97.
Taylor, B. (2001) "The Management of Labour in Japanese Manufacturing Plants in China," *International Journal of Human Resource Management*, 12 (4), 601–20.
The Sunday Times Magazine (2004) October 17, p. 52.
Thompson, J. D. (1967) *Organisations in Action: Social Science Bases of Administrative Theory*, New York: McGraw-Hill.
Timmons, J. A. (1999) *New Venture Creation: Entrepreneurship for the 21st Century*, Singapore: Irwin/McGraw-Hill.
Triandis, H. C. (1994) *Cross Cultural Industrial and Organizational Psychology*, California: Consulting Psychology Press.
Tung, R. L. (2007) "The Human Resource Challenge to Outward Foreign Direct Investment Aspirations from Emerging Economies: The Case of China," *International Journal of Human Resource Management*, 18 (5), 869–89.
Vanhonacker, W. (1997) "Entering China: An Unconventional Approach," *Harvard Business Review*, XII (2), 19–32.
Vanhonacker W. (2004) "Factory and Manager in an Era of Reform," *The China Quarterly*, 242–64.
Von Hippel, E. (1988) *The Sources of Innovation*, New York: Oxford University Press.
Walder, A. (1995) "Local Government as Industrial Firms: An Organisational Analysis of China's Transitional Economy," *American Journal of Sociology*, 101, 263–301.
Wallin, M. W. and von Krogh, G. (2010) "Organizing for Open Innovation: Focus on the Integration of Knowledge," *Organizational Dynamics*, 39 (2), 145–54.
Wang, J., Wang, G. G., Ruona, W. E. A. and Rojewski, J. W. (2005) "Confucian Values and the Implications for International HRD," *Human Resource Development International*, 8 (3), 311–26.
Wang, H. and Han, G. (2008) "Local Government's "Black Box" in Small and Medium-Sized Private Enterprises' Trans-Ownership M&A Failure," *Journal of Small Business and Enterprise Development*, 15 (4), 719–32.
Wang, T.-K. (2001) *The First Breakthrough of Enterprise Reform in the Textile Industry*, Beijing: The Forum of Minister and Academician.
Wang, Z. M. (2000) "Economic Reform Foundation's President Shangquan Gao on Organisational Reform and Sustainable Business Development," *Academy of Management Executive*, 14 (1), 8.
Wang, Z. M. and Zang, Z. (2005) "Strategic Human Resource, Innovation and Entrepreneurship Fit: A Cross-regional Comparative Model," *Institutional Journal of Manpower*, 26 (6), 544–59.

Bibliography

Warner, M. (1991) "Labour-management Relations in the People's Republic of China: The Role of the Trade Unions," *International Journal of Human Resource Management*, 2 (2), 205–21.

Warner, M. (1992) *How Chinese Managers Learn: Management and Industrial Training in China*, London: Macmillan.

Warner, M. (1999) *China's Managerial Revolution*, London: Frank Cass.

Warner, M. (2002a) "Conclusion: The Future of Chinese Management," *Asia Pacific Business Review*, 9 (2), 205–24.

Warner, M. (2002b) "Introduction: Chinese Management in Perspective," *Asia Pacific Business Review*, 9 (2), 1–21.

Warner, M. (2004) "Late Development Experience and the Evolution of Transnational Firms in the People's Republic of China," *Asia Pacific Business Review*, 10 (3/4), 324–45.

Waterman, R. H., Peters, T. J. and Phillips, J. R. (1980) "The 7-S Framework—Structure is not Organization," *Business Horizons*, 273–6.

Watson, T. J. (2002) *Organizing and Managing Work*, London: Financial Times Prentice Hall.

Weber, M. (1983) *Max Weber on Capitalism, Bureaucracy and Religion: A Selection of Texts, Edited and in Part Newly Translated by Stanislav Andreski*, London: Allen & Unwin.

Wedeman, A. H. (2003) *From Mao to Market: Rent Seeking, Local Protectionism, and Marketization in China*, Cambridge: Cambridge University Press.

Weidenbaum, M. (1996) "The Chinese Family Business Enterprise," *California Management Review*, 38 (4), 141–56.

Weitzman, M. and Xu, C. (1994) "Chinese Township–Village Enterprises as Vaguely Defined Cooperatives," *Journal of Comparative Economics*, 18 (2), 410–37.

Wen, W. (2004) "Bankruptcy, Sale and Mergers as a Route to the Reform of Chinese SOEs," *China Economic Review*, 15 (3), 249–67.

West, M. and Patterson, M. (1998) "Profitable Personnel," *People Management*, 8 (1), 28–31.

Whyte, M. K. (1995) "The Social Roots of China's Economic Development," *The China Quarterly*, 144 (3), 999–1019.

Wickham, P. A. (2006) *Strategic Entrepreneurship*, fourth edition, Harlow: Pearson Education.

Wiklund, J., Patzelt, H. and Shepherd, D. A. (2009) "Building an Integrative Model of Small Business Growth," *Small Business Economics*, 32, 351–74.

Wolf, C. (1988) *Market and Government—Trade-off Two Imperfect Options*, Beijing: China Development Press, pp. 55–7.

Wong, A. L. Y. and Salter, J. R. (2002) "Executive Development in China: Is There any in a Western Sense?," *International Journal of Human Resource Management*, 13 (2), 338–60.

Wong, Y. H. and Chan, R. Y.-K. (1999) "Relationship Marketing in China: Guanxi, Favouritism and Adaptation," *Journal of Business Ethics*, 22, 107–18.

Woodward, J. (1970) *Industrial Organizations: Theory and Practice*, London: Oxford University Press.

Wu, Jing-lin (1985) *Economic Mechanisms and Coordinated Reforms, Anthology of Wu Jinglian*, Tai Yuan: Shanxi People Press.

Wu, Jing-lian (1993) *The Theory of "Rent Seeking Activities" and Some Negative Effect of China's Economy*, second edition, Beijing: China Finance and Economy Press.

Wu, Jing-lian (2003) *Contemporary China's Economic Reforms*, Shanghai: Shanghai Yuandong Press.

Wu, W., Wu, C. and Rui, O. M. (2012) "Ownership and the Value of Political Connections: Evidence from China," *European Financial Management*, 18 (4), 695–729.

Wu, Yan-rui (1995) "Productivity Growth, Technological Progress, and Technical Efficiency Change in China: A Three Sector Analysis," *Journal of Comparative Economics*, 21 (2), 207–30.

Xie, Q. H. and Lin, Y. F. (1992) *The Theory and Practice of State Assets Management*, China: Economic Science Press.

Xin, K. R. and Pearce, J. L. (1996) "Guanxi: Connections as Substitutes for Formal Institutional Support," *Academy of Management Journal*, 39, 1641–58.

Xu, F. (2000) *Women Migrant Workers in China's Economic Reform*, New York: Macmillan.

Xu, Xin-peng and Voon, J. P. (2003) "Regional Integration in China," *Economics Letters*, 79 (1), 35–42.

Xue, Mu-qiao (1979) *The Study on the Problems in China's Socialist Economy*, Beijing: The People Press, p. 185.

Yan, D. and Warner, M. (2001) "Sino-Foreign Joint Ventures versus Wholly Foreign Owned Enterprises in the People's Republic of China," *Working Paper*, No. 11, Cambridge: The Judge Institute of Management Studies, p. 31.

Yang, K. M. (2002) "Double Entrepreneurship in China's Economic Reform: An Analytical Framework," *Journal of Political and Military Sociology*, 30 (1), 134–48.

Yang, K. M. (2004) "Institutional Holes and Entrepreneurship in China," *The Sociology Review*, 52 (3), 371–89.

Yang, K. M. (2007) *Entrepreneurship in China*, Aldershot: Ashgate.

Yang, J. (2002), "Market Power in China: Manifestations, Effects and Legislation," *Review of Industrial Organisation*, 21,167–83.

Yang, J. Y. and Li, J. T. (2008) "The Development of Entrepreneurship in China," *Asia Pacific Journal of Management*, 25 (2), 335–59.

Yang, M.-M. (1994) *Gifts, Favours and Banquets: The Art of Social Relationships in China*, New York: Corner University Press.

Yano, G. and Shiraishi, M. (2004) "Efficiency of Chinese Township and Village Enterprises and Property Rights in the 1990s: Case Study of Wuxi," *Comparative Economic Studies*, 46 (2), 311–40.

Yin, R. K. (1994) *Case Study Research: Design and Methods*, third edition, London: Sage, pp. 110–11.

Yin, R. K. (2003) *Case Study Research: Design and Methods*, third edition, London: Sage.

Ying, H. (2002) "Business Ethics: Is It Useful?—An Empirical Study of Chinese Enterprise," *Business Ethics: A European Review*, 11 (4), 335–42.

Young, A. (2000) "The Razor's Edge: Distortions and Incremental Reform in the People's Republic of China," *Quarterly Journal of Economics*, 115 (4), 1091–135.

Yun, G. P. and Chen, Q. Z. (2000) *Study of Chinese Enterprises' Management in East-South Asia*, Beijing: Economies and Management Press.

Zahra, S. A. (1993) "Environment, Corporate Entrepreneurship, and Financial Performance: A Taxonomic Approach," *Journal of Business Venturing*, 8 (4), 319–40.

Zahra, S. A. and Covin, J. (1995) "Contextual Influences on the Corporate Entrepreneurship Company Performance Relationship in Established Firms: A Longitudinal Analysis," *Journal of Business Venturing*, 10, 43–58.

Zhang, H. W. (2002) *The Development Report of Private Enterprise in China 2001*, Beijing: Social Sciences Academic Press.

Zhang, L. (2003) *Make the Strong Stronger: 21st Century Business Overview*, Beijing: Higher Education Publications.

Zhang, Xing-quan (2000) "Housing Reform and the New Governance of Housing in Urban China," *International Journal of Public Sector Management*, 13 (6), 519–25.

Zhang, Z. (1999) "Rural Industrialization in China: From Backyard Furnaces to Township and Village Enterprises," *East Asia*, 18 (2), 61–87.

Zhang, Z.-Y. and Zheng, H.-H. (2008) *The Restrospect and Prospect of 30-year Reforms of State-owned Enterprises in China*, Beijing: The People Press.

Zhao, M. (2006) "Conducting R&D in Countries with Weak Intellectual Property Rights Protection," *Management Science*, 52, 1185–99.

Zheng, P. (2012) "The Contrasting Strategies of Owner-Managed and Foreign-Engaged Joint Ventures under Market Socialism in China," *International Entrepreneurship and Management Journal*, 3.

Zheng, P. (2013) "Entrepreneurial Growth and Ownership under Market Socialism in China – A Longitudinal Case Study of Small Business Growth," *Journal of General Management*, 38 (2), 5–37.

Zheng, P. and Scase, R. (2013) "The Restructuring of Market Socialism: The Contribution of 'Agency' theoretical perspective," *Thunderbird International Business Review*, 55 (1), 103–14.

Zhou, Z. (1988) "Chinese Accounting Systems and Practices," *Accounting, Organisations & Society*, 13 (2), 207–24.

Zhu, Z.-L. (2006) *The Security of Chinese Industries after WTO Accession*, Shanghai: Shanghai Finance and Economy Press.

Zou, D.-T. and Ouyang, R.-H. (2008) *30 Years of Reform of Ownership in China (1978–2008)*, Beijing: Social Sciences Academic Press.

Zuo, Z. (2001) "Characteristics and Origin of Pearl River Delta Model," *Journal of Economics & Management Strategy*, 10 (3), 435–61.

Index

Note: Italic page numbers denote figures and tables

Administration and Inspection Committee of State Assets (AICSA) 63–4, 65–6, 67–8, 70, 71, 113, 152–3
administrative decentralization (1958–78) 2–4
American–Chinese joint venture *see* DSF case study

banking, reform of 8
brand management 103–4

case studies: comparative analysis of 112–28; DAL, private-owned company 82–98; DSF, foreign joint venture 100–11; LTG, state-owned company 61–77; McKinsey 7 S framework 141–7; selection of 148–9; utility of 139–40
Central Banking System 8
"China Model" 13, 52, 132, 133, 134
Chinese market socialism 1–2; challenges facing 19–22; emerging trends in 129–36; evolution of economic reforms 2–10; foreign direct investment and economic development 14–19; government institutions, role of 10–12; key characteristics of 12–14; regulation and deregulation, paradoxes in 23; summary 23–4
Chinese organizational behavior *see* Guanxi networks
collective-owned enterprises (COEs) 6, 9, 10, 41; privatization of 48
Communist Party of China (CPC) 26–8, 132; administrative structure 10–12; market socialism advocated by 12–14

competitiveness 153
contingency theory 137–8
"contract farms" 34
contract responsibility system 30, 34
"copycat" image 135
Corporate Law of Sino Joint Ventures 39–40
Corporation Law (1994) 31, 54
corporatization processes 31–2
corporatization reforms 31
corruption 31, 52–3, 134
crisis of legitimacy 133–5

DAL case study 82–4; alliance with Japanese company 85–6; business reputation 95–6; business strategy 84–5; communication structure 89–90; finance 90–1; job specialization 87–8; Labor Union 90; leadership style 93–5; learning culture 95; management philosophies 94–5; network access to resources 95–7; organizational structure 86–7; training programs 91–2; work relations 88–9
data analysis 150–1
data collection 149–50
decentralization (1958–78) 2–4
decision-making processes, state-owned enterprises 70
deregulation 23; incremental approach 26
DSF case study 100–2; communication systems 102–3; education level of key personnel 104; Enterprise Resource Planning (ERP) 110; human-resource issues 104–6; leadership style 106–8; organizational culture 108–9; planning system 103; Western style of

management 109; work environment 108
DSF Club 102–3
"dual-track economic system" 6–7

Economic Development Zones (EDZs) 6, 14, 16, 17, 40
economic growth 129–30, 132, 134–5
economic reforms, evolution of 2; phase 1, administrative decentralization (1958–78) 2–4; phase 2, incremental reforms (1979–93) 4–7; phase 3, growth of reforms since 1994 7–10
employment 9
Enterprise Resource Planning (ERP) 110
enterprise types 9–10, 39–42
entrepreneurial growth: development of the private sector 34–9; indigenous Chinese entrepreneurs 47; role of government policies 26–8
entrepreneurial process model 46–50
entrepreneurs 82; legislation recognising 98; representation in National People's Congress 97, 133–4; suspicions toward 97–8
entrepreneurship 25; and cultural convergence 51–2; drivers and barriers to SOE 78–9; and growth 44–50; *see also* DAL case study
external resources 51–2

family culture 94–5
fieldwork investigation 149–50
financial reforms 8
financial resources, access to 96–7
firm growth 44–6
foreign direct investment (FDI): and economic development 14–19, 135; and expansion of joint ventures 39–40, 47, 55
Foreign Enterprise Law 129
foreign exchange system, reform of 8
foreign joint ventures (FJVs) 41–2, 55–6, 110–11; cultural values 120; expansion of 39–40; human resource issues 117; impact of 47–8; leadership style 118, 119–20; management style 118; organizational culture 121–2; organizational profile *127*; skills/resources 125–6; staff 116–17; strategy 113–14; structure 115; systems 115–16; *see also* DSF case study

foreign trade composition *39*
Foreign Trade Laws 129
Free Trade Zones (FTZs) 17

GATT (General Agreement on Tariffs and Trade) 18
globalization 53–5
"going global" strategy 131–2
government institutions 10–12
government policies 26–8
Guanxi networks 50–1; and development of market socialism 52–3; and firm growth 55–6

Haier Corporation 33–4

ideologies within Communist Party 11
incremental reforms (1979–93) 4; free-market trade 5–6; non-state economic-growth measures 5; regional development areas 6–7
Incremental Reforms Strategy (1976) 4
indigenous Chinese entrepreneurs, growth of 47
individualism 145
industrial production 34–5, *36–8*
innovation 135–6
insider control 31
institutional change 25
integral reforms, theory of 7–8
"intrapreneuraship" 124

joint ventures *see* foreign joint ventures (FJVs)

Labor Law 68, 116–17
Labor Union 68, 90
leadership style 118–20, 125, 144, 147; and entrepreneurship growth 45, 46; in foreign-owned joint ventures 106–8; in private-owned enterprises 93–5; in state-owned enterprises 74–7, 80
learning culture/learning organization 34, 46, 59, 95, 121–2, 125, 126
legitimacy crisis 133–5
LTG case study: history 61–2; Labor Union 68; leadership 74–7; political education 76; recruitment 72–4; strategy 113

management philosophies 118; foreign joint ventures 100, 106, 109, 120, 122; private-owned enterprises 94–5; state-owned enterprises 76, 120

Index

management practice 56–60
management selection 21
management theory and practice 43–4; Chinese organizational behavior, Guanxi networks 50–6; entrepreneurship 44–50
managerial evolution, Haier Corporation 33–4
market-economy reforms 7–8
market socialism and Guanxi 52–3
McKinsey 7-S framework 141–2; shared values 144–6, 147; skills 146, 147; staff 143–4, 147; strategy 143, 146; structure 142, 146; style 144, 147; systems 142–3, 146–7
mergers and acquisitions (M&As) 41, 48, 54, 63, 80–1, 124, 131–2
"mixed-ownership" enterprises 5
mottos 94–5

national cultures, impact of 145
National People's Congress (NPC) 97
networks, using to access resources 95–7
non-state economy 4; growth 5, 7; stages in development of 34–5

Open Door Policy 14, 15, 17, 26
organizational behavior "Guanxi networks" 50–1
organizational change 28–30, 50, 67–8, 138
organizational culture 144–6, 147
owner-managed entrepreneurial firms *see* private-owned enterprises (POEs)
ownership 25

person culture 145
planned and market economy, coexistence of 13
"political elite" system 133
political reform issues 133
power culture 144
power distance 145
private-owned enterprises (POEs) 42, 54–5; development of 34–9; institutional components 57–9; leadership style 118–19; organizational culture *122*; organizational profile *127*; shared values 120, 121; skills/resources 123, 125; staff 116, 117; strategy 113, 114; structure 115; systems 115–16; *see also* DAL case study
private sector vs. public sector growth *39*
privatization 25, 32–3

privatization of collective-owned enterprises 48
process management 108
public-sector versus private-sector growth *39*

Quality Management System (QMS) 69

recruitment and selection 121, 143–4, 147; in foreign-owned joint ventures 104; private-owned enterprises 91, 92–3; state-owned enterprises 72–4, 80, 124, 130–1
"reforms in all-round-way": measures and schemes 8–10; theory of 7–8
regulation 23, 134
research: future research 153–4; limitations 151–3; operational measures 140–1
resource access: external resources 51–2; finance 96–7; raw materials 95–6; supportive government policies 98
resource-based view (RBV) of the firm 49–50
restructuring of state-owned enterprises 48–50
retail commercial sales *6*
role culture 144–5

shared values 120–2, 144–6
Shenzen economic zone 12
social security, reform of 9
socialism, redefinition of 12–13
socialist ideology 13–14; and reform 76–7, 119; training programs 27
soft budget constraints 20
spiritual civilization 13–14
staff 116–18, 147; autonomy 109, 116, 122; development 92; *see also* recruitment and selection
state-owned enterprises (SOEs) 41; control by Communist Party 77–8; drivers and barriers to entrepreneurship 78–9; institutional components *57–9*; leadership style 118, 119; losses of 20, 29; main indicators 9–10; management style 117–18; organizational culture *122*; organizational profile *127*; policy recommendations 79–81; reform of 8–9, 54; resistance to change 124–5; restructuring of 28–33, 48–50; shared values 120–1; skills/resources 123–4; staff benefits 116–17; strategy of

112–13, 114–15; structure 115; systems 116; three stages of reform 20–1; *see also* LTG case study style *see* leadership style
super-ordinate goals (shared values) 144–6
systems 115–16

task culture 145
tax evasion 30
tax holidays, foreign joint ventures 40, 101
taxation reforms 8
textile industry 126–7, 148
township village enterprises (TVEs) 4, 5, 34–5

training: foreign-owned joint ventures 103–4, 105, 107, 110–11, 117; private-owned enterprises 91–2; state-owned enterprises 74, 80, 81

uncertainty avoidance 145

WTO (World Trade Organization) 12, 15, 18, 141, 148; tariff commitments 18–19, 127

Xiaoping, Deng 1, 5, 7, 11–12, 14, 17, 26, 33, 35, 43, 134, 157